The Theory of Everything and the Man Who Could Save the Earth

The Theory of Everything and the Man Who Could Save the Earth

All but the World Is Loving 2

Dennis Zamudio Flores

PARTRIDGE
A Penguin Random House Company

Print information available on the last page.

To order additional copies of this book, contact
Toll Free 800 101 2657 (Singapore)
Toll Free 1 800 81 7340 (Malaysia)
orders.singapore@partridgepublishing.com

www.partridgepublishing.com/singapore

Contents

Foreword

The book(s) that the author believed that great men is longing for; The second edition of All But the World is Loving ISBN 9781434983824, refer or known as Book 1, The Theory of Everything and The Man Who Could Save The Earth (all but the world is loving 2), were reciprocally complimented each other, wherein, its primary objective is to provide information on a certain subject and that the author believed to be critically misconstrued or taken for granted; say the compelling reasons or the truth about climate change or global warming phenomenon in particular, the inhabitant of this planet need to deal with. It include the natural sciences in general, and its phenomena in particular, thus works on topics such as Philosophy, Metaphysics, Physics or Natural Sciences; Cosmology and or Astronomy, *Geology, *Hydrology, and *Meteorology (*__with regards to global warming of its impending catastrophe__). In addition, to counter skepticism or to defeat anachronism, it uncovered the link between science and religion in a certain aspect, are among others.

It says that the physical environment and its natural phenomena is the fundamental basis of our life, survival and existence, thus understanding its immense but not very complex processes is therefore aiding us to lighten the task of surviving, and or duty and operation attributed to us human beings, is the primary concern of this tenet dedicated in this world. We have to remember that Science and Religion is essential tool to obtain knowledge or wisdom, however, while in one hand it says that if we perceived life on purely scientific aspect, we may end up losing one' soul as those noble people or of the teaching of the church from the past and the present time does, strives hard for us to achieved. However, if, or to inclined too much on religion, with the current trend or activity upon the Earth, we might end up losing the beauty of nature, or the death of inhabitant and the habitable planet itself. Therefore to achieve its goal, to support and compliment, and to affirm the idea in the face of challenges and impugns, the author employs the Mono principle that lay down the theory of everything and these uncover unexplained phenomena, superfluous or superstitious belief, thus, rather, that is to overcome or defeat skeptics.

However the rule, the influence and or beauty of religions and churches in a certain life, and that motivates a person's character into their benevolence towards themselves and others, provide us room to explore a might be *amusement and solace of one soul (***because human thought to survive a would be perpetual life through the mind***) that more than this (material world) can offer or expresses. And for this reason, the writing's desires' to settle down argument, the reason that keep us apart or secluded or isolates from each other into an acceptable manner and that sure leads into (science and religion) harmonious relationship. With the fundamental or the origin and operation of the universe unfolded, it aim and hope for a civilized world and that are free from predilection or partiality, parsimony and injustices.

Propaedeutic

*The information contain in this writing's absolutely author's idea. The fact, rather, the notions that the author trying to believe is that it might share the same thought to many; at this point in time however, specifically in the year 2012, except for an appreciation letter from a royal couple from one of the kingdom in the west where the money is, rather, where the best of world's education exist and the great thinkers flourish, wherein, it considered as the author's theodicy, has neither declared as official's statement from any governing bodies nor receives citation this far from any authoritative assemblies. Thus, it is the individual responsibility to examine the fact in order to discern or note the differences and or similarities regarding the veracity of every claim of both parties in any subject involve. The fact that the idea might share the same principle to others, however, may deviates from what one's expected. And consequently, can be disadvantageous or detrimental in some extent or offensive to a person of a certain belief and reputation, and that the author express regret on this matter. Nevertheless, from the author's perspective, this writing has been carried out on purpose and that, rather, at least to save the earth, our habitable planet, from a possible or an imminent destruction, alongside, rather, therefore saving the environment's an intended outcome and to survive a human life as its utmost desire. Thus, impropriety or impudence that may lead to antagonisms or adverse emotions is not to demean a person character, personality and belief but to hold the balance (**emotional and mental stability**), to clarify issues and concern and that is for everyone's good sake's harmonious relationship or co-existence and moderation. And this conclude, rather desire that Neutrality* *with the inclination on noble things and deed shall manifest and prevail on one's heart and mind, and this is **(the)** God that reflects the theory of Quintessence, wherein the fundamentals rooted or promulgated by John The Beloved **(on His book of Revelation)**, considered in here as the true Vicar of Christ, the Jesus of Nazarene.*

DEDICATION

This book is lovingly dedicated to Jesus of Nazarene, to the Middle East, and with equal opportunity to the Israelites and Palestine people, as well as the Churches and Religion, specifically Pope Benedict and Pope Francis of the Catholic faith, and as applicable to other congregation and religious sectarian's preachers.

Likewise, this treatise's a pledge to the devotions and affair of the world of astronomy and geological services (NASA, CERN- the Large Hadron Collider, USGS etc.). And all effort and struggle of all environmental advocates all over the world; individuals like His Royal Highness Prince Charles of England for His Saving the Rainforest project, The Honorable Al Gore of his Inconvenient Truth of Global Warming issues, the French President Francois Hollande of his invaluable effort to combat climate change, and with the same privileges to the United Nations Climate Change Panel or IPCC and other private institutions or NGO's.

*Furthermore, it devout well to the Skeptics and Thinker (**Francisco Sanches – French/Portuguese Philosopher and Physician; Nostradamus author of the book Centuries 1555, Baruch "Benedict the Blessed" de Spinoza, Dutch Philosopher; John the Beloved, author of the Book of Revelation of the Catholic Christian Bible and considered in here as the Vicar of Christ, the Jesus of Nazarene; all are of Jewish bloodline and (or royal) origin.***

***Special mentions to Dr. Jose Rizal, the Philippines National Hero, Charles Darwin, author of Evolution Theory, Isaac Newton, author of Universal Gravitation, Galileo Galilei, the Italian astronomer and physicist, Nicolaus Copernicus Polish astronomer and or Stephen Hawking author of several books (Brief History of Time) who revisited the theory of Black Hole;** And of the world (great) Chess players, the educational institutions of their respective discipline and especially of that Philosophy of its branches and attributes, the Metaphysics and Natural Science in particular, such as Geology, Hydrology, Meteorology and the Weather Bureau, as well as Cosmology, Astronomy and Physics.*

INTRODUCTION 1

The Philosophy

The greatest wealth a person could have is wisdom. The optimal possession that bequeath knowledge and that bequest health and power that in a material aspect may obtain world's life's pleasure. And on one's thought, the *Spirits (*noble deeds and or non-guilty of sin) that comforts and or the solace of soul in the demise of flesh, motivated, rather, with the aim of human survival through the mind (transmigration as the like of Pythagoras [He remembered everything how he first had been Aethelides, then Euphorbus, then Hermotimus, then Pyrrhus, the Delian diver; when Pyrrhus died he became Pythagoras. source: Diogenes Laertius, Live of Philosopher, VIII 4-5] or life after death or the resurrection – as the account of Jesus of Nazarene on the later era and the author experiences especially on a doleful scene in some instances remembering circumstances had happened exactly on the same manner).

Specifically, Spirit as the virtue, such as love and help and it turn to noble things, the Holy Spirits that manifest in the actuality of (noble) deed such as loving and helping one another, thus, non-guilty of sin in life's tenure is a solace of one's thought and or emotion especially in time of grief and fear and that makes the difference in favor, or in reward being faithful (intellectual) or as the advocates of Truth. Early on this thing is that we have to learn and teach our children to "Love" and do noble things with passion because it is, rather, these

1

are the only way to find the Happiness in life and hereafter and this scientifically, nay, a person can see a precept on L. Ron Hubbard's 21 Moral Code.

*Wisdom can be acquire and or achieve in two things; can be through self-mastery via proper channel or the formal education, and by experience thru the actual or practical means. While in one hand, achieving wisdom through education is all true in a rhetoric writings that **(edify or)** encourage intellectual, moral and spiritual improvement or "rarefication". The practical experience on the other, widely manifest on rationalism and or logical reasoning in which applies to all walks of life; the erudite and ignorant, the royals and commoners, rich and or poor, and those actions nevertheless leads to one's noble deed. And it is notable however, that without the knowledge of the former, experience may go through a hard time. And in relation to the subject matter, Philosophy, or the love and pursuit of wisdom by intellectual means and moral self-discipline, fortunately stands on both, and or works simultaneously, and apparently the reason on why a philosopher, of whom perceived or well known as a person who love to argue, rather, a certain practitioner of philosophy – the loving for noble deed and honor, claimed that the greatest thing in life is to learn the moral Philosophy wherein it encompasses all the field of discipline and that include being the intermediary of antagonism in between science and religion. For obtaining the Truth according to them, sets the thought of a person's free thus, relieve a burden (anxiety) on one's life, and comfort the soul from the fear of dying, therefore succeeds in gaining the true meaning of life's happiness. It holds on to the saying that "it is better for one man who practiced philosophy than ten who taught it". Law is a philosophy of life, or should we say that God and the Truth attributed to their nature is the philosophy of the existence of the universe?*

Surprisingly, the Spinoza's system or principle, attributed to a Jewish-Dutch philosopher Baruch "the Blessed" Spinoza 1632-1677, best known for his work on Ethics, and that he tried to explain how people can best find happiness, and that is to be found in the intellectual love of God and or Nature which humans attain through reason and understanding, And he argued that God and nature are the Thing. And on 27 July 1656, at the age of 23, Baruch faced expulsion from the Jewish community in Amsterdam as a consequence of his works. Nevertheless, when he died, he was considered a saint by the general Christian *population and was buried in holy ground. In addition, he claimed that he did not believe in the validity of sense perception to gain knowledge and he believed "geometry" was the perfect model for philosophy [**source: Wikipedia**].*

Nevertheless, as far as the comparison of philosophy is concern, and that adopting and or working with life's consequence, I wish to add that everyone should play the board game "Chess" where in this treatise believed that this game is more suitable, if not depicting the real game of life or survival and existence. The same thing apply on dealing with the nature or global warming inconvenience or difficulty, be wary that playing chess with computer generated opponent requires no emotion but a sharp memory recall, nevertheless, manipulative skill's an advantage or essence in any given circumstances and this overrule the convenience of the few (global warming denier) but for every common good.

The fact that everything, or science in particular, is in harmony with mathematics, where in the later depicted as reasoning, thus, in a way or strict sense to other, consider as philosophy as well. Say, in one thing, if a person interprets the creation theory in Genesis literally, and that takes place in a matter of six days, was numbered. And on the other, scientifically speaking, in which I considered attributed to dichotomy or transmutation, is in fact governed and or regulated by numbers. Time is math. Temperature is math. Consequence is math. All is numbered even up to the proposition of Michio Kaku, the Japanese-American physicist and TV presenter that says; "impossible is nothing," in a sense govern by a number, and it's all true in politics that says "nothing is impossible" coincidentally govern by the figure starting from, or made up of zero's.

*In Book 1 however, I submit with a French /Portuguese Physician and Philosopher, and like Spinoza of a Jewish origin, his name was Francisco Sanches, 1550-1623. Surprisingly, rather the irony was that with its wit notable for medicinal practice and educator, unfortunately considered by the church as the most ruinous of the skeptic. Notable for his writing That Nothing is Known, and that he said, certainty cannot be achieved through numbers or mathematics (**later was supported by succeeding French philosopher named Denis Diderot 1713-1784, co-founder, chief editor and contributor to the Encyclopedie, as He warned His fellow philosopher against an**)* *overemphasis on Mathematics and against the blind optimism that sees in the growth of physical knowledge an automatic social and human progress. He rejected the Idea of Progress. In His opinion, the aim of progressing through technology was doomed to fail [source Wikipedia]. Where in this treatise totally concurred only if the "Progress" mentioned is against, or incompliance especially with the work of nature in general aspect),* especially, rather as I see it, though mental challenges flashes and flares up one's thinking or reasoning, however, when it comes to an *immense object, astounding force or strenuous matter like celestial body or galaxy, numbers are mere assumption [***citations follows on the article of the origin of galaxy]***. In fairness, or giving Spinoza the benefit of the doubt, and that in one hand, since geometry proves and improves by mathematics, is in fact resembling or depicting a real object and constitute by configuration, therefore it is an arrangement, and indeed an arrangement or geometry is a philosophy with the manner of actuality, where in, nay, on the other hand, say in ethics, and psychology are philosophy of the mind, is purely an abstract idea and reasoning ability, and that tell us, rather depict as the counterpart of realism. Nevertheless, subscribing faithfully to ethics, sure lead one into a modest life and that an indicative of an organized and systematic way of living therefore geometricize.

Anyway, if Spinoza thought of the subject matter as to aid one's capability, or to stimulate and hyper the senses as to enhance betterment of the person's rationality and nobility, He's therefore correct in this case. And hardly that Spinoza was all alone in this notion, for the Cartesian system or Cartesian Dualism, attributed to Rene Descartes 1596-1650, French philosopher and mathematician, precisely if not absolutely concurred or harmonize his idea with the former. The fact that mathematical order of the universe is independent of sense, mainly because the senses that well-coordinated with thought is purely dependent **(of its development)** on the circumstances **[including threat on its existence]** of what a reality or a material thing in particular, or world in general, of its mechanical operation the universe can offer, and that specifically the Evolution of things or universal event that play a significant part as mnemonic or an essential tool of human thought or knowledge, understanding or comprehension. In this case, since the Theory of Evolution, a notion postulated and advances by Charles Robert Darwin, British Naturalist 1809–1882, *provided this writing a great insight, leads to think, and that failed to satisfied skeptics* **(specifically the irreducibly or intricately complex organ like the Eye; Molecular biology revealed that each human eye has over 100 million rods and handles 1.5 million simultaneous messages, has automatic focusing and has 6 million cones that can distinguish among seven million colors)**, *or foible on its fundamentals, unfortunately, a would be essence or importance of the tenet may be smother as the Theory of Evolution conceded; "If it could be demonstrated that any complex organ existed which could not possibly have been formed by numerous, successive, slight modifications, my theory would absolutely breakdown." And He confided to a friend, "to this day the eye causes me a cold shudder." source: www.Y-origin.com*

Indeed **(the consequence of philosophy is that)**, *claiming or talking things that you can't prove is like taking matters against yourself. In this regard, since the reality or facts of the Theory of Evolution by Darwin and His proponent such as Huxley, though arguable, is undeniable, to the point that it may be consider as a Paradigm for "future" research and development. And that if the complexity of the eyes' problematic, with the best of my knowledge and experience, I'd rather share my idea as to aid His notion with an impeccable, best or suitable representation on the following:*

Snake may have eyes but has no vision or it cannot see things, however, the sense of movement or motion coming from another party, are precise or effective in such a range or distance. In this case, due to "unfortunate" circumstances or malady, say brain lapses, mechanical or congenital **[innate]** *defect, specifically, human with impaired vision, however, sense perception will adopt on the circumstances similar to the entity, which is the snake in this case. In other words, if a certain command or operation* **(on specific purpose desired or determine of the will therefore developed and manifest)** *of a particular cell or sensory element, failed to carried out its duty or definitive function, may serve another purpose instead, or may create or alter development and operation which is all true on (all living) things as it may increase the ability of the other sense(s)* **[sense-compensate or sense-brain generative coordination]** *as it, or that may satisfy or utilize what a circumstances has have to offer, and this, the primary objective is of surviving or for one's own existence.*

*Say intelligence: how could one lead into inventions; i.e. as a result, while in one hand nature's event, such as flood, landslide earthquake etc. formed a ditched or holes in the surface of the earth, on the other, necessity, human makes pot. Nature or rain provides water in that hole as well as men on the pot. While nature's shape that hole in a relatively harder surface such as rock, man makes a stove on the counterpart. And while nature provides heat by volcanic activity, man makes fire, and the similarity on these entity, or its parallelism is that both can boiled one's egg. While some entities capable of thinking has **desire**, which is the (most) important aspect of the matter, others relied only on what the circumstances (nature, heat, temperature) has had to offer and that one can see what makes the difference.*

*As Aristotle believed that intellectual purposes [final causes], guided all natural processes, noting that "no animals has, at the same time, both tusks and horns." He suggested that Nature, giving no animal both horns and tusks, was staving off vanity, and giving creatures faculties only to such degree as they are necessary. Noting that ruminants had multiple stomachs and weak teeth, he supposed the first was to compensate for the latter, with nature trying to preserve a *type of balance [***compliments or citations on the following theory of quintessence: adlib; It is a blessing, rather, If men had wings, it is hard to figure out how far a Greek or an English playboys will go, perhaps the rules and venue of the Olympic will be quite different as we have today; as the Greek struggle on economy as we had observe to this day of writing, the English has a sound one on the contrary, and this tenet want to know if this is an indication that Greeks spend a lot on women that they counterpart do? It is notable that while most of the aquatic species had its fins, sure there is one with wings, and it is true with the colony of ants as well. In this case, was it safe to assume that if someone opted for a certain way of life, say sex over the essence of having wings, therefore it depicts and or manifest to what we have or what are we on today, and could this be our inherited sin? Or should I say unlike birds, men prefer to stay at home (thus unable to developed) and use no wings at all due to jealousy or being possessive and or laziness? I mean, I'm now on my fourth and second decade working overseas, and that despite the fact of the best of education and or citations received,*** *the Philippines Economic Team is still trying to find its rhythm, and that means while looking for the trouble, the economy is still hanging on a thread. You'll find the economy recuperating, and then struggle on nature's calamity and *corruption (*bank secrecy law is a perfect cover up of a black money and crook thus, must be revised in favor of the legitimate, or in a total clean up drive for money laundering scheme or scam, must be abolished. In good faith, to update, verify or monitor its status, overseas bank account holder's name [at least] must be submitted back to the commissioned body of a government of its country of origin). In this case, was the culture of corruption can also be traces or rooted back to the geographic identity of a community or country wherein a tropical places are more vulnerable if not common to such concern more than the places having with an extreme weather condition or pattern where they take no chances against nature? If this assumption on Greek economy however is correct, pardon Mama Mary and pray for me. Indeed, man was made to impress women, and woman live to attract men, and the love or attraction that binds them one, is the reason they multiplies].*

In other words, like a child growing up, Experience precedes human Astuteness, and this to lighten up the task of surviving. Basically, the honing of intelligence is the method, or if not the product of inscription of artistic surviving skills that would have been adapted to circumstances at any given time, and certainly, had been developed overtime. While no doubt that human being possess the most intelligent processor, which is the brain, however, If Aristotle is right in this case, wouldn't be safe to suppose, that human origin or on its early form may be a nocturnal creature or specifically might have *poor eyesight or impaired vision however could have the stringer, sound and strong sense of motion or a more sensitive feeling or interaction with the nature, and this is true or more likely the other way around as this feature manifest in most, if not some or selected species; *say due to poor nutrition or hygiene, and that deduces the quality of a human cell or perhaps the cells and or its attribute that human has adopted to, though or somehow applicable or viable to form a human being, with the environment as a factor, is weak in a certain place, but highly reliable or desirable in the other, and that may lead us to come up *with the idea of different species or race in different parts of the world that in a certain period, era or eon, that permits or owe from the **Circumstances, and that could be credited to natural selection process [**and one of these is the Temperature, rather the most essential element or component to produce life is pressure or heat coming from the sunlight or the general source of heat in the solar system, and volcanic activity contributed well by sun's courtesy; {nature's} reproduction process is in fact the act of proving a certain species or element's superiority over the other and the struggle or lovemaking {synthesis} in between them form a coherent whole – formation of a compound from a particular or simpler compounds or elements], or synthesis of molecules or organism or cell or genes that constitute of the human species considered as the most intelligent, however dormant due to ignorance, arrives massively in most places of the Earth. In scientific view, it is very interesting to learn a human form could be found in another habitable planet like ours. Nevertheless, the notion that human coming into existence, is like the saying that goes like of shooting an arrow to asteroid Pluto (relatively takes a longer time to develop, and that is only by Accident, before discovering their potential to procreate or to learn to reproduce thru sexual means, could be the beginning of an end of evolution or reproduction the original way, wherein human form could had been started in a bizarre feature or appearances, much more to suggest that everything on this world or human being to be specific, originate from the disparity in Temperature [during a trip, actual observation was on the North plain of Saudi Arabia close to the border with Iraq] heat against cold produces water then algae that turn into fungus or mushroom, and so on, given the chance, the group, or the combination of genes could had been a lateral or unilinear or universal transfer. And with the ideal or corroborative circumstances, produces what the circumstances could offer, therefore bear or yield of what we are, or what we have today. Indeed it was crude, but was it not correct that in the Bible Old Testament and that said "a man comes from the dust, and on the dust he shall return"? A preposition of the context, suggest that the concept of religion today, is a science aspect of the ancestral time. In this case, Sexual Intercourse, considered in here as the original or inherited sin that was mentioned on the Old Testament and countered by Jesus*

of Nazarene on the New Testament by promulgating the greatest of the sin which is the [deliberate] destruction of one's own Spirit or the [good sense] quality trait of a human being [character], specifically the brain (wherein too much a fasting deduces or diminishes millions of brain cell, the reason in here that Jesus of Nazarene let his apostles carried out fast not) that leads a person away from discharging a noble work or the Holy Spirit), and it hit the target bull's eye, in a strict sense could or might be true in this aspect. In technical aspect, human evolution could be that of a sledge on the primitive time, then introduce a horse drawn cart, then a conventional or manual cranking engine, turn into a remote controlled operation and or now a driverless car and that is through human innovative character. Nevertheless, nature or biodiversity, or entities incapable of thinking or duplicating human works, carried out self-transformation or evolution by itself thru the virtue of Temperature and or corroborative circumstances.

And this, by experience, or human using tool and or makes comparison – mathematical knowledge, and later years learned the language of nature's philosophy, and that the function or quality of the brain sure improve overtime, as we can observe in human kind that is good in adaptation to environment, such as "great" ability to reproduce {**while human being goes as they will, animals with limited capability mate only on season**} and to take care of themselves and offspring among other. And in this case, nay, indeed, it is not surprising if not safe to assume that human species undergoes evolution which is absolutely comprehensible through the methodology of sciences, and the problem lies on the people that doesn't want to believe in the truth of this matter or the truth of the nature that really exist. And nevertheless, some animals alike, inhabited places that provide and suit with their basic need such as habitat, food or nutrition, thus may improve cells or genetics for the quest of what we called pleasure and satisfaction (human invents or creates technology to improves life's aspect; some men become blinded with power, wealth and pleasure that leads to insatiable quenched for improvement. The tendency to be on top of the other is like of those suffering from attention deficit disorder that they may not aware of), if these things in strict sense differ from survival and existence.

And regarding the significance of this subject, or the eye in particular, may however do well, rather, can we make its philosophy brighter or easily perceptible by correlating this notion to the concept of the "Fall of Man" also called as the "Original Sin" (interpreted in here as the [pervert] sexual conduct) inscribed on Genesis 3 of the old testament, and given emphasis on Matthew 6, Luke 11 or Mark 9:47 of the new one. In other words, rather in strict sense, wasn't the **EYE** *(vision) that causes us to sin, and that indulge* ***creatures** *and champion by the human race of the sexual pleasure [* ***usually, animals mate or desired sex on season only, may not really on the right place but more likely to be in the right time]** *and that hyper the growth of population that leads to poverty and higher rate of mortality due to cataclysm or nature catastrophe, thus, ancestral people initiated population control by circumcision, the inexpensive method, and or literal or available scientific idea on that time where in its method is a single cause having a lifetime measure (like fasting on food, aim toward a goal directly as anti-austerity measure and sexual harassment). And that, nay, was it not the concern, or the law, or the covenant of circumcision* **[for the "inherited sin" in this case is the "sexual enthusiasm" that hardly explain if not figurative language by the author of the book of Genesis of its philosophical idea]?** *To circumcise* **[is to repel or hold back or to decry the degree of sexual desire as explained on Book 1 or All But The Word is Loving, as well]** *or not to circumcise* **[is to protrude sexual enthusiasm]** *is the heated argument* **{in Antioch}** *between the apostles Peter and converted Paul. In one hand, rather, the later insisted that it is not necessary to carried out this ritual to Gentiles or non-Jew where I believed He succeeded in enticing, rather, persuading western and the great land dwellers in this case, and on the other, it is a blessing that circumcision was greatly implemented akin to one's pride and was triumphant in emphasizing it in the land called the "aquatic triplicity", and that with, or as far as the current economic performance is concern, is really unambiguous to figure out the outcome. I mean, if the people in here were circumcised, and yet do have the struggling economy on today, tomorrow's gloomy for sure, I mean, much more if it suggests or insisted otherwise. Nevertheless, thanks to Saint Peter and the clergy in this case, but should they found out that this writing's correct, and that with regards to over population that slow, drag and pull the economy down, would have the law be amended to a rigid or rigorous or to at least maximum safety measure which* *has been carried out as early as the Father, or Abrahamic time with the best of the idea such as circumcision, or philosophy or law and circumstances they had on their time have to offer. We have to note however that it is the right of a person or a child to be circumcised or not to be circumcised until he finds a reason (hygiene, urinary trachea infection UTI, HIV) to have one. And being uncircumcised, beware that this idea will accused and or ridicule you on this place thus, a subject of teasing, not just until your death, but up to your third generation. But behold, as far as the comparison regarding performances' concern, one should stick on the very natural idea, and be undaunted, because by the numbers, he can be wife's "inner" satisfaction and pride, some say a secret of woman happiness.*

Furthermore, reflection or interpretation on this subject comes like no easy for this treatise. Actually, rather in a sense, is taboo to the conservative, but it seems like a joke or ridiculous to other. And materialistic or realistic view does really need a trained eye to arrive on this thing, and that teleological understanding of the nature of one's philosophy may have an intended and essential role to play in the society. In other words, uncovering arcana, a cabalistic or figurative language, to the point of deciphering a hieroglyphic writing, in the present time, could be the triumph of Wisdom if not the last bastion of our knowledge. And in relation to this, though being mentioned in the prayer gathering in almost every chance; it took the author more than twelve years to recognize that this philosophy, or law or covenant of circumcision of the ancient time had been reprimanded by no less than Jesus of Nazarene thru John the beloved that expressed on John 6:63 and says; "It is the Spirit that gives life, the flesh counts/ offers nothing [or **circumcision in particular, however Fasting may be effective in a certain time on holding back sexual desire but could be detrimental to brain cell, may or thus deduces the quality of thinking and therefore reduce significantly the power of mind has had to offer]**. *The words I have spoken to you is the Spirit and they are life; 64; Yet, there are some of you who do not believe". This particular subject (of sexual desire or circumcision) of cause and effect according to Jesus of Nazarene, of his superior mind ability is "cheap". The essence of rational thinking and superior ability and that leads to noble deeds, this tenet believed is the "sound" quality of one's brain.*

Moreover, it is indeed notable that while most of the aquatic or marine species had its fins, sure there is one with wings and it is true with the colony of ants as well. In this case, was it safe to assume that if someone opted for a certain way of life, say the pleasure of sex over the essence of having wings, therefore it depicts or manifest to what we got or what we are on today. And could this be our inherited sins from our ancestors, or was it Jesus that correct that we are losing the moral ground and that must be corrected through the efficacy of faith or the noble of scientific, yet moral intellectualism or the other way around, that is moral and yet scientific intellectualism. And this is the methodology of self-preservation wherein it dissuades *evil (*which is the result of ignorance, backward or inadequate understanding) and that is the intellectual love of God and Nature. And depending on the degree one may possess, these entities may acquire the prowess of mind?

*In saying this, is that it is the **original sin (of flesh)** mentioned in the old testament, which was interpreted in these books as the "sexual enthusiasm" **(of men),** and personally gives trouble to the thinking of the like of Jesus Nazarene that he countered it by promulgating the **greatest of the sin** was in fact the one that destroys the Spirit or the noble qualities of an individual, specifically the wisdom **(thought)** or the person's ability to do the Holy Spirit or holy work such as helping or loving each other, wherein, the abuse of drugs and alcohol that impedes the person ability to discharge the Holy Spirit (noble deed) is the most detestable thing against a person himself. The Philosophy in this case however particular and specific, is in fact depicts with equal opportunity with the universal Philosophy shared and advances by some of the great Greek ancient philosophers such as Thales, Anaximander, Heraclitus or Empedocles saying that the origin of the universe starts from water, air, fire and or earth, and these are against or to denied the mythological god of ancient Greek and their belief. And though meet challenges from the skeptics by the like of Parmenides, nevertheless gives this author the idea of real God's Nature and this consolidated with the writings on the **Revelation on the New Testament, authored by John the Beloved considered in here as the great of the Apostles and the true Vicar of Christ (see also Book 1 for additional input).** And in addition to an evolutionary fact, is that to assume that human being might be crawling then by what the hands now, can be a possibility. And who can discount a certain* species of their intelligence parallel or equal to human, but it is the "hands" in particular and *"discipline" (***wit or intellectual ability or satisfaction to live and to survive***) in general aspect that makes the difference. And the anthropologist of their theory of [**human**] evolution may have the lead and could respond to this quest. And though some people ridiculed these personalities, we can't deny the fact of their great contributions to the society in general and in our knowledge in particular. According to Huxley, one of the advocates of Darwin, "we should make it clear on this generation that if the Truth maligns, is not just a blunder but a crime". This writing believed that this is correct. We are on ourselves to our believing, but the truth that the nature governs us is actually a fact, and **working against (****literally means a one way and tremendous force of nature***) is a ***sin (*****term used by the ancestral people***) and that sure would meet the consequence leading to a disaster and or one's death eventually.

The Truth about the reality of God and Nature was unfolded as early or beyond 1000 BC wherein this era, and this writing believed that civilization was already thriving in places like Europe, or at least at the time of Prophet Isaiah on the Bible Old Testament where He founded the real concept and essence and moral obligation of church and religion. And the great question however is that, was it not the (**awe-inspiring and wonder of**) Nature (**and this include nature cataclysm**) that the people on the Old Testament was referring to, of God. And as this was learned, Jesus of Nazarene countered old believing to the point of probing this thing by braving the death for His resurrection in order to alter the so called belief (Abrahamic God), and so the idea of many philosophers and thinkers like Socrates, Spinoza, Sanches, Rizal or Newton, Copernicus, Galileo, Darwin to name a few. Though technical aspect or scientific theory and or terminology was not available at that time, however, and these conclude and or proved that Jesus of Nazarene also called as Christ, was the most *faithful or *intelligent among them all, to the point He was considered as the Son of God (**words that may be used on different occasion or time might share the same meaning on today; with or depending on "gestures" of an Arab speakers, term may dodge or varied slightly on its definite or specific meaning. Say the word "faith" doesn't just confined nor subscribes to literal meaning of "believing in things that you cannot**

prove or see", but sometimes it use to describe the *[awe inspiring]* **degree of a person intellectualism or ability to discharge work- see also Book 1 for additional input).**

What this writing can conclude is that the people or inhabitant at any point in time, wanted to be free, have pleasure and be satisfied; what the authority suggests is to govern and upheld this freedom with ease and that will yield a comfortable way of life for them, the ruler, to the point that they may subscribe to any method they think will work effectively. However, this writing only concern is that this matter, the teaching and governance should not be compromise the mechanical or scientific aspect of living, to the point that it may or would expose biodiversity in danger. It is a great statement, but in strict sense, rather in fact, everything on this world is a factor of life. Treat the Nature or the Earth as the precious thing that support and provides life, thwarted therefore the global warming because it is the indication of the slow death of biodiversity as this writing firmly believed is the same thing as the planet Venus then.

INTRODUCTION 2

The Comparison

Comparison or Analogy is a form or method of Measurement; An essential tool or weighing instrument upon the intellect. And it is the greatest asset of the philosophy of life. Judgment, parallelism, equation or comparison develop and beget wisdom in every day of living, now and then.

But what provides the passion to think of this idea leading into this writing? And it was because of the author personal experience on witnessing a transformation of compounded cells described as slimy gel with black color dotted in it and rested on a leaf, into a probable life of a certain species. By the Sun's spectrum as its essence in particular, and with the collaboration of the environment in general, the perfect circumstances, or frequency or distance of the sunlight in particular, tend it to vibrates as it was the breath of life, just enough to improved its size and condition on a very discrete value. And screening the sunlight ceased it (vibration). And in addition, with a couple of leaves attached to its stem identified locally as Pili nut, serve as the body of a certain type of mantis, is a rare, but was really great insight.

Of this observation at an early age, it had been impressed like a seal, or the impression that had been molded in my thought may last as long as I live, and that the Sun's heat or pressure and or its frequencies with the collaboration of a cold in particular, or ideal environment temperature and its perfect circumstances in general, reshapes or forms, gives life and breath to a creature.

In saying this, rather, straight forward was that we can claim that planets were in fact passionately crafted by the sun spectrum; citation shortly on the following article, the Theory of Everything – the origin of planet. In this case, we can derive a conclusion that a certain species is made up, or could be a synthesis, or is a product of a compound cell or multiple cell membrane and or organism **[whether an attribute is a conductor or procreative cell, neutral or dead or a non- conductive cell that may however contribute to form a viable one and become an integral part of a living organism; early on this thing we can conclude that living organism or human in particular is a cross breed, compounded or formed out of multiple organism by jointing or mating two more agreeable cells]** *originated, derived or deduced from a collaborative environment and circumstances and that include the existence of attributes that was, or may had been set apart by an immense margin of time. In this writing, the Origin of Life resembled like of the oceans; comes from a sea, that comes from a river that may come from a lake and its tributaries and that comes from a spring then sustain by the trees or rainforest and or ice cap deposit or mountain dew that comes from a gas rarefication process or as a product between the disparity of hot and cold temperature* **[cloud seeding or clouds is the less denser element that evaporates, while water or drop of rain is the heavier substance. In this regard, see the following on the theory of the creation or formation of a planet and the creation of the universe or see Book 1 for additional input]**. *So the puzzle or question of the origin of life as whether it is an evolutionary accident or an intelligent design may lead to think of a much greater approach, perception and or comparison, and that concern about the *outgoing planet like Venus, and the incoming one such as Mars. In here nevertheless, or the side information on this idea is that the planet Mercury is pre-supposed to be the moon of the former* **[*from the firmament that was cold in temperature, creates the original gas nebula, then it turn to water or ice, then earth as housing that eventually become the belting region or shell. And as the circumstances, distance or space between the two body permitted, creates **core** *{**that serve as the "intimate" link or junction between the two body by sense or sensing the degree of temperature: global warming or high in temperature is to attract or indulge more intensity otherwise tells in contrast}* **by the relentless drive of the sun, thus the bed or belting region of the planet revolves around its core, and this to provide** *room for operation or prevent friction that may lead the planet from disintegration. Therefore, by the given circumstances from the sun's revolution, planets in the solar system is in fact originated, reshaped commutes or purified inside the sun's whirlpool or current, leading or back to the sun's chamber or its black hole for fusion. It is noteworthy that the sun we see all day is in fact one of the dual port or "Suction Chamber" of this body, therefore everything on its web is subject for suction, thus, to mitigate global warming is to repel this causative]. Citations will follow on the Theory of Everything; a must see Book 1 for additional input].*

*An overview of this subject is that the methodology of gravitations, or the gas suction process of the solar/sun system that used to fuel itself, and that, all along the current, such as the planets and their satellites, on a normal course of action or procedure **(universal gravitation),** one after the other, where in the body was originated is subjected through a coned shape patterned **(of the principle of a whirlpool or procession - and this operation must be understood the relationship of the bodies, wherein the planet's inside of the cone shape sun's frequency leading to the core)** and might or shall end up to the core of the Sun for nuclear fusion. And these bodies standard operation **(universal gravitation – a must see Book 1 for comprehensive and or genuine input; the fulfillment of Isaac Newton Theory),** produces heat or gases that floats, diversify and therefore exist in the firmament. And at the same time gases from the chamber dissipated through the equilateral area or on the celestial equator of the body by an action of a self-pumping centrifugal force to equate or to bring about the system in *equilibrium for its existence **[*Equilibrium is the essence if not the reason for a matter to exist in an unspecified time, and although everything undergoes transformations, the purest of the element shall exist in perpetuity (gas to liquid to solid to liquid and gas) where in life in particular, or all of the matter as a whole, originated, proceeds and resolve and or regenerated].***

It is notable and that, say the whole process of the solar system resemble the operation of an aircraft engine or the human digestive system; while the quality of compression or degree of heat is attribute to its density, floating of the body *itself in the space is in fact its Existence. That could be plain and simple, yet this writing hope that it is not a sullen to suffix in the synopsis, teleology, or the philosophy on Genesis of the Old Testament or of its creation concept as well as in addition to affix as a prelude to Global warming theory and that the main goal is to suffice with at least enough idea to meet the present needs or requirement to work passionately on this matter (**to lay down fundamentals of the theory with the purpose of** [defeating skeptics that works against] **mitigating global warming and that is saving or helping the earth's repel attraction coming from the sun**). And was it too early to assume that riches abound on this world will end up nothing if we will not contend this phenomenon? Or was it not surprising for Diderot, a French philosopher and writer, to assume that progress is doom to fail? Come to worst, one can tell to other or to ignorant person that a moral teaching's concern's only of the soul, and it is good and the right thing in the first place, but a not so correct teaching or a wrong fundamentals that neglects or taken for granted the essence of life or the mechanic of existence, say the nature as a whole, sure shares the responsibility of misleading the people or persons involve after all.*

Say the reformation initiated by Jesus of Nazarene that bid or cost His life was about blindly leading and following a not so correct teaching or fundamentals, may had unhappy but meaningful ending in a certain case at least, but the consequence, or should it comes to worst, blindly leading and following a certain belief that is contrary to nature creationism and this writing believed Jesus of Nazarene stands for, will lead us to nowhere or uncertain future leading to its death. And that is the tragic aspect or element of ignorance. In addition to Huxley's, "Nothing in this world is more dangerous than sincere ignorance and conscientious stupidity" says Martin Luther king Jr.

The great question would be that; if the body or biodiversity, or the planet's slowly heading dead, what would be the purpose of the essence of the noble deeds to the point of the comfort of the soul or the shot or the promises of life after death if no one in this world (or wherein the biggest congregation that promotes the essence of perpetual life) is concern and could live in the future? The pitfall could be that, rather, if the Theologian suggests that God doesn't interfere on the human affair because of the free will, then it is the people's duty to work for and help our self and save the planet.

Nevertheless, for God's generous, we can start a new one, say on the planet Mars and we can prove this notion and see on the planet Venus that must had been ended its biodiversity as it is apparent that temperature is unbearable, thus, no life exist. While the former is not surprising that we can view the same thing but uninhabited at this point in time, and the fact that the duo had an opposite atmospheric condition **[hot and cold]**, and these reflects of habitable planet Earth as it is rest or caught in between. In other words, rather, therefore life might have been originated, and that depending on its discipline, evolves and developed overtime, and this, if the planet atmospheric condition in particular, and the cosmic system in general, permitted, and could had been perished as it satisfied the contrary.

And in this case, I'll take this opportunity to reasess the **[earth]** planetary condition as to thwart the global warming saga or its mayhem attributed to this event in particular, in order to delay a presupposed event, or would be consequence, however can be view as nothing but a natural course to others. But nevertheless, and that global warming, sure will hyper the increment of planet's temperature, and like Venus, therefore commends the end of the biodiversity or life in the planet soon. In this case, a must see concept on Moon and Earth operation on the following or see Book 1 for additional input.

In this regard, by the race on space exploration in general, or by invading the planet Mars in particular, this treatise trying to believed is that advance or developed countries like the United States or countries alike of whom discovered, introduces the **[massive]** production and uses of petrol products and these at least works against the planet stability and existence or worst destroys the body in general aspect, may had the strong leads on this matter. Nevertheless, cutting corners or taking environment for granted will not solve the problem at this point or in this case, and that not to duplicate technical or mechanical lapses, or error on teaching or philosophy, or and not to decry the essence of nature, and that without any pride or compliment neither meant to brag, I wish to bring this idea with them in any planet they can find suitable for life and living. Apology is much better than possessing power for pride, may not be consider late *at this point, however, compensation or treatment shall be, if they started it not tomorrow but right now. In other words, **[developed]** countries shall unravel themselves from the liability of inducing global warming as explained entirely on this tenet, and the educational body, religion in particular, to reconsider the fact, nay, to recheck the idea or teaching that may **[indirectly]** compromise or advocates, rather invites the idea that may cause the trouble, specifically, may works against humanity, biodiversity and the planet existence. Insurance works on a certain case, but of course no one should sell defective products, or marketing devices beyond its capability to perform, is therefore a fraud.*

In this case, the author trying to convey is that no one shall be a hostage of a certain belief and or fear out of assumption, but to live in Love and Truth, of God and Nature which is the principle or fundamentals of living. Life is a memory recall. It is like a game of Chess, all but a comparison; the gambit and the witty stands last and survived.

INTRODUCTION 3

Einstein and Hawking and Sanches and Spinoza and or Celeste and Upton

To support and or compliment the above idea, fortunately, this writing provides the *Theory of Everything in general (and that idea is what we have observe on today such as body of galaxy), or literally (of what) a Fine Tune Universe" in particular. However we cannot discount the possibility that in earlier time sure a certain body went through a turbulent state before the nature provide us a better room for or of living [*see also Book 1 regarding the origin and or the creation of the universe, principle of operation and or existence as well as planet's natural phenomena]. In other words, is that in one hand, to uncover the truth scientifically, or the fact and or proof based on nature or natural circumstances that may satisfy one's expectation, and to provide a theory that will serve as universal model, wherein the goal is on adapting to the system of life such as philosophy, science, engineering discipline or medicine among other, as well as, rather, if these things differ from the course of nature or the natural sciences. On the other hand, propositions, or skeptics that were unable to produce material or empirical evidence, wherein this writing understand that is not [necessary] to give up a certain faith or knowledge and or belief, nevertheless, since Kate Upton "staring contest" will not change the "Reality" on the ground, specifically an adverse effect of global warming, one should have to bring into light, and that is on Arianny Celeste's "Submission" to what is not just essential, but perhaps we can consider as the Truth throughout.

And these are for the sake of unity and existence, for the common good or the welfare of the masses as well as the safety of the planet itself. The fact that even the great warrior falls on Celeste's category, mainly because in reality of the material world, is that life, or living is desirable than death, logic is advantageous than conjecture, even in a game of chance, more "suited" is favorable and that procure high stake, therefore the realism or reality must supersedes fiction.

The proposition's opened up the door or paved the way to an infinite idea wherein this writing tend to deliver and share the gist for some of great men from the past and present time does. And Albert Einstein in one hand, who said that "science comes first because only the discovery of the universe have lasting meaning," strove hard for the unification of the law of physics, while Stephen Hawking on the other, who said that "philosophy is dead" because He believes philosophers "have not kept up with modern development in science", which is, rather could be true in a certain aspect, however might be gross, if not an exaggerated statement from the later, this treatise could say, because this idea believed that science's thrive unless, rather, only after the philosophy has been established, nevertheless, do longing for the theory of everything to put forward which is the aim if not the passion of those great men as well as this writing. And in addition, the philosophy of Francisco Sanches of the methodology of knowing the truth and that leads in repulsion of Aristotle' doctrine, or the method of syllogism, as well as Baruch Spinoza of his view on ethics, trying to find its place in philosophical as well as in scientific arena.

INTRODUCTION 4

The Skeptics

Why Philosophy, (Quintessence) and why's the Theory of Everything? Or what constitute the essence of, rather, what is the significance of restructuring fundamentals that has been neglected by time? To be particular, with the shrewdness of ancient and renaissance philosophers and or scientists, and with the great advantage on the field and laboratories of the counterpart or contemporary personality at the present time, what we think of the missing link and that we are unable to produce a theory that will be consider a perfect model that may reflects the universal truth or its established fact.

*Basically, the skeptic or a sophist makes a wave on the ground of the following; rather, thrive at the time of inconsistency and ambiguousness, confusions and or feeble-mindedness, far-fetched ideas, dissension, antagonism and or ambivalence. And in addition, nay, let alone the "tawdriness" and "surreptitiousness". And this writing sorry for these words but we need to identify the consequence and or the reason or the truth behind the failure in our quest, and that the fact that we are indeed polarized couldn't be enough to describe the astounding force towards dissidence or against the maxim. The fact, rather according to A.W.R. Potter and H. Robinson, lecturer in geology and formerly head of Department of Geography and Geology, The Polytechnic Huddersfield and co-author of M and E Handbook titled Geology, said that **"It should be noted that there are many theories in the field but none of them is entirely satisfactory or meets all the objections which are put forward,"*** *of his comments regarding the origin of the earth and nature of the universe. Absolutely and unambiguously, this is the reality in the ground that we need to subdue. Specifically, a theory, methodology or practice that is considered to be without (**scientific**) foundation (**whether it subscribe or does conform to unknown truth**) is therefore (**considered**) an inference (**category**) to say the most, or pseudoscience and or hearsay or conjecture at least, or fairly, everything maybe treated as an assumption.*

*In this view, nevertheless, whether the subject matter is all mathematics, science or religion, regardless of circumstances, Philosophy is simply the method of discovering or knowing the Truth, and astoundingly, like any other method, through and or by means of Comparison (**No kidding, it is a blessing that most of the philosophers are polymath; mathematicians, physicists and medic, scientists or astronomer let alone a humorous person, and that "dodging" or "variation" on the subject is an advantage making the matter more interesting, otherwise working on these things would be "dry" and or "boring" and that, more likely to find men outnumbered by those coming from a cockpit arena or saloon. And who would love Philosophy alone in the first place, for most of the time it works counter to our passion, and your writing might be put on the list of those tenet no one love to read. And though Philosophy was defined as the love and pursuit of wisdom by intellectual means and moral self- discipline, and that knowledge, or the wisdom begot truth, and the truth sets us free. But in strict sense, rather, in fact, it requires great sacrifices, which means detaching oneself from "worldly matters", and in strict or a certain case limits our freedom of thought, expressions and deeds and that is not easy thing to do on this era. And on this matter, Hawking might be right on saying that Philosophy could be a thing of the past, but in fact to consider Philosophy as the fundamental of living is not just correct but an essence.***

Despite of the fact that prophets or philosophers lead a noble way of life, as much of their work, they are condemned persons and Jesus of Nazarene also called as Christ was one and the greatest of those; it was doleful and deplorable that He was despised by the authoritarian

church, of his own people, disciples and nearest of his kin because
these people opt to live in denials and that, however of the stern belief
and somehow the *safety [*from condemnation, excommunication or
face death to the grounds of treason-apostasy] and or pleasure of life).
In other words, and that the best of the philosophers or prophets' recognitions
and proliferations can get, is measured on how plausible and conspicuous
a Comparison or Measurement they labeled; It is the impact on the masses;
ingenuity or uniqueness, the validity or fact, value and or quality, and the
purpose and the applicability of a certain idea.

   Like the variation in an opening move of a board game Chess, and usually
that move was named after the (great) player of who's initiated, and get hold
on this as effective and successful way or technique against an opponent, the
"variant or variety of comparison and or measurement" may subscribe to any
other method available in the field, and that depend on the author experience
or upbringing, or their respective era, career or discipline, the educational
attainment and the degree of knowledge and intellectualism and that's true,
rather, sure a certain characteristic's manifest on someone's work. This writing
believed that it is, but should it be safe to claim for other that **[playing]** the
board game Chess is unique, and it is one of the perfect illustrative instance
of the realism of Philosophy? With the fact that Philosophy is applicable in
everyone or in all aspect of life, Method of Comparison may however depend on
one's discipline and that pledge or bind, but not limited to prophet's parables or
proverbs, or philosopher's figurative language, scientist's humorous statement,
nay, theory and experimentation, **[Socrates and Sanches]** method of deduction
or **[Aristotle]** syllogism approached and geometry or mathematics **[advanced**
by the like of Spinoza and Descartes]. Likewise, experiment or actual or
natural event, say on the book of John's Revelation, animals behavior like roaring
of a lion, the agility and swiftness of a horse or cheetah or the characteristic of a
snake, and while nature such as water and sunlight are some of those. And that,
whatever the circumstances and timeline can offer, is all for the sake of a certain
belief, or truth as the author see it, and that to impart wisdom, knowledge or
comprehension or to exercise full potential into one's own sublimity especially
on the younger or future generation. Thus, it is notable, that it was and it will
ever be the best thing's to study and acquired in life is the **(moral)** Philosophy.

At one point, it **(tend to)** *reveals oneself who they are, assess what they want, or the quality of one's life or contentment and the purpose of heading one's life. And the catch's that central idea share of one's trained thought, is surviving life with ease, say an aspiration of an aesthetics or comfortable life, to the point of facing death without the trouble or consternation, wherein this treatise believed to be the summit's purpose of a (noble) person. In other words, nay, this treatise believed that those who carried out this thing in a passionate way, the climax is very rewarding, to the point, rather, and that death for them is nothing, because as proven by the different account on books and personal testimony, or with the role of powerful mass media like movie, or say an ancient tenet and that in a way or another, sure inspired this writing. And that as I see it, purifies the Soul by the Holy Spirits or simply the reality or actuality of one's noble deeds, and it is notable that this "honorable work" feeds nourishment into one's soul [and* **as maintenance for a purified thought, Prayer among others, provides an essential nutrients for the soul that a body alone may not be able to produce]** *as the *sun or galaxy fuel with the purified gases to exist in the firmament [****citations on the following- creation of the universe or see Book 1 for additional input]***, and so the Soul is, "therefore thy desire's shall be done and thus, might live by thy will eternally". The aim or ultimate goal of a faithful or intellectual being [***or person's survival through the mind by the noble deed]***, and this was the case whom I'm trying to believed when the apostles asked Jesus of Nazareth also called as Christ, for a greater faith, and that quoted on Luke 17:6; "If you have faith as big as a mustard seed, you could say to this mulberry tree, 'Pull yourself up by the roots and plant yourself in the sea' and it will obey you." Likewise, stated on Matthew 10:28, Luke 12:2-7 and said "Do not be afraid of those who kill the body but cannot kill the soul; rather be afraid of God, who can destroy both body and soul in hell." In this regard, the author defined the word "Faith" as the *power of the believer [****the prowess of mind; though this gift might be obtain by any individual, however, uniqueness may differ or vary depending on the way of life or in particular, right from the start of conception which require the proper nutrients-nourishment and tenderness and care]***, in order **to do things [*****miracle; such as healing but then again through one's faith and will - brain regeneration or reinvigorating a higher level or degree of "wired brained component" triggering the point of cure therefore*** *healed - it is the power of mind of the able body and the essential {noble}* *deeds]* for ***God's glory *[***The truth, common good and or welfare of* *the masses-essence or significance of one or people's desire].* In this case, *therefore being Faithful is to unravel oneself from resentment and or guilt,* *and faith is the intelligence possess by an individual working against detestable* *things. Though religious connotation is undeniable, Faith is the intellectualism,* *or to be faithful is therefore being knowledgeable in literal aspect [see Book 1* *for additional input].*

INTRODUCTION 5

The Metaphysics

Quintessence basically sounds more logical in science and or metaphysics, if one considered these subjects as two different things. However, when talking about the nature of reality, or between mind and matter, substance and attribute and fact and value and these simply called Metaphysics. And the thought of Religion is something within, and it goes in parallel. Was it too early to pronounce that metaphysics or science and religion, and that depending on the degree of education or discipline, knowledge or comprehension or belief that divide each other, nevertheless in perfect harmony, as far as the affair in philosophy is involve? Likewise, would it violate or be unethical to consider something like a certain belief, or would be wrong to assume that Prophets were in fact the Philosopher, as well? Or being specific, was it not the one of whom we call Prophet of the ancient time is the Philosopher of today, or the other way around?

Philosophy in a sense's like a board game called Chess, or Checkers, it is a "game" of mind, and like archers and cue artists or golfers, when put into practice; the mind or its ability to adapt with the circumstances; the perception, say rationalism and that "discipline" in a sense complement on exemplar blood circulatory system, must be well defined or precisely coordinated with the force that is absolutely proportional with the factors; the wind, the angle and the quality of the surface and or accessories. And it is notable however, that we can however manipulate numbers or mathematics but Philosophy, that is really *well accounted. Too, we have to remember if not notable, and that however sluggish and sturdy, the fact that as early as first century Before Christ [BC], a civilization somehow, radiates in places like the North African country of today and flourished especially in (Western) Europe and that characterized with the shrewd writings of their great thinkers, and imbued us with the tangible and magnificent civil structure and that stand with the test of time and or nature. And in this case, gives this writing an idea that in a certain point of time, these are one of those, if not considered as the most ideal places to live and could be the main reason to inhabited by the early dwellers, thus it is not surprising to assume that a Creationism or its Philosophical attributes or History like the Genesis of the old testament begins, and that men from the past and future time, does is to fight for possession (of an ideal place to live) and one's advantage. Indeed, with the best experience or idea the early dwellers or emigrants had acquired, sure does include the topographic study of a prospective place(s) and that include the safety aspects, economic, the study of earth sciences, such as biodiversity, aquatic feature, botanical aspect, And wow, while one can think that earth's a paradise at the time, the geographic location that include the *earthquake free zone in particular [*due to uninterrupted or concentrated solar frequency, where in the Sun consider as the life-giving body or God; See the Moon, Earth and Global warming articles for additional input], were a vital aspect that a middle eastern race had been considered thus resides in this place. And in addition, nay, furthermore, Atomism theory in ancient time in which resembled the view of the present chemistry, surprisingly amazing but introduced as early as 4th century BC where in the application of scientific method is rare, or thinking and uses of such as conventional cell phone, was I believed may not yet a subject of discussion if not just a dream of a future.*

INTRODUCTION 6

Justice for Jesus of Nazarene and the Like of (Christ) the Reformist

Besides being consider as a prophet in some other religious congregation, to think that Jesus of Nazarene also called as the Jesus Christ, as indeed a Reformist is unequivocal thing or truth. The Crucifixion is in fact a daring "Experiment" to prove, to teach or share with His people of His acquired knowledge or wisdom that He believed is more valuable than the teaching of their ancestors, and that results or a success of this "experimental or innovation" expect from His people to carried out reform, and that is absolutely for their own good (sake), nothing more and nothing less. Specifically, the real reason, or the significance behind Christ's sacrifices was that to redeemed His people, the Israelites or the Jews from a possible backlash or condemnation for a great erroneous teaching and or belief.

If you are one of these personality, a devout Christian in general aspect, or in particular a layman, clergy or preacher, imagine yourself trapped in a ludicrous or compromising situation, and that is to learn that Jesus of Nazarene also called as Christ, was considered a pantheist person then, and with the best of the author knowledge and belief, though Jesus doesn't want to put a burden on his people (emotional and psychological anxiety on devotee, especially the radical and extremist believers) but a reformist that tend to affirm the what he thought a correct teaching, or specifically to defeat Anachronism, perhaps if not precisely a superfluous or "supernumerary theurgy". After an astounding hard time, everyone expect theodicy, but this is not to demean these people or religion

30

*and belief, but to share the Truth in everyone as Jesus of Nazarene did in the past, and tried to impart and prove the worth of the idea at all cost, thought against his own people's will and their staunch belief or devotion to the God of Israel and that is the God of Abraham, Isaac and Jacob, Christ own bloodline and royal ancestors. Christ is not asking for a total conversion but a slight, essential yet a very significant modification and perception and that is not to rely very much about a powerful, "magical", creationist nature of God and with, or literally for all of this, is for the people's survival (**or planet and biodiversity in general aspect; Blasphemy or profane utterance concerning God and sacred rights and entity, is sure not the author forte; however, thinking that a supernatural assistance would come to our aid in case of a great disaster, and that [therefore excessive belief that lead to disorientation and] disappointment, upon the destruction of the planet and death of inhabitants to be specific, is somehow the ancestor's excessive "Teaching or belief" could at least be held guilty or responsible or if not culpable in this case, therefore condemn. And this is the main reason that Jesus of Nazarene submit his own life on the cross in an anticipation and or to redeem his own people from the disgrace [or backlash from a not so correct teaching or excessive belief).***

*Correspondingly, theoretically Quintessence, in a sense, or literally on metaphysics, speaks out about the fifth of the elements of matter and the quartet namely; air, water, earth and fire. It goes with its definition as the pure, highly concentrated essence of a thing. Quintessence thought to be the substance (Temperature) of the heavenly bodies and latent in all things or in all form of matter. In this concept, it is analogous to Anaximander's "Apeiron," Empedocles' forces of Love and Strife, or Parmenides "The One," Anaxagoras' "Nous," and or Heraclitus "Logos." Perhaps it is most likely similar or tells more about the concept of "*Brahma" in India or Hinduism [*the holy or sacred power that is the source and sustainer of the universe], and this writing couldn't be problematic, rather, it is a great relief if the God in Exodus 3:14 of the Christian holy bible, the Old testament, wherein, God said to Moses, "I Am Who I Am," speaks out of the same notion or element, unfortunately, holds not, as the Theists' believed. However this writing holds on to this principle, saying; "to know one's flesh is to cut through it" thus, opened up the idea that this may be the reason* *or concern of Jesus of Nazarene, also called as Christ, that stands on His own, and with his superb intellectual ability brazed the death to prove His *point* **[*additional input in Book 1- The Original Sin against The Greatest of the Sin]**. *And that, this treatise firmly believed, in one point, though preponderance, ideal and *applicable [****applicability's universal, generative and in strict sense without time constraint is the reason of its existence all around the globe; the fact that he emphasized the essence of a moral deed, specifically the value of their ancestor's noble deed, he underlined however the significance of scientific knowledge. Nevertheless, with all the knowledge and belief of this tenet, it is poignant that it was, or the core of the idea was misinterpreted by the very believer of the church]***, *morally principled, sublimed, promotes* **[gender]** *equality and rationalism and adheres to logical reason such as obtaining proper education among others, yet, His "Rhetoric Idea" to tell it honestly and straight forward, considering the circumstances or elements therein; tenacious or obstinacy, stern and or disdainful mentality, spontaneous feeling and or lynch or tumultuous mob and more serious concern is being belligerent mentality, which seems to be immanent and perdurable, was a *Conceited view or notion at the time. And that means, most advance and or scientific, if not a farfetched idea to a commoner and that reflects that Jesus was indeed an "erudite and or knowledgeable" person* **[that might be acquired from other culture or civilization through migration or traveling and learning from another country such as Greece and Egypt and most probably Turkey, where in John the Beloved, of whom He entrusted Mary, his mother settled in, after the crucifixion (adlib: the later scene depicts, that Jesus Christ has no extended family to cling to or close relatives to rely on. In other words, rather in addition, to brave the death, this treatise understood that besides John the Beloved, Jesus is unlikely to have a wife or close relatives that may add to His emotional burden when carried out the trial or experimentation of death through the cross in order to prove life after, that may, rather therefore fulfill and or bust Israeli culture of "superflousness or excessiveness"), or had been to others places such Europe or Rome in particular, where in civilization's thriving at that era; though self-mastery or read up works are not discounted. In strict sense however, rather in second thought, locally educated and that without the personal experience or knowledge** *of reliable information or any other method of comparison regarding a certain culture and or tradition, is difficult to discern whether such teaching or belief is indeed correct, ideal or factual, applicable and morally principled. His work on healing and miracle save him from being labeled as wind talker]* or "highly" educated one, and or no doubt a super intellectual person to the point that He was perceived as the *Son of a living God mainly because of His extra ordinary abilities (*son of a living God is a phrase used to described an entity or a person and that person is above the norm; appraisal or hype expression; rational, noble, divine, generous or intellectual; exaggerated as it used informal such as joke to "play" with someone who does a noble and or unexpected heroism).* Or on the other view, though the essence's unequivocal, the significance of His idea's promulgation's too early to release at that point, or one should say it is the wrong place and at the wrong time. Nevertheless, since it's His point in time, and the fact that a new teaching was indeed necessary, or in particular social reform was invited if not demanded by the circumstances, thus, His turn on that era therefore takes place. And the irony, rather, fortunately or coincidentally fulfilled the presumption of the preceding thinkers or the ancestral Prophets that, too, like Jesus of Nazarene longing for social reform, and that faithful prophet's divination has carried out with high accuracy or precision.

Studying history or philosophy's great question would be that; though He wasn't the first, wasn't Jesus of Nazarene, also called as Christ's the greatest of the philosopher, reformist and humanist, or prophet to the point of considering the son of God because of His greatness and peculiarity, that had ever written. And that, in a sense, rather, somehow and someway holds, or reflects also of that *pantheism belief [*citation's shortly on the following]* wherein, on His time considered guilty as the Atheist person leading into His crucifixion and death?, Based on actual events, preceding Seer, that somehow concern with the "environment" or a certain teaching, the law in particular, could had been prophecies those things attributed to the coming of Jesus of Nazarene also called as Christ.

In one point, though may not be absolutely the same, one, or can we tell a parallelism on Socrates fate, a Greek ancient philosopher c.469 BC – 399

*BC who was tried for defying the Greek gods in pursuit of goodness and [**that**] corrupting the minds of Athenian youth by his attempt to improve the sense of justice, and that irritated some people and subsequently put him to death by [**administering**] poison. And in this case, according to Robin Waterfield [**Why Socrates Died: Dispelling the Myths**], Socrates was a voluntary *scapegoat [****a must see All But the World is Loving ISBN 9781434983824 or Book 1: The reason of the death of Christ in the Ultimate Theory on Global Warming article**]; His death in one hand, was the purifying remedy for Athens misfortunes, and a *token [****a rooster**] of appreciation for Asclepius, the Greek god for curing illness, would represent a cure for the ailment of Athens [**source: Wikipedia/ American heritage Dictionary**] and that is Athenians belief on mythological god.*

*While on the other hand, Jesus of Nazareth who was condemned by His fellowmen, and suffered at the hands of Roman soldiers and died on the cross speaks out of absolutely the same thing for Israelites. Prior to crucifixion, given a brief view of Jesus trial, it is logical that Herod and Pilate found that He was not guilty of any crime. The former treated Jesus with contempt, wherein the later found Jesus of Nazarene of much a lesser offense than death penalty as demanded by His own people [**In a modern court trial, accused or accusation of blasphemy could be improbable lest is hard to prove by the authority then except of course from the jury of the fury of tumultuous mob or lynching that happens in or at any point of time. Jesus Christ were most probably guilty of usurpation of authority's premises or property by teaching in the synagogue without the authority's approval at least, and inciting sedition at most as Jesus ensnare on a hyperbole statement written on Luke 12:51-53 and Matthew 10:34-36 that says; "He come not to bring peace but a sword and that He will set division among them", and this, the author understands that a 'speaker mean this figure' as a result of dissenting opinion from initiating reform out of stern and tenacious belief – we have to be very clear that Jesus of Nazarene would like to impart "perpetual knowledge" leading to law reformation, and that with his unique intelligence or faith, bid his life to prove things right as he saw it, or as he knew its essential to humankind and will save the face of Israel from a possible world's**]* condemnation at least, or retaliation at most and worst, once the Truth or the concept of true teaching of "God" takes place; believe on these thing for one may have the comfort of the soul, and "courage and Intelligence – the faith", may procure or pave the way for the life after death. These aspect is through the noble deeds; while the former is an open ended opportunity for everyone, say, every soul can obtain the gift without any discrimination, the life after death chance's dim for it requires the "greater faith", {this was make the apostle's sad} but as He said, do not lose hope but try your very best or acquire faith which leads one's noble deed as it deem necessary for the soul to procure life or resurrection]. Nevertheless, on crucifixion, it was preposterous if not a blatant misjudgment setting Barabbas, a tumult and a murderer, free, in lay of Him. The tawdry scene is not just a concern, rather in fact reflects a negative aspect of human nature especially on these places. But the "calibrated" concealment of fact or *cover up in between the faculty of Jews and Romans [*note from the author that if the notion is in fact the truth actually, Jesus Christ was correct that in strict sense, somehow they share the responsibility or they might be liable of the nature's future consequence or effect, thus initiates reform. And thought to be great but not really strange, that the misjudgment over the natural habitat or scientific shortcoming that leads to global warming phenomenon is one, yet a serious concern, that will be added, whether you like it or not, to your liabilities thus another burden, as well as a liabilities and a burden to those who's belief was pattern in yours; with that great magnitude of not so correct teaching or mendacity to say the least, according to Samuel Foote "He is not only dull in himself, but cause dullness in others".

What this writing can or is trying to say is that to commit mistakes is purely human traits, and to correct this is a civilized manner. In other words, if we indulge our self with the teaching that doesn't exist, it not just impedes the educational progress, rather invites shortcoming and failure, but a chronic psychological defect, and that logically compromise morality, and definitely, rather, in a certain aspect the moral principle could be problematic. In this case think of the fate of ancient Greek philosopher named Socrates, then the so *called Prophets, as well as Jesus of Nazarene also called as Christ of the Old and New Testament respectively, then the French Doctor Nostradamus, the Italian Astronomer named Galileo Galilei, and or the Dutch Philosopher named Baruch Spinoza among other, and that authorities then eliminated these personalities as an option or opted for an "easy way out" rather than embracing the fact, not knowing that when it comes to Nature, taking for granted or cutting corners, lest negligence is the most dangerous path the human could take.*

This notion's desire's an eye opener and might be if not sure unpleasant, and that "feigning" could be applicable then, but on this era breaking rules to gain an advantage, misleading, deceiving or cheating cannot overrule the Truth and the Fact. Specifically in my country, The Philippines, and that it takes more than a hundred islands to learn that we had been subdivided by water, which is a fact, could had been unfolded at the time of the assumed national hero named Jose Rizal, thus, might dodge the consequence or fury brought out by natural calamities, this as a result of reliable education or information regarding the essence of nature. But unfortunately the helpless reformist was sentence to death by firing squad. And who's to blame of such lapses, or just simply charge it to the experience of ignorance, and men, just ignore it? Thus nature (of experience) require us men to be properly educated because "backwardness" not just divide men (psychologically, from pressure or tension to affiliate into [a much "stronger"] organization and a way beneficial to a person in a certain aspect or interest to the point of one's survival. In this case [restriction], the social life of the youth suffers most. And indeed their future or life sure will be compromise on nature recourse. Outdated teaching (that hinder or restrict the social norm) paves the way for a (young) reformist, and wrong concept of that idea begets a rebel one), but a very dangerous trait as far as human existence is concern. Backwardness couldn't be problematic if those men are not feeling insecure. They can live and die into their believing as long as they bothered no one, rather as long as they attuned to the demand of a civilized world or adhere to the rule of law. Unless noble men alter its course, things will go as what it indicated. And as this writing see it, war is imminent and looming and they are grooming it. This is in addition to the greater threat of global warming or intense nature cataclysm, wherein scientific education or essential knowledge in defense of the danger, is the threshold of the very survival of planet and humanity. In other words, or in totality, stamping out backwardness and that leads into planet rehabilitation are all cure of the menaces. Malala's demand for education is indeed correct in this case.

What this writing believed is that in one hand, Jesus of Nazarene, also called as Christ, was denied by his own people and crucified to death, and this holds or keep the old believing and teaching or law intact; on the other hand, religions or belief that fundamentals are dependent on the old teaching of His people were consider him as either a great Prophet to the point that he was the son of the living God, and this accolade, compliment and commended that "Old" believing, teaching and or law. In a sense if not unequivocally the truth of the matter, depicts therefore the Anti-Christ. And Jesus of Nazarene instituted or promulgated a new teaching that he knew then is the essence of the present time. It is not that bad or there is no harm to insist and or practice the orthodox belief, but to be an Anti-Christ which is against the essence of a new teaching (that project the essence of nature) is a different thing, because the trouble started when this matter of belief compromise the physical aspect of human survival and planetary existence and nature or biodiversity in general form. And this writing concludes that taking nature for granted is that it shall work counter to all of us and we are all loser in this case. And this writing believed that this is the idea that John the Beloved, considered in here as the Vicar of Christ, unfolded on his Book of Revelation; the true aspect of God as described and justified on the theory of Quintessence [later on this part]; fearing for their safety, leave their beloved hometown called Jerusalem, but still His passion to write and promulgate His "vision" has been carried out. And this writing's concerned, is like literally playing with fire if not working on inside the Lion's den. I'm writing this thing on Jesus of Nazarene 2013 birthday and was it a coincidence that John the Beloved prophecies the author and the idea of this Tenet on His Book of Revelation, and so Nostradamus on his Century of where the author would came from. And if so doing, that indeed this is the Truth, please help this writing o' God.

And this treatise pleads to my love one in the Church, please do not wait to see that men weakens or taken down one by one by the natural disasters and war. Nature disasters that happens almost every day prove things out; air upheavals were pungent, earthquakes were violent and there's a fire everywhere, nowadays rains were severe and there's a great intrusion of water such as floods, and or tsunamis. There's a fire in every heart of mankind and the war could be imminent, in Jerusalem? All the entities are becoming common and continue to thrive, and literally a great fire could be a serious concern in the future. In fact, weather disasters occur almost daily or more frequently. Can't we comprehend, rather, was it an obliviousness, and that even in the very beginning of the history of the earlier civilization, the pagans (in the Americans) and or gentiles as well as those people imprinted on the Holy Book, attended to nature by pleasing it with "sacrifices" (of course not necessary to relive or carried out these rituals on this point of time) to the point that, nay, it is because they attributed nature repercussion to their sins. Specifically the unregulated sex or sexual perverts, thus initiated reform by the method of literal circumcision of genital as to decrease the manifestation of sexual drive or libido, and this as birth or population control in order to minimize "collateral damages"- In this case, Social Science indicates that uncivilized people, men are promiscuous thus circumcised, and women are frail and "sick" (and to learn that in some culture women undergoes female genital mutilation is deplorable if not disgusting), therefore live under the rule of men, and they prefer or opted for a comfortable life, where in retard by heavy population. This, in addition of being prone or expose to natural calamity and that case might claim numerous lives thus sorry for outrageous sexual potency therefore offers sacrifices and fast, which is, rather somehow correct in this case. However, Jesus of Nazarene tried to evaluate and or modified these things and He said on John 6:63 that "it is the Spirit that gives life, flesh offers nothing". And these treatise's literal interpretation is *that it is the essence of logical reason against the desire of flesh or sexual enthuse in particular, which is the *cause and or triumph of sins of the old teaching* [Genesis' Old Testament depicts that the pervert sexual manner of men gives trouble on upbringing the community and that sex is the original or reason of sin and hard time as well as the cause of death; these philosophy were 500 years apart], *and that to correct or counter, Jesus of Nazarene promotes rational thinking, to the point of proving the prowess of mind or intellect by Faith or Spiritual healing – intellectualism and or moral philosophy's education and or discipline. This treatise were learned and never surprise that an anti- Semitics remarks were said that Semites are greedy and sly, and as far as this treatise is concern, mainly because unaware, they actually work ahead with the nature, and that is brotherhood's survival* {thus developed the attitude of being on top of the other and that depicts a "first born child or son mentality" {{mean, proud and or superior over the other and with that is the emotional and psychological aspect, that most probably because of the existing and continued threat on their people and sovereignty and or rooted from the atrocities they had been through or suffered, and that because, as this writing see it, literally they, or their race could had been weak, compare to meanest neighborhood}}, *and that means to acquire the first and or of the great share of the harvest or graces, or the first in line to the throne or heir}, and in this case, on a "different approach or perspective" which is, rather, could had been applicable and effective in a certain way of life, whether it is the culture, places and on a particular era, and that makes the difference compare to what we believe today by means of a more advance method and technology. To work with things or to comply with nature without the auspicious of God is saddening, if not too harsh to us believers, but to come out on idea like this, is to have a trained eye is not enough to say, but one's desire and will to "change the atmosphere", which is in corroboration if not complimented with what was written; and that faith or believing to a new teaching is like "buying a land without owning it", or giving a good account for oneself without expecting interest or reward and that to help yourself, or to "knock someone's door for you to open", is the same as to give oneself for war for their beloved country, is a plain motivation and concrete model, and is synonymous on giving up the ghost or get rid of anxiety* *and that is to face one's work and give way to the Fact or Reality. And we wish well on working on this matter without compromising Spiritual aspect or any abstract idea that we ought to believe to guide us in an honorable or noble way of life and its magnanimity. Nevertheless, though the core of the idea may offend others, but the sole purpose of this writing in this case is that in behalf of the Truth, to get rid of any excuses and that to understand that Nature's govern us is in fact the reality of our existence. And to comprehend on its manner is for the welfare of the biodiversity and common good specifically. This treatise understand, that mostly those people that enjoys the wealth or product but in expense of nature, and those who live by the law and or book or religion is the first to cry foul and most likely to shun this calling which is true in all the reformist's account of suffering, in all of the time, from the past as well as the present does. One can challenge the idea, as Jesus Christ did in the past, and He said that, "I didn't come to abolish the Law, but to fulfill it", yet, no one is sure to what does it takes, or how much degree of suffering may incurs, for us to allow changes. The world suffers the brunt of nature cataclysm; typhoon {Haiyan or Yolanda – world strongest 2013} in Philippines, Asian tsunami on 2004 and earthquakes and flooding as well as drought. Jesus Christ set up reform according to the present need or circumstances. Life's change, or nothing endures but change, but the Truth is in fact Consistent, therefore anyone who works against, this treatise assure, and that will suffer the consequence in the future at their intended time as control by the "Quintessence"(see the Quintessence's theory on the following). What we sowed is what we would reap in the future, and whatever will be will be as a reward or consequence of someone's deed [accumulated karma], and some factor of losses can be attributed to a wrong belief or principles and that will leads to erroneous, injustice or inadequate action, let alone the self-interest if these things are differ from one another. See also Book 1, The Earth, The Global Warming and The Revelation and the Black Hole Theory for additional input]. And their much devotion protecting one's "legacy" was troubling that it may serve as a precedent or simply of a political motivation, one way or the other, and that pleasing the crowd in return for their support and cooperation, while the other party is of protecting the interest and or belief.*

*Furthermore, if not had been dodged or averted, almost the same fate of that Aristotle 384 BC-322 BC, a Greek philosopher and polymath [**a student of Plato and teacher of Alexander the Great**], might had suffer. And a reference to Athens's prior trial and execution of Aristotle said: "I will not allow the Athenians to sin twice against Philosophy". A little more of this, well resembling the history or event, *John the Beloved also called as the Evangelist, and the Divine, and in here, He was assumed that he was indeed the greatest of the apostles of Christ, in addition to being the youngest, the most trusted, the intelligent, and the celibate one among other. With Mary, the mother of Jesus Christ of whom He entrusted to him (John) then move to Ephesus, the Asia Minor or in the present day Western Turkey, most probably to avoid and or evade the authority in Jerusalem. And that besides evangelization, the *vexatious theme {*an experienced or learned, scientific, yet an introduction to a (semi) pantheist view of future things or the divination with the view or sentiment of anti-Semitics, and like others, that sure be scrutinized thus, migration to other place is a clear contingency plan and measure} of John's writing especially of the Book of Revelation, could be one of the serious concern; This thing give this writing a hint, and that, if their migration was pre-arranged, and that was before the **actual crucifixion <continuation shortly> (**citation; the whole theme of this event was the institution of Jesus Christ's Church, and that since John the Beloved fully comprehended and adopted well on Christ idea, therefore consider on this treatise as the Vicar of Christ, the greatest reformer and founder of church and religion; As this treatise see a not so correct interpretation regarding "Peter the Rock" on the bible of the New Testament, and that, with my all my knowledge and belief, wherein the "Rock" is in fact the "Rome" itself with the church foundation built on John the Beloved's concept {In saying this, rather in addition, with the experience in the Middle East, and the way that Jesus of Nazarene ***emphasized [***characterized by harsh and or hyper words], the essence of family or against divorce in particular, gender equality and or women empowerment and moral values, and that, nay, nevertheless, missing or deleted "key" or essential* *text in the Bible could had been shaded or shadowed the probability of the fact that Mama Mary, the mother of Jesus was more likely to be a widow, or a divorced mother of one, if not her husband Saint Joseph, and that aside from them may have another family and or both, or at least the variance within these scenes, holds the possibility, and this scroll, or this assumption hope not bother the believer or advocates of monogamy or church, but only for history's sake and that the fact that this culture still exist in a community or country that was pattern to this costume, supports this claim or somehow does conclude some literal aspect of the history in the bible}).*

Interesting indeed, but the great questions were; why uses a Figurative Language and a delegation to Saint Peter, these, in addition to why the church {or school} to be set up in Rome? With the corroborative account in the Bible, reasons could be one or might be the total of the following; First, besides that "figurative language" provokes thought, stimulating, challenging and exciting, it (figurative language) used to conceal things, and this set to be a cover up thus proceed with the plans and denied or mislead the authority of scrutinizing them therefore evades the hostile situation, or it because that the people in Jerusalem would not allow Jesus of Nazarene to set His church, or not actually a church alone but a school of Thought or Religion, likewise, Philosophy or Law and Science or Medicine as in *Faith Healing (*Intellectual - Medicinal practice or healing is depending on the degree of a person ability and that is through Faithfulness or Intelligence among other; as we can conclude Europeans expand its empire for education as business then, and now business as education. And the concept and potential of the system's application is so great that a celebrated preachers, author or spiritual advisers, religions and or with the concept on non-religion base organization, or education in general aspect's wealth sure owes a royalty to Jesus of Nazarene then, if not to the Catholic church with John the Beloved's concept on today), and that will teach the essence of life and mind, would frustrate a might be attempt to stop them from so doing for the very main reason and that was to compromise the Jewish belief and or the ratification of the law to be specific therefore

Romans might destroys synagogue. Second, a delegation to Peter most probably because John the Beloved though faithful or intelligent, was inexperience, sure too young and tender and the side plan to take care of Jesus' mother, Maria is one of those. Third, Peter struggle but pursue the plan of evangelization (in Europe which is more liberal and or educated, could be funded by the donation from the Jewish community right there and somehow in Israel who was convinced and or believe in his teaching and or wanted the reform), and the reason why stays in Rome in the first place, it's clear that people migrated to other places or country because of economic, social norm and or unrest.

Another thing was that neither Herod nor Pilate condemned Jesus, wherein fact, the former was pleased of him and sure believed and or convinced them of Jesus' work and concern that they become "friends" right at the time of trial is another. And one can sense the potential of a business in a learning institution that is unparalleled in here in addition or simply another thing. Fifth and or last but not least, was that to set up the church in Jerusalem is like setting up church in Saudi Arabia (It is "a blow on the moon" but it is not that impossible; Saudi's in fact a benevolent people and we see a great transformation on them working hard against impartiality; for not all of us can afford to go to other Christian country, this writing wish from them is to reconsider and allows us Christians to have a church or a monastery built even in remote area or places of their choice [Church and Priest are important to us Catholic so as the Mosque and Imam to our Muslim brothers. Bible or Koran should be preached by those who have the authority or regulated and commissioned by the hierarchy of this religion and that "exploitation of belief" in any form must be protected by the church, thus carried out amendment therefore self-corrected - Preachers from any congregation has the great responsibility to correct doubtful writings then; specifically a certain passages on Koran that says it is justifiable for the believers to kill the infidels, or the radical interpretation of the word "jihad", or to make peace not to unbelievers are some of those, wherein this writing believes a purely human thought or emotion against a devious character and threat (from a disgruntled or disappointed view- an Arab or cultural speakers or wording has a different connotation from the rest of the continent as far as their uses or choices of vocabulary, depending or varied on occasion, is concern - say figurative, strong and abrupt in sense. And the pitfall is that words can be interpreted differently in different region. We have to note that even the most beautiful law provision that had been drafted now and then, would or could had been amended by a brilliant reformist to suit on the current generation preferences and betterment, thus Old Testament beget the New Testament, and begets different interpretations (Saint Jame's version, Christian Science, Church of Christ) from different scholars leading to the creations of thousands of religion. And hoping for the rightful one may had been unfolded on this case. The horses used to tilt the field then, but now carried out by the big boy's toy. Things changed and changed happens), **troubling the Muslims and the world today]. Nevertheless, carried out pilgrims on at least Christian designated or accepted holiday like Christmas is the greatest gift we could have from the {holy} land, we expat consider as {second} home; local or domestic tourist benefits local merchants thus contributes on domestic growth. But the catch's or the essence and that Muslim believe in God and so do Christians are, it is trouncing, rather, this writing suggest why we don't cut our losses or set aside pride for we share a common values and this we can express the beauty aspect of religion in full potential and that is, as far as one's belief and security are concern, possess no harm at all. And peace as bequeath to mankind by God, the ultimate goal speaks about co-existence and love.)" And the reason that Jesus of Nazarene could, or one of those that has been mesmerized by the Rome could had showed interest on Italian's great thinker like Lucretius the Poet, ca.99 BC, the author of the poem "On the Nature of Things". Indeed, this place or Italy in particular, is a home of not just the intellectual and brilliant artists, but also of the beauty of fashion and the passion of love and romance. But don't forget England where the money is, and go to France to have some fun, said Hagar the Viking.**

Furthermore, aside from nature consequence (say inclination, nay, the more believing in something we can't prove [and that assumed that will save us from cataclysm], the more we compromise the safety of

the planet and inhabitants), what would be the essence on the lateral transfer of Peter the Apostle designation's to John the Beloved? Well in a personal perspective, with the veracity of this discovery [decoded the writings on the testament the author believed] or proposition, with the old law or teaching, it may turn out to be a little uncomfortable to the former to stay in post, say for "delicadeza"– and this is dare to say of church's "aggiornamento" or upgrading to a transparent, faithful, focus and better services. And that include the massive demonstration against the global warming and its consequence, which is clearly depicted, as far as the author is concern, rather, as this writing see it on John's Church concept or his writing. Was it not the idea or reason on several occasions, and that for they cannot accept the New Teaching; we have to note that there was a point on Jesus of Nazarene's time that except of the apostles, all of his disciple turn their back from Him (and the should be account or text of this event in the Bible's New Testament is the author really missing for, wherein experience on sharing this concept to the community, and that, after finding the idea's probability or its presumption, turn a happy atmosphere into a gloomy one which reflects of the same scenario then). And in another, according to Him, superseding the old believing, or Law, Matthew 5:17 is not the whole thing but it is the fulfillment. And in a certain occasion, He speak of the parable of a "New Wine" that is inappropriate to put on in an "Old Wine's Skin" simply for the reason that the scientific fact of today will work not against outdated teaching, because what it's on stake is the very existence of humanity. ({Christ} figurative language make the conversation more interesting, nevertheless, the phrase above in particular, depicts and that while the true fundamental remain to be the central idea, recent scientific time is a contemporarily of modern law). **With spurious or false-hearted thing and that alone could be a ground for the loss of courage and confidence of the faithful to the church or religion? today; for this treatise hope for the better, therefore one could work hard not to wait or reach the tripping and or flash point {In this proposition, Pope Benedict XVI on His resignation is not a faultiness, this treatise could say, only or perhaps, rather, perhaps or only the fundamentalist isn't that brave enough to implement reform, I suspect. And the question that on what's right do this treatise in to demand reform, is that as a/we Filipino Catholic**

working overseas, is/are on the frontline particularly in the middle east, and being a citizen of this world, is on the battle zone against the nature upheavals specially in the Philippines. The church in this case should reconsider Catholic in particular, and Christians around the world in general of its contributions on its progress, thus this treatise firmly believe of its right to demand reform for its own good, welfare and or safety through the acquisition of essential and indispensable, and that is the "inexorable perpetual knowledge" of nature as well as religion which concern the comfort of one's soul and for the most faithful of a shot of life after death; With this aspect, I love to see my church initiating reform and that is making no room or excuses to someone else's or congregation of exploitation, say in expense if not taking advantage of those "widows and or weak citizen of the society" and that makes preacher or "politicians" that those who gain power out of the support of religion, holds a comfortable life in exchange of those who persevere in the name of religion and in believing God. And this is the tipping point; to gain sympathy upon denying the truth of the subject matter, skeptics and churchmen alike (specifically in Jesus time and resemble of the like of Greek philosopher Socrates), might accuses this writing of an atheistic belief, wherein to revise or fulfill the law from the apparent manifestation of social injustice tainted and or severed by corruption, are just another weak excuses against the authority, of whom, rather, which is or was taken for granted now and then due to (author) pure philosophical context (that may weakens religious position), law and or inclination to religious subject matter and which is, nay, this mean a poor technical or scientific knowhow and or lapses from the society lest the authority itself (that cover up a certain interest). Specifically, while knowledge of science medicinal practice or faith healing in the church is very particular, ethics or values can be obtain of either way of teaching, conventional or scientific, wherein science or scientist somehow had different approach and or concept. Nevertheless, in reality in the world, both concept subscribe in one truth thus can consider as one. But we have to note that things are different on today. We have different perspective on our present time, thus distinct and definite approach. We have to join hands and work really hard and determined to establish the truth and its manifestation because ours, human being and biodiversity's safety or existence, and existence and safety of our planet are at stake, if not totally at risk.

This writing believed, and that though a lot of people represent and advocate this idea, the problem lies on the incompetent authority when the politics and self-interest takes place. And that is when institution that protects and secure the right of an individual, stand loose guard when the safety and or career is concern and or might be compromise. In other words, building up culture that is hard to resist, and that tend people to become a hypocrite for survival (at least a separate state of church and religion – while the natural calamity is to survive people with the government affair, religion is to decry people for their small faith that beget the nature upheaval as punishment), and or other make a living out it, and or worst is extremist's willing to sacrifice their life for their believing, can only be counter if someone is willing to risk the same thing. And the sad thing is that the later leads to losses not just because of the fear of their life and or the extremist, but on a much stubborn thing called "psychological hostage". And on this matter, I would like to echo once again Martin Luther King Jr. and that he said, "Nothing in the world is more dangerous than sincere ignorance and conscientious stupidity."

With all the knowledge we have, the advance technology and the keen scientific investigation of fact, are we with, or familiar with the saying that "it is better for you to have one man die for the people, instead of the whole nation destroyed?"; a pro-Semitic remark or a simple denial of truth or just a plain selfishness which is common to a ruler that knows may sacrifice the way of living and belief of his people?

In contrast with what the former United States President George W. Bush said in the past that he can't compromise the American way of life, is indeed we must not, but the way the circumstances of global warming goes, or doing nothing to offset the consequence of nature catastrophe in particular, is he does. We should learn from the items 7th, 11th and 12th of the 21's L. Ron Hubbard's moral code that says "Seek to live with the

Truth; do not harm a person of good will and safeguard and improve your environment." And nevertheless, we can conclude that these people that work against this idea could be liable of the consequence or danger of nature, and that compromising oneself upon denying the truth that resulted from the so called " forced or in purposed" ignorance, as Huxley said "is not just a blunder but a crime".

Can you relate, rather, this claim or proposition is no strange when it comes on mitigating global warming phenomenon, unless that inhabitant or everyone in this planet {such as religion or church, much more of the oil producer, scientist or geologist and cosmologist among other, western dweller or developed countries and [individual] economics}, concede, the fight against it is not just great, tough and a hard one, but extremely difficult to carried out. And unfortunately, nay, the truth on this writing, according to one reader's report of Book1, could be the truth throughout, thus this idea hope and expect from the authority and individual of either science and religion that matters on this subject, is to investigate the veracity of this claim, and should find out an essence, however hard to implement, hope to refute not but adopt and carried out the necessary measure instead, and or carried out alternative in order to prevent further damage and suffering from nature catastrophe and or to avert unrest such as war. Pride, self-interest, ignorance, devotion and or extremism and economic downfall and or emotional distress, might however painful and dangerous to tackle, but learning to know the truth and love of the essence of nature is no threat to any entities but another or a certain knowledge of human survival and existence.

In saying this is to imagine how vast the idea is on this treatise, thinking that, besides being German nationals, Martin Luther the reformist, Hitler the nationalist (however his character tainted with the extreme fascism and infamous with the holocaust which was as this writing saw it, a radical or an extreme advocate of Christ's idea of Socialism. And this treatise conclude that as he found an obstinate Jew's attitude, his [socialist] idea was to protect his people [from being *rated as second class citizen to migrant Jews and held hostage {psychological, political and or economic} in which had, this treatise believed a questionable belief to Hitler himself, where in the Christian teaching now and then, is in strict sense and surprisingly the socialist form of government on today, and one can consider Hitler is the most notorious crusader of the history so far],* **and in a way or in a sense, is to serve justice to Jesus of Nazarene as well. And it got what it takes for someone to be nailed down and that is against the fundamentalism or the greatest extent of theism, where in, depending on the degree of the truth they had uncover and share, Jesus Christ and the trio of character mentioned above, and the like of the advocates suffers the same fate. And with Jesus of Nazarene, these people share a great role in the history of the world, being a Christian or a reformist. And Christianity simply means reformation wherein this personalities stands on their principle and that, as this treatise saw it, is for the good of their people, and perhaps the idea is for the good of the people all around the world.**

And the "disappointment" toward a certain goal might be the reason of a precarious or precept, risky and drastic decision. And before condemning a person, the question would that be, if the reformist deserves only to die in a cross in lay on up keeping a covenant with a flawed philosophy and belief? And knowing this perception begets a question if the Germans in particular, are affable and or impatient of silly things, and that reflects of one's intelligence that decries affectation? One can tell a mean person, but were the most intelligent the Germans or the French? (Angela Merkel for instance is doing a great job that no one or never in the history of women did in the past). Should we say Religion in the absence of technical or scientific aspect then, or the other way around, and that could be more significant, which is the current trend on technical and scientific perspective with the morally principled, and that was taught by religion on today?}. However in this case, as the English mathematician, philosopher and noble laureate Bertrand Russell, 1872- 1970 said, "It is undesirable to believe a proposition when there is no ground whatever for supposing it true".

And the really great questions are; is your church's an advocate of Truth? The Truth that Jesus of Nazarene would like on his people and the world to uncover and set up free? In this case, will someone opt for a Theism belief that makes us unjustifiable and in strict sense, insecure? All along, the negligence's of the essence of nature that is in fact destroys the earth? Or over someone that care for Jesus of Nazarene, where this writing firmly believed, and that though the Pantheist overtones present, nevertheless, credence and certainty that advocates the essence of life, the love, the truth of nature and the comfort of one's soul's the way out of this troubled world? And through John the Beloved, the idea of Quintessence that promotes co-existence or equilibrium which is the fundamental of perpetual life would make the circuits complete? In this case it is apparent, nay, your response is where the panacea or trouble came from, and who the culprits that make us unrest. Make peace therefore my friend [see also Book 1 for additional input]– The idea on how the Jerusalem would have lasting and meaningful peace, is to set it free and become the third and neutral place or city along, rather, that go-between Palestine and Israel state. Sure it will avert a great war.

In Book 1, Faith or *faithfulness defined as the intelligence [*focus, deep penetrating enhancing; in other hand, nay in contrast, that is to believe in things you cannot prove or see is a blind faith], and that is the prowess of mind or the power of a person with the spiritual or religious overtone and that said in one hand to advocate noble things and repel evil deed on the other is the sole way to obtain. This writing's mean is that existence or reality applies to what matter or has life and or being, however the comfort of the soul and or life after death that could be obtain through noble works is what the church promotes and that is Morality. And realism, rather, to accept the reality of nature as a part of one's life's not a frailty trait or feebleness in human thought or affair, it is because of its concern or significance to the welfare of humanity. And a true knowledge is in fact an adherence with the Truth of the matter therefore elevating its status, specifically upgrading church's services to the utmost, these, in respect with John the Beloved idea or the concept of the church on his Revelation which was of Jesus, *nevertheless, reflects of Prophet Isaiah. It is perfect if they find this writing's right that John the Beloved was akin to Jesus wherein, the author middle east experience, believed, that He was the *child [*not John the Baptist] of whom Mary the mother of Jesus visited, and that the royal or "faithful" blood exist therein, therefore correct. In this case, anything that John was said, or must say through the church, every faithful or believer must obey. Someone could have excuses, but we should not make mistake about it, and that anyone who works against or denied the truth about John's teaching and its desire, which is in fact the truth upon Jesus of Nazarene, are sure the anti-Christ. Written on John 21, chapter 20-24, the promise of Christ's return was in fact pre-arranged and or pre- agreement between Peter the apostle and Jesus of Nazarene, where in this treatise believed must be honored. A must see Book 1 for additional input} <continuation> from previous page)* *then it is most probable that Jesus was aware of this place, the Ephesus wherein, one of the great ancient Greek philosopher named Heraclitus 535 BC – 475 BC, famous for His Flux and Fire philosophy and known for His rigid moralism and asceticism, originated. In relation to this, knowing a philosopher like Heraclitus leads to some of His prominent contemporaries such as Thales, Anaximenes, Anaximander, Pythagoras and especially Empedocles 490 BC – 430 BC {known for his writings "On Nature" and "Purifications" and believed to worked miracles by magic, and that he could control the winds and allegedly restore to life a woman who had seemed dead for thirty days}, to name a few, and that pave the way of being highly educated on that time especially on the subject of Philosophy. In addition, closeness that binds them, it is not surprising then to assume that Jesus of Nazareth and John the Beloved can be akin or blood related personalities. And both, nay, should the notion above is arguable, may not however lost the significance of the theme as the Jerusalem was under the colony of the Greeks then, before it pledge alliance to Romans, and in this case may however learned from Lucretius 99 BC – 55 BC a Roman poet and author of the philosophical epic De Rerum Natura or In the Nature of the Universe, wherein the later tenure's very close to the duo. And like Heraclitus, knowing Lucretius will lead you right away to Epicurus 341 BC - 270 BC a Greek philosopher known for His thought as Epicureanism or the Happiness to be the highest good **(On his crucifixion, Jesus Christ of**

his "signature robe" in which at the time we can consider expensive, and that the Roman soldiers used to gamble with it, depicts of him as an epicure person). *And that will point out towards Democritus, a Greek philosopher c. 460 BC – 370 BC and Leucippus His mentor of their atomism view that counter Eleatic philosophy of Parmenides 515 BC or its paradoxes' say or show that "the opposite is occasionally true and that we must beware of logical pitfalls" and His notion that "nothing ever change" could have been change after his "One". Furthermore, renaissance era reflects of that Desiderius Erasmus 1466 – 1536 the Dutch humanist, Catholic priest, social critic, teacher and theologian, it goes as well as to Baruch Spinoza 1632 – 1677 Jewish-Dutch philosopher* **[admired by the then Albert Einstein 1879 -1955, the German born of Jewish bloodline theoretical physicist, and hail at the same time by the Philosopher named Georg Wilhelm Friedrich 1770-1831 saying; "You are either a Spinozist or not a philosopher at all" source: Wikipedia]**, *wherein, the former, though He was critical of the Church, Erasmus remained committed to reforming the Church from within, while the later, Spinoza, notably most as free thinker and of His shrewd writings and principle that enrage Jewish community in Amsterdam and that leads to his expulsion and or anathema. And this thing goes as well to Friedrich Nietzsche, German philosopher and poet, upon misinterpretation of his [beautiful] art works. And one can take a closer look on these great men [Jesus of Nazarene on the cross; Jose Rizal on his Last Farewell; {Mi Ultimo Adios}, Nietzsche poem; Thus Spake Zarathustra] as they appealed the truth, and that truth banks solely on the Truth and Love of Nature. It is a common understanding that the significant, or impact on one's life in general aspect of religion, is essential, nevertheless [deliberately in worst case], represent something contrary to the truth and or nature therefore must initiate reform. In saying this is that to think that we sinned and or we are sinner is correct, nonetheless, we have to make it clear, rather to be free of anxiety or guilt and in a point held hostage of this, and that knowing Jesus of Nazarene was in fact crucified not truly because of our sins* **(we have to note that on the Old Testament that sex or *sexual desire [*or the truth about sexual attraction is to prove masculinity or superiority, one, over the other and that leads to reproduction] is the root or the original sin the reason people dies; see also All But the World is Loving, the "old" or original against the "new" greatest of the sin)** *but* mainly because He uncovered the Truth of a flawed religious belief and or law and that His own people, the Israelites, wanted to cover up thus maintain the old teaching. For good, or for John the Beloved sake, this must be corrected because no one should exploit God or Jesus Christ in lay of a "supposed noble deed". And in strict sense, according to Saint Thomas Aquinas, this is [pretension] immorality; the end justifies the means. At the end, a great but unequivocal statement is that, Nature will judge our incompetence.

And with all of this, Jesus of Nazarene also called as Christ, with the nature of a "backward time" or a hostile environment we could say, as one, yet a hard or harsh factor, and hardly, that this writing to be all alone, it could claim on these finding, and that as far as the experience in the middle east is concern, He *struggled or works really hard on these things [**Christians are the ambassador of faith in the Middle East; they do understand that it is a law not to practice religion in public other than Islam, particularly in Saudi Arabia, but in strict sense, rather, unequivocally, the actual circumstances suppress the freedom of religion, and that, monopoly like in business, turn out of a higher price of services and commodities and induce hypocrisy (obedience's mostly an external compliance) among others and not so surprising that breeds fundamentalist, and the extremism is the dangerous idea out of this thing. It's not the religion nor the teaching of the noble men that create chaos, but the hated preaching** [say "inproportionate comparison" from other culture somehow or someway denotes animosity] **and "partisan mentality" that one think he/she is superior if affiliated to a much bigger or radical group with a certain view** [if it's not the rationality that manifest to an individual, and or justice being serve or the rule of law govern mankind {because weak group or individuals tend to consolidate}, in strict sense, rather, it may turn out that religious group are indeed a sort of {collegiate} fraternity]. **And this creates division and unrest because freedom, equality and co-existent has been and being democratically promoted globally, rather, globally, being promoted democratically. Since you came and visits foreign land, wasn't fair that you had been treated a "free men" in them, and while on your premises others are consider prisoner? Law is perfect, or could be perfected, but it's the actual deed that one can**

*judge a person, and or the person's manner being a member of a group,
of or with a common value that binds them along. Things, law or ruling
of the past could be a fundamental, but this day, arms of the law can
reach and can be serve to anyone in anywhere that may works against
it. Indeed, moral and scientific education is essential. Was it (equality
and education - knowledge) not the life and the battle cry of Malala?
Without love, your women will seek comfort in the foreign land, and
the heart that full of jealous is the apple of the eye, rather, the subject
of interest or entices by or of "Satan". And the winner of the best policy
on good education and governance goes to United Kingdom or perhaps
Denmark and countries alike],* surmounting almost every consequence that
put forward on His way, and one of these most enduring event was to "serve his
term ahead of time". And that means until His people conceded or embrace the
Truth that matter on Christ's teaching. And in His humbleness or with his virtue
of humility, the love for His people, and reverence to the holy land, Jerusalem,
is not necessary to hail Jesus of Nazarene himself but His desire is to believe in
the veracity on what is He preaching therefore freed them from the unnecessary
binding from the old law and that shall set them free from any anxiety (Law of
Moses or Ten Commandments was the fundamental of the law of today. Law of
today subscribe to it. But this treatise believed that the law of today is the most
beautiful law ever written, so far. Maybe hard to keep one's culture in adapting
changes, and govern by the recent law, nevertheless transformation toward a
certain goal might be an essential in compliance with the work of nature for the
sake of humanity). This is in apprehension, or a precursor or in anticipation
against a possible *retribution or a will be punishment from "another party".
*According to the theme of the history, this is due to the flawed or a superfluous
if not a preposterous teaching or belief of Israelites that Jesus of Nazareth tried
to counter, fulfill and or supersedes, however postulating his idea, and that to
most of them viewed as conceited *[keywords or phrases such as: I, and the
Father is one; or whatever you ask in my name, shall be given to you]*,
and to the obstinate attitude and traditional or orthodox belief, consider as
obnoxious one. And the most controversial aspect wherein the Israelites consider
as blasphemous or proud and arrogant, and in strict sense and that Christ
teaching or John the Beloved writings was in fact an introduction to pantheism
view, where in figuratively express in Lord's Prayer that says "Holy be thy Name,

thy kingdom come" (agreement or coming out of a new form of prayer (wording and or expression) means that the people, or the apostles particularly, has been convinced of a certain reform or teaching), thus, not just being denied but lead to Christ conviction and death.

As this treatise see it, Israelites are indeed an astute people [or clever enough to protect or preserve the orthodox belief], for the time of Jesus of Nazarene, and that to reject His scientific idea [of course that, or they thought might compromise the "Abrahamic belief" however, at this point of time that they discovered and knew that science work for them, and them work scientifically, this writing wish and hoping from them of a change of heart even only for the sake of scientific knowledge and that means safety and preservation, for it is not just a panacea or providence on this world but scientific progress that people may express full potential in living with the nature, therefore preserve its essence. And believing in God and people's noble's work, thus comfort its soul at the demise of flesh and a shot of life after death to the most of the faithful. In a way, however that claim denotes inequality, this treatise understand how sweet it is to be called the chosen people of God, and hope they too, realize how hard it is to be chosen to speak, as Jesus of Nazarene and other philosopher's did, write these things, banking only on the literal Nature of the Truth about the Truth of the Nature and that means people will decides our own fate and time and nature will decide people's destiny and may settle the differences. And a not so many moral works decides the comfort of concern soul; for it is the immaculate of the thought or mind that is devoid with encumbrances, the comfort of the soul lies, where in, on loving the truth with passion, or obedience to work on noble deeds with one's full judgment, is the rational and the right thing to do. And on one hand, those who value the significance of good things are to establish the tranquility of the heart and are the essence of the real peace of mind. While on the other, and that, by the simple submission of the will, and that rely on an empty fundamentals which is frailty in nature, and so on obedience only for the external compliance, one may be deprive of the gift, for one may had been submit or committed to the provision of the law that was, or perhaps at fault], *though undeniable, they, especially the authority, refuse to believe in faith healing wherein that era is the only way or means to prove things scientifically, mainly because of inadequate or in an absence of technical support or matter in general aspect. Aside from social stigma from either ruling forces, or colonizer or race and host country to the emigrants, and that Jesus Christ found a probable consequence from a much more conspicuous, reliable or plausible teaching or knowledge that He knows may fade-in and arise eventually. This is besides from the assumption that Romans wherein they are under colony at the time, will destroy their sacred temple should they found out that the teaching of Jesus is more reliable or actually the fact or the truth and reality, this according to High Priest named Caiaphas that was seems agitated of the circumstances, and because of these reasons made him the decision of sacrificing Jesus Christ [**John 11, 49-52; a must see Book 1 for additional input**]. Jesus of Nazarene nevertheless braved, and carried out these things only to save, or to share or to assume a would be suffering, rather, in behalf of His people's pride or dignity and or humiliation to say the least, that they shall be, as Jesus of Nazareth see the way it is, will be experiencing [**eventually**], and that for the Love of His people and the Holy Land, therefore carried out "redemption and salvation". Amazingly, nay, peculiarly, this one's ahead of time and that shows of Jesus of Nazareth' intellectualism, courageousness and audaciousness. And in relation to this, pardon me if this contradict other's assumption, but the reason of the holocaust that takes place in Europe, and that proclaiming "Jewish intellectualism is dead" by propagandist, could be one of Jesus concern, besides, the "manner" showing by the neighborhoods, might invites or encourage the "theme" of anti-Semitics as well, and we have to note on this era, as this treatise conclude, and that with the advance and developing technology, the aftermath of confrontation could be more wretched and doleful to the point that comment or anti -Semitic remarks will be even more harsher, and that clearly depicts that problem is being recycle and or as the saying goes that history repeat itself is true, in this case, notably this time with an elevated degree of hostility. Believe it or not, watching several times on the National Geographic channel the Hitler's life and history, and that lead to conclusion that the holocaust could had been fanned if not passions by Jesus of Nazarene or Jesus Christ activism or reformation (social reform). However, the unintended emigration or depiction, if this is the case of the theoretical Physicist named Albert Einstein in United*

States could have infuriated Adolf Hitler more, but most likely it provides a sanctuary for the Holy Land by providing the host country with the god-like machine called Atomic Bomb. And in this case, as explained in Book 1 and that it suggests, rather, it is far better to "offer" hands to the neighborhood and live in peace as favorable and earn a concrete outcome, than to delved into the color of politics; ought to understand those people (Palestine) that you thought doesn't understand you. The author wondered why on what was the passion that leads Saint Paul and other apostle, to search for Jewish people in every corner of the continent to spread the "good news" (or new teaching) and that left unanswered until I challenged the words of Jesus and literally proved me of Him to be true, thus share this one to you. A "Three States" solution, and that Jerusalem as the capital of the Holy Land, as John the Beloved suggests on His Book of Revelation, could be better if not desirable alternative. And to live by the ancestral law and tradition, must reinstate a king in honor of the greatness of your people and of the life of Jesus of Nazarene, the son of Mary and Joseph, a descendant of King David. And what can I say or can I add more but whether it is the World War, Holocaust or the Global Warming cataclysm, I think it is best for us that every time that things we believe it is going the way it is, we have to, or we should have learn to read the writings on the wall.

And to conclude, this noble deed or the sacrifice or crucifixion specifically, where in at this point in time, one can consider as inhuman, undignified or disgusting event, nevertheless, the concept or process of redemption and salvation, or on acquiring great knowledge and that started and takes place right in their homeland in what they call a holy one, should not vexed the Israelites nor spurned and earned Jesus affront, or treat Him like of a sinister, but in a sense, though might be spiritually painful mostly to Conservative clerics, and may cost fundamentalist's pride. But **the catch's, or the essence with the sublime or maxim on Christ teaching, is that Acceptances' could be a Panacea or a Providence in this world or the all the world to come.** Thus modification of a certain view or understanding, or law, or updating or upgrading knowledge and skill required to do things correctly, is the badly needed antidote in this case. Indeed, peace in the Middle East, in particular, or the Neutral World in general, would bring a new life and perspective. To implement this thing is all what the Scribes are looking for a great leader, and for the commoners to *foster. And for the generation and or the youth of today, it might be disdainful to other, but the Truth, and that, always remember that law of nature and its perpetual process, struggle and change, provides the very circumstances of all nature to exist. While living things or people's life is surviving, noble deed's God Spirit – and it is the comfort of the soul and is purely spirit – It is the soul or spirit that feel the sensation (comfort of the soul by being guiltless or a mind that is unperturbed), suffer and endure the *pain (*disruption of normal blood circulation) of flesh. Noble work is the comfort of living, and noble deed or thought, say non-guilty of a sin is the comfort of one soul. God in strict sense, is the transforming power, a prevailing natural phenomena and cycle of a transitory states; a dominant and *one way purification process (*helping or loving one another) wherein everyone must adhere. And literally, anyone that will go against (the noble deeds or circumstances – the common principle of nature such as **cosmic principle [**single pile of gasses all along the current feeding into the combustion chamber, say of a galaxy or sun; a must see article on the Origin of the Universe on Book 1 – All But the world is Loving ; please note that with this book, the ingenuity of the idea can answers all the queries that'll be put forward or its primary aim is indeed to defeat skeptics]) is sure will commit sin, otherwise live on their own (body such as galaxy, nevertheless principle or fundamental of Existence is the same all throughout the universe) and or face the consequence and die as per the law of nature of existence, or life's surviving according to the law of the land, which ever come first. Education is a must, as Francisco Sanches, c.1550 – 1623, French – Portuguese philosopher and physician said, you have to read books and compare it with the facts throughout your life; and only the discovery of the nature of the universe had long and lasting meaning, Albert Einstein quoted as saying.*

In either way, Israel should be very grateful to Jesus of Nazarene at most, and being fortunate and proud out of fulfilling the prophecy and that bringing forth the greatest Prophet has ever lived, at least. This treatise believed, and that if not to prove the truth on one's noble deeds and that may *comfort the "soul" on the afterlife, the crucifixion of Jesus Christ was indeed a gaffe (*in saying this is that early on the year 2000, the author had the vision and very brief conversation of Jesus Christ, and that His couple of associates *standing alongside – all dressed in white robe, and Jesus in a typical Arab one-finger sandals. Though fascinated, I make all the effort and tried really hard but I saw no facial images or had not shown due to circumstances; their faces shining so bright in sparkling white or brilliantly glittering flashes that I manage only to look at their toe, appeared to be a resurrected soul and or glorified bodies. While on the 4ᵗʰ month of 2013, the author Christ's vision takes place* [while covered with bath towel to minimize brightness, and an input from a compact disc player with the music playing on a muted sound, and that right after a plain conversation from a flat mate regarding the truth {as the author see it and with great knowledge and confidence I believed, that had been delivered and shared, of Christ perspective and instances; reform, sacrifices} from the screen of the television set, Christ, the author believed, the image of Him appeared. The instances above tell of two things, and that while the scene on the later was that the author believed the reason his image depicted and or appeared, apparition takes place when the author challenge Christ, and that, in no way he can prove his own words that was written in the Bible in which the author found and or proved the contrary]; *On His ordeal appeared that His left eye was badly wounded and virtually, if not highly assumed that is totally blinded. Atop of His both ears depicted substantial wounds. And despite with the unkemptness, the image show of His real identity or outward look figuring that He look more likely of the late King Saud* [or Prince Salman bin Abdul-Aziz al Saud] *of Saudi Arabia but had a ridge or a little oversized nose. Tingling, but the great scene from the author's memory and experience, and that sure can share before everyone else's).*

Certainly, the whole truth is really inconvenient most especially to conservative, much more with an obstinate attitude, might be upsetting in one point or could be disturbing to other, mainly because, if a certain law of religion is not the law of the land or its respective government, such as, rather, specifically, the monarchy form of government, and that without the fundamentals of true nature of God, is therefore, rather in a sense, or in a way, is a falsehood doctrine. And that preachers in different sect, in strict sense if not definitely commits a fraudulent activity in a way that things they might be talking about cannot be prove as it compliment what has Jesus of Nazarene said about this thing and that, "they cannot even turn a black hair into gray", somehow guides through a noble way *of life which is good, but in this case, theme might fall as one of those educational entity therefore submit to respective authority as governing body. This treatise firmly believed that this was the idea of Spinoza when he wanted to take the political power away from the church and give it to the king and that angered the church and accused him of being an atheist. Apparently, and that without their control, separation of the church from the state is some kind of problematic to the former because of the manner they will handle the situation or affair, primarily of financial matter that comes mostly from the people's wealth. And since the ancestral law's applicable to a church's monarchy form of government like the Vatican State, Kingdom of Saudi Arabia or the United Kingdom of England, otherwise, like any other learning institution, the church and its law which may fall on this category, is not the ruling government itself, however enjoy the protection from the state as well, therefore must pay the tax like the commoner or its citizen, otherwise, is to "Redefine" its status quo as purely charitable institution that exempt them from the liability of paying taxes provided by the states' constitution. As far as the tax collection is concern, even the Israelites on the Biblical time grumbles in this matter. In a way, rather, in other words, provided that their earnings, collections or donation as they call it, a *transparent financial matter [*__the idea of Jesus of Nazarene stated on Matthew 6:1-4 for the secluded or the solemnity of the clandestine of one's charitable works may only applied to individual donor, but this treatise believed that transparency and well accounted activity on this kind of institution especially if one does not have the burden of paying the taxes, and that avoiding scrutiny's to declare asset and or liabilities for good. This concern applies to all community of religions because it may serve a perfect cover to money laundering activity or unscrupulous individual that would like to evade the burden from paying taxes]__ regulated by the government itself, absolutely leads to charitable work, otherwise, rather, they should pay taxes as Jesus of Nazarene did in his time; Matthew 17: 27- Payment of the Temple Tax; Though informal, they preached and practices healing and that consider as education or learning institution on either era, and this, one can consider as the School of Religion, as well as Medicinal practice on scientific field, in which, or both are branches of Philosophy. And with regards to the truth of the matter, it is notable that the degree of the event in case of defiance, and or its outcome is without a doubt, unpredictable if the tenacity of* *a panderer and prideful takes place. Nobody ask for, nor looking for trouble, but the challenge this treatise ought to possess, is that of Christ's work and sacrifices, do we think a gambit will trade its piece without its gain at the end, or a quant trade-off for less or in favor of the undesirable? Absolutely, as far as this treatise is concern, derision or anti- Zionism, or *anti-Semitism [*to tell it straight forward, the way that Jesus of Nazarene criticized the authority on His era was actually an anti- Semitic remarks, nevertheless, the desire or purpose of the modification of the teaching, or law reformation was purely pro-Semitic, which is true with all the Prophets and reformist of their respective era and so this treatise were if someone found it alongside at least, or one of them at most] or Atheism overtones is out of the question, but this writing seek only for the truth in favor of the welfare of humanity in particular, or habitat, nature and planet existence in general aspect. And in addition, while it is a plus serving Justice for Christ and the like of Him, say on His apostles that suffers persecution on their era, and in a sense, Spinoza of the renaissance, His Pomp therefore will flourish anew as a result. In this case [as expounded well in Book 1] this writing see no despondence nor berates the Israelites as they play the part very well in proving, as well as the fulfillment of the most significant and essential teaching and knowledge of humankind called "redemption" from the concept of original sin and "salvation" which was primarily dedicated to his people, the Israelites. However, along the way, besides indoctrination, with the package, say healing, wherein He commissioned the apostles, found out that the teaching was applicable to the gentiles or non-Jew as well, thus shares the good news or doctrine of deliverance from *destruction, and that though thought to be great, aside from *spiritual concern, in a certain point, scientific connotation in strict sense, implying about the trouble of global warming thus, changes is not just essential but a must and a necessity.*

And in another view, if we will take a closer look on the event, what this writing shared is all about spirituality, or the mind and its thought, and moral formation is one of the outcomes. But on the other, if we will change the angle of perspective, what this writing found out and can tell that the "history," or the "theme of the whole event" specifically the crucifixion, was indeed a great "Experiment". Experiment to prove a certain idea, no more than a laboratory *trial wherein, rather it seems the life at stake, is that failure is not an option or there should be no room for failure. The supposed or reputed "test" where in provided with the greatest entities or accessories and that include the life of a being, Jesus of Nazarene, or the literal and spiritual aspect of humankind, and that hope from the greatest teacher ever written of human race, could have shared us the Value and Essence of a true Knowledge and Wisdom of life. And it is amazing that the idea was really great, great that it took almost the entire history of humankind and that aim however to bequeath wisdom from one generation to another, and that to survive humankind by his own spirit through the mind as desires on the summit. Was it not the point of the great Greek philosopher named Pythagoras? And thought to be great, at this point, yet will be expounded on the later part, and that, from an slender view, the very limited and awkward scientific concept of the teaching, nevertheless prelude, derived from, or suffixes the idea of the global warming in particular and the nature's [**universal, cosmic and or humankind**] philosophy in general. And as a result, as far as the subject or natural science is concern, may produce a perfect model for a perpetual knowledge, and that dedicated for the protruding generation to live with "nature", the spiritual and material aspect, in full potential. Anyway, this treatise conclude that every man and every entity is a part of this world, therefore a part of a history; and while Heraclitus saw that everyone as world's collaborator, one can say that everything in this world connived, and one says, all is one. Nevertheless, this treatise hoping that eventually or sooner, religions should realize and value the essence of nature and the consequence's attributed to it, or at least be aware of its worst capacity in the highest degree, and that is the danger it possess; as the former United States President Lincoln, and though hesitated, the Pharaoh in Egypt at the time of Moses, saw the essence of ending the slavery, and as this treatise believed, as well as the consequence of not ending it, for they might thought that it was imminent, and or the worst things is yet to come, thus initiated reform, a countermove or counterbalance [**Quintessence**] if not a countenance of the truth of the social affair. They are indeed a gambit. Consolation of the *church* **[it is notable that the supposed John's Church, the church this treatise believed instituted by Jesus of Nazarene** {on the cross; the third of the seven last words}, **primarily, is the service of the people afflicted by nature calamity in general, and social concern as the widow and orphans in**

particular aspect. In saying this is to express concern as Jesus had for his mother and that with the "backward" culture exist, being a widow (without a family) in the middle east is a life that is hard to bear; it's like a woman drifting in the sea, she tends on either holding on anything to stay afloat or hold her feet into the fire] *or the comfort of the faithful in religion is not a bad idea but in fact a moral and noble thing or essential matter we can say, nevertheless, for it was taught the essence of free will, where in God doesn't mend with the affair of men, and thus, this treatise's concern is that, at this point, no faithfulness's therefore is enough to alter the course of nature but to have the scientific knowledge to live with it. And it is funny, but with the overwhelming forces and wonder of nature, only, or at least men can plant a tree and take care of its rainforest and ceased activity underground in order to aid the planet mitigates the global warming and that retard its submissions on its creator which is the Sun, [***as explained entirely on this book; see the theory on the creation of moon and planet articles on the following and also in Book 1 for additional input]*** therefore prolong the life and or biodiversity of this celestial body and saves humankind.*

And we can conclude that the Truth of the fundamentals of life and its operation, cannot be altered by either faithfulness nor intelligence alone, but at any given or respective time, the Messiah, prophet, philosopher or scientist is set to introduce, impose or carried out reform as it deemed essential demanded by the very circumstances in the planet. Hail this treatise is to the like of His Excellency Francois Hollande, Al Gore and in a way for Prince Charles of saving the rainforest and all the nature advocates throughout the world who works hard to save the environment and the earth.

INTRODUCTION 7

The Theory of Quintessence

Neutrality (spacing or interval or sufficient freedom from external pressure to develop) is the religion of the universe and co-existence is the mantra. People around the world have diverse culture and different belief. On coming into existence, their respective principle believed that they may have different fundamentals, which is not as it should be, and this is obvious amiss. In one hand, the church as trusty institution and on the other is science and that though comes with a substantial cost, is dependable as far as the medicinal practice or hospitalization and healing process is concern. Over the former, science at this point is more reliable; though faith (intellect) healing or miracle is popular, it is rare nowadays because, nay, except the moral formation, or of upholding the moral principle which is sporadically failing or falling short, she or the church fails to live up with the teaching of Jesus of Nazarene as far as the medicine or faith healing is concern. This writing aim is not to demean an institution, but help them to reasses the subject matter. In one hand, it helps to uncover fraudulent activity of preachers that making a fast and enjoy hefty bucks from the unscrupulous member of a certain congregation. To give, or not to give donations, is none of my business one can say. But with the thousands of religion across the globe, imagine how vast the wealth of these people that would or should have make a dough to fill the empty stomach of the poor and that in a strict sense have taken away by those "religions" away from them. Sublime teaching is a noble thing but logical pitfall (corrupt, abusive and or exploitation among other) is once again a real concern. Another tragic treatise,

64

nevertheless, with their balls on the right place, this writing's desire's from the authority to look deeper into this case **(fraud on a false claim or otherwise in a sense's learning institution therefore their duty to pay taxes must be uphold by the government; We have to note that Jesus of Nazarene himself pay tax)**. *And on the other hand, this idea would like to introduce once again that Philosophy as the fundamental, and Science and Religion, if these things differ from the former or with each other, will work all along with each other. In this case, the article offers a bright and balance perspective and approach, and that for us to know and learned the common principle of survival and perpetual existence of soul, and or flesh for the most, and or those who are faithful (brave and intelligent) enough to fulfill or carried out what is necessary and or required, in order to survive one's body and soul?*

Basically, the Quintessence is where the "Void" is, or the home where all of the elements rest **(and as the Greek philosopher named Parmenides c. 515- 510 BCE, famous for His Eleatic philosophy, contends; if it is the void, what is the void? If what is, is, then what is, has always been what it is and will not cease being what it is; And as to defeat or get rid of a tough or insurmountable skeptics like Parmenides, or perhaps in a way to counter Francisco Sanches 1550-1623, a French - Portuguese of a Jewish origin, That Nothing is Known's philosophy)**. *The Fifth element is the "grave" of, or to the space which is made up of degree or layers of different gasses accessible through conduction or the application of different degree of Temperature or the nature's capacity to carried out transformation process, has had to offer* **(atomism in other scientific term; wherein literally "dark "contracting matter that depicts or reflects of a cold, an immense, densely or crude gases and that exist in the absence of literally "light inflationary" body of gases counterpart, such as galaxy and sun. And more of the ice, such as dried or contracted ice and that cryogenically treated as hard or as to become a diamond itself and the later consider as one of the heavy or refused materials upon rarefication by cryogenic method or extreme coldness application that define the contraction bonding method and that eliminates feeble (vulnerable to the changes in temperature) matter of the element such as gas and or water and that describe the nature of the degree of hardness of a certain material** *as a result).* *Quintessence is in fact the neutral point where conductions begin. Quintessence works like of a semi-conductor works and that finely regulated by Time and Temperature. Innate and phlegmatic, consider dormant and or latent, it is temporarily quiescent, however its duty is at work and its work is in progress as well. And depending on the circumstances, the Pressure (**density/ mass/quality/quantity**) particularly, the said element will manifest, regroup and respond to the call of nature and that is measured by the Time and or (**degree of**) Temperature, and it is true the other way around or one way or the other (**diminution to neutral point to manifestation to diminution to neutral point**). Thus consider not only an integral part, the presence of quintessence's element exist absolutely in all entities and is living in every soul and in every material thing on earth and or in the universe.*

*In a sense, Quintessence, retains the idea of Greek philosopher Heraclitus 525 BC – 475 BC, that thinks that God, which doesn't mean the Greek gods or personal entity. And in here, nor the God of great religions but somehow carried out comparison regarding propositions according to thy belief; Say Quintessence is a process of *karma or destiny [***Hinduism: the total effect of a person's actions or conduct; and its beautiful with the aspect of "Trimurti" which is the triad of Gods consisting of Brahma the creator, Vishnu the preserver, and Shiva the destroyer as the three highest manifestation of the one ultimate reality. And the holy Trinity of the Catholic doctrine which is consists of the Father, the creator, and the Son as the Redeemer, and the Holy Spirit, the Sanctifying power to work on noble deeds and that is against the detestable things in which all leads to God's glory or the manifestation of the Truth of the reality**]. In this case, wasn't surprising that Jesus of Nazarene braved and conquered the face of death in order to correct the flawed Israel's belief? How about the wit of the philosophers like Socrates, Spinoza or Sanches or Galileo and Copernicus and Leibnitz, or Albert Einstein of his famous Space Time - the four dimensional continuum of one temporal and three spatial coordinate in which any event or physical object is located.*

In one hand, successive phases of noble deeds glean the holiness or comfort of the soul, or the "shot" of life after death, while on the other, incarceration to the point of the death of one's soul is the consequence of detestable action and that is the Neutralization, the objective and main duty of the fifth element, the Quintessence. In other words, the question on how the quintessence or neutral point exist or can it be created, is that it is the outcome (or product) of the dispute (or the settlement upon the struggle) between opposing forces of matter **(and or deed, mind and spirit)** *and or element such as hot and cold, light and darkness or of good and evil such as being mean or unpleasant and unfair practices thus create space or spacing between opposing forces. And the idea of Heraclitus of the essence of war could be that, rather, because He believed, and that strife is, or creates justice and that all things come into being and pass away through strife* **(source: thebigview.com).** *Nevertheless, rational mind or intellectualism* **(sensible mind and judgment)** *promotes self-justice, co-existence or equality and these averts literal war hence begets peace therefore eluded struggle (on the part of the live, the human aspect) and leave it by the nature themselves. Neutrality, rather practical application of neutralism in strict sense, rather aware or not, is in fact widely practice in human's day by day living, and that implementation in or of the law of the like of mid- eastern dweller, or Islam religion in particular. For instance, a divorced woman/wife wouldn't be able to reconcile with her former or "estranged" husband unless she get married with another man and divorced him before she can have her former husband to rejuvenate. Blood money or compensation, or loving or present's giving, are some of those neutral desire or practices.*

In one hand, Neutrality or co-existence's view or attitude really works or beneficial to one's own existence. And on the other, the Natural Order of nature and life in which we can consider in uncivilized world as crucial, is the survival of the fittest **(one's existence is either the outcome/product or the remains between opposing forces; say the art of sex or sexual intercourse/ reproduction [sexual reproduction is to prove virility or masculinity, vigor and or potency over the other], or strife and or war in between elements. In between rigid or rigorous strife, the space that is tolerable by the certain element or human in this aspect is therefore our time of existence. But still the so called "strife" is taking shape all of the places and all the time and in strict sense, that only survives the fittest).** *In other words, nay, therefore we can conclude that while a human thought control its action, Quintessence monitors, supervises and or regulate; as admonishes* *individual or entity as it should, or must be or as a necessity, and aware or not, proceeds accountability depending on the gravity of the event or one's action. Should we say Miracle in this case, and that, with one's power (**scientific/ intellectualism or faithfulness for the advocates of religions),** and deeds, in the right place and at the right time, things happened and some of them miraculously coincides. And the great question is why if there's Quintessence, why there's an evil (**deed)?** Or to relive this idea is that century before the time of Jesus of Nazarene also called as Christ, civilization was already thriving in Europe, specifically Greece, wherein the like of philosopher Epicurus (**341 BC - 270 BC)** promulgated his idea about (**Greek mythological)** god and that he said: "Is God willing to prevent evil, but not able? Then He is impotent. Is He able, but not willing? Then He is malevolent. Is He both able and willing? Whence then is evil?"*

*In one point, rather, in this case that God allowed the good and evil to co-exist, therefore the God we knew in this case is Neutral, or a neutral entity but at work in duty and its work in progress, which is in fact, rather, absolutely the idea and fundamentals of the messages on the Revelation of John the Beloved, consider in here as the true vicar of Jesus Christ. And the fact that it is the (**human)** soul who's responsible (**for accounting)** its deed, therefore God is purely spiritual (mind) wherein in only by the power of his spirit can people worship Him as He really is, which was emphasized on John 4:24 and His first letter 4:12 of the New Testament Bible and that says; No one has ever seen God, but if we love one another, God lives in union with us and his love is made perfect in us (**John's proposition should be interpreted on today, hope to help the author two decade experience in this ancestral land, and that since mid-eastern people doesn't consider Jesus of Nazarene also called as Christ as the "truly" son of omnipotent God, will turn out that the "son of God" term was in fact a local dialect, which is a figure of speech or a local hyperbole word or figurative language and that means supernatural and or extraordinary and the commoner uses the phrase widely as an "expression" or a mantra).** Where in the literal concept of the word "Love" from religion, is in fact the word Attraction in scientific term, can be explain on both ways of scientific and religious aspect with different connotation on different purpose and or occasion. And this* *conclude that these subjects, the Science and Religion, are in fact linked and or one, and this writing see it, as far as the ancient wisdom and the knowledge at hand, is concern therefore must be harmonize for good. A must see article on Universal Gravitation in Book 1 for an extended version and or additional input; specifically, the methodology of natural conception (**of untouched or a virgin woman in particular**) that causes the origin of matter, life and the universe and the link between the subject of science and religion. Wherein this treatise hold on that ancient or archaic book is in fact a scientific matter or revolution on that era with the best the circumstances or knowledge has had to offer; it could be a philosophy on moral deeds, law on social reform and medical and nature sciences and some of them on engineering discipline or mathematics with the greatest inclination to uncover the secrets of natural phenomena. Was those things said above differs on what we have today?*

And in another point, though manifests universally and or present in everything, Quintessence does not implicate itself wholly with the affair of an individual, subjects, element or component. In other words, nay, however, in a discreet or calibrated manner, commence in parallel with the entity, and that as the circumstances satisfied, Quintessence involve itself in full potential, and this, to stave off vanity or hold off preponderate, and this to ponder and bring Peace, its primary, general and absolute purpose; and the Peace is the Quintessence or the Neutral point, thus, no struggle especially in the human affair, therefore everyone's faith or believing should, or can co-exist equally. In saying this is to retard proposition that a certain congregation is better than the other or an individual better than one, except for their generosity or willingness for the counterpart to survive.

*While everything and everyone is subject to Quintessence's Law, the catch's on loving or imitating God who is Neutral, is allowing other or every entity to exist with equal opportunity. While, rather, mostly if not in strict sense, human affair is bound or subject in particular or specific law of existence, and the division of properties or the line of defense and or responsibility according to their "might" among other, are some of those. For these reasons, Quintessence's the purest of the element; with the slightest degree of impurity (**evil or unnecessary**), will tend or have the chance to destroy that entity or enliven according to its (**noble**)*

purpose. *Everything will be humble before the Quintessence, and only the*
*Truth (*the circumstances in the shortcoming or absence of human thought and
affair) shall live in itself. Even in the slightest degree of inequality, specifically
in the case that it's the woman who cries, the law or kingdom transformation
is therefore imminent.

   Well, a person "skilled" enough can play with a "thing" or two for a while,
but all the time and sure not all along. In other words, say, his or her will, a
person can choose their respective destiny, but it is worth remembering as well,
that by a person's deeds or action, the Quintessence decides their fate. Specifically,
if not strange, the irony of the Quintessence is that, it is not just, only the person
involve or who does commits sin will suffer the consequence of its action, but
along the way a vulnerable acquaintances, community or a high end entity
such as the source of income or provider will feel the brunt or sin's burden. And
in this case, rather, with the knowledge of the nature of Quintessence which
we can consider as the "Greatest of the Gambit" and a deep penetrating agent
with absolute precision – No matter how huge and complicated the situation
might be, it finds a way, and conducts through the highest or deepest degree of
the possible options. If someone carried out a noble deed or start to compromise
one self, the Quintessence shall work accordingly. In this case, nay, so that
while one commits sin, must be aware or should learn to identify indication
that Quintessence's somehow is taking its shape and turn. And as the saying
goes, learn to read the writings on the wall, therefore one must ceased or turn
its back from wicked or evil's way; Was it not the point or concern when
Jesus of Nazarene said that a pain on a finger, can be feel on the whole body?
Principal and corroborators of sins are both liable of wrongdoing, but beware
that the later may suffers more than the former, thus, do not degrade yourself
or compromise your future on this category, or being the initiator of detestable
thing neither, for the comfort of the soul in the time of death is much greater than
the comfort oneself in flesh can obtain in this material life, or its the "comfort
of the unknown" as the greatest reward of success or the most fascinating things
a human can experience in his/her tenure. The psychological aspect of the law
which most of us view or consider a ruling from God is not doing something bad
because we afraid of Him who is all knowing and powerful, but because we do
not do something detestable because it is the right thing to do for our survival

[body] and existence [the afterlife-soul-thought through the mind], therefore we must love God in this case.

Pride creates division, sometimes if not most of it, leads someone astray *{Literally or in fact, for it blocked the intensity of blood circulation upon the brain, should I say that prideful people are most likely to suffer cardiovascular or brain related trouble or diseases? The right amount of nourishment and the ability of the person's part of the brain to trigger the appropriate or healing point of a certain ailment, where in chronic diseases requires a higher degree of the faithfulness or intellectualism, can cure diseases, and it is the wonder of faith healing}.* And it is notable that no one can "buy off"- there's no option but a noble deed, and no days can borrowed and no one can "buy time"- and that however long and how far it would take, Quintessence strikes anywhere at any time, at any cost and that sometimes it is poignant that, depending on the degree of evil's astuteness, it sacrifices, or it takes few good men to stave off the vanity of one or others; Can you believe, rather, this treatise believed that on September 11 2001, it takes hundreds of precious American lives to grant the prayers of women in Afghanistan. And the list will go on such as the story of a couple from a war torn country only to reunite after several years in the other. And a Pakistani friend of mine tells the story of a couple denied with a child and finds one in the middle of the sea, but on the child-parents dissimilar feature, the authority traced and reunited the child to biological parents. In this case, exercise the virtue of patience and sublime deeds; because these are the most important aspect and very interesting portion and feature of the Quintessence; it works with you when you carried out these things with passion, thus prayer or desires therefore shall be granted. On the other hand, do not be surprise to see some good men suffer at the hand of the evil one, they might be the collateral damage, but be proud of the *magnanimity of the former {**happy are those who dedicated their life for the good of others, their soul shall be comforted on the afterlife therefore received what God has promised}**, everything or every matter including abstract idea that can reach up by Thought through the mind, is treated just and fair, and that considering its existence, the same or parallel to Quintessence's itself.

It is noteworthy that one should feel free and comfortable with working on the principle of Quintessence; if a person or an entity, or when you are with the truth, you are at peace **(the treat of harm or death has no power over it, the great reward of learning Philosophy; the Metaphysics or Theological Science, the first philosophy and the knowledge of being in the highest degree of abstraction).** *If then you are with peace with someone else's, you must be neutral, and that you possessed the virtue or essence of the Quintessence. It getting closer, for God is the Truth, God is Omnipotent, God is Omnipresent and God is Omniscient. If the Quintessence is Neutral then I am who I am, and If God is Just, therefore Neutral, if there is Neutrality then there is Peace, then it is the Philosophy of life whatever you may believing,* **{"John 4:24; for God is Spirit and only by the power of his *Spirit can people worship him as he really is." *Spirit is a good and noble traits such as lovable and just; and the Holy Spirit is the action word or verbal form of Spirit such as loving},** *and that Peace is the Quintessence of life. And while the noble deeds are the comfort of the soul of its most can achieve, to the point of the promises of life after death, or soul's transmigration to the faithful, of its summit, and the consolation of moral thought and deed in this life at least, and God, which is or whom is neutral and just, therefore is Quintessence. It is the Equilibrium and that exist, beget peace and everyone could freely express one's potential or free will, however only, or subject to quintessence' toleration or moderation and that clearly depicts that except of the noble works, no absolute freedom on deed or thought, for everyone is subject to God's or quintessence accountability. And so do have limitation, we should be grateful however for it is the greatest gift of the mind; rational, sound, faithful and or intellectual, and that to achieve its full potential trained upon by the Holy Spirit or the power of the mind to choose good over evil things, and these has been taught extensively by Jesus of Nazarene, also called as Christ, therefore, rather, at least to live with His teaching is a, or the noble thing to do.*

And the wonder of passion that drives this concept is on John's Revelation 10 and 11, considering His loyalty, not just only to Jesus of Nazarene, but His shrewdness that depicts fidelity and faithfulness to the Truth and essence of the New Teaching that depicts and complies the true services to human and its nature that is universally applicable, as

well as their personal cause and believing, and that was the love of their people and the holy land, deemed on this writing with the best of its knowledge and belief, and that, while Peter the Apostle as the guardian of the church, John the Beloved is the real Vicar of Christ. These as to modify and restructure, and or consolidate the church that was stated on Revelation 10 specifically verses 10-11 that said "Once again you must proclaim God's message about many nations, races, languages, and kings". And as the later unfolded and professed the concept of a true Christian Church [and that was initiated on John 19:25-27 and complimented in the writings on John 21:22 as well as on Revelation 10:1-11] therefore, John must be the One, until Jesus Christ's promises' return.

Furthermore, Quintessence works like the principle of an antibody works, and acting like an immune system acts, or works like policing the street in preventing crime. Employed in a human aspect in particular, however its application or duties bound to, rather, does include the cosmoses or universe in general. Whatever the applied process or interactions might be; e.g. gravitation, magnetism and or repulsion, attractions or loving, or a maintenance work as to repair a cell or tissue of a system, whether, nay, to the point leading to the introductions of *atomism theory of the subatomic particles, specifically the electron of the Elementary particles and proton and neutron of the Hadrons particles (*Introduced by Leucippus 440 BC, and carried out by Democritus His disciple 460 BC – 370 BC, to Epicurus the laughing philosopher 341-270 BC and Lucretius a Roman poet c. 99-55 BCE, the author of "On the Nature of the Universe" [De Rerum Natura], and handed down to John Dalton an English chemist 1766-1844, whom formulated the atomic theory).

Quintessence in a sense neither work or wills from anyone or anything, but on the pre-established harmony, obey or proceeds only on the call or on what the circumstances has had to offer, most especially when it comes to the changes in *"Temperature" [*compounded technical term which is applicable on both literal {say human on illness or earth on global warming; as the people of this earth abuses the environment therefore the quintessence *commence its duty as well}, and on spiritual aspect as someone does evil things therefore the Quintessence commence to neutralize him/ her], as it works like a person's conscience as procreator and at the same time an eliminator or an antimatter in a firmament or huge celestial body like a galaxy, but surprisingly, its main purpose is not to destroy but to set or achieve its goal or place as peacemaker or moderator **(It holds the Fire and Flux and The Unity of the Opposite philosophy of Heraclitus, wherein a Fire or Heat as non- destructive but mere transforming power and the Uncertainty Principle of the German Physicist named Werner Karl Heisenberg 1901-1976 which states that "it is impossible to correctly determine the position and speed of a subatomic particle like the electron": The things is that light against light, say galaxy against another body of galaxy might destroy each other, and literally extinguishing each other's fire, shall create dark matter, thus as a result of having no light. And it's true the other way around and that is dark matter against dark matter which is in extreme cold creates friction [big bang in a way] that creates light or body of galaxy wherein we can consider the origin of the universe. And from here we have to note that either of the element, dark and light matter totally take control of the system, is therefore no life as human being would exist, and life to exist in this universe we need the light and dark matter to co-exist. The product of the disparity in temperature** (sensitivity or the intensity of radioactive force or chemical reaction) **and the allotted time of settlement say multi-billions of years had our life in this world created. The history of our life is like a tiny speck on the vast land, but as far as the universe's circumstances and or time is concern, it doesn't make sense; dark matter or temperature as it nature, creates the potent cell and this creates the big bang, big bang or friction creates galaxy, galaxy created the sun, the sun created the planet or earth and its biodiversity; product or environment created from circumstances' magnanimity, by evolution or chance, considered or known by the so called "faithful" as "The will of God" and that is according to the ancient thinker).**

    The neutral degree or positioning essential to balance the system in as much as to achieve an absolute proportion to avoid collapse of the entire system and *that for its own existence. However, as far as the body existence is concern, Quintessence is not an obsolete factor, for a body that has beginning therefore has an end. The fact that its quality is persevering and persistent, circumstances in a sense is not in the Quintessence control, as everything sets by the Quintessence itself temporarily, and that it will others to disintegrate as necessary and or resolve as essential, or as to give way to other. Magnifying this concept, the "innate" characteristic of a Quintessence resembled absolutely of a human trait and that is the "scapegoat mentality" which is attributed to its astuteness of its survival and existence skills, and besides of its stereotype manner, genetically, it is perfectly and perpetually bound to procreate. In other words, things exist in the demise or absence of others, and others exist along with others, everything is in proportion and with equal treatment. In this case, the progress of Time, and the variation in Temperature, the Quintessence, merged and conducted thru the elements. It can be express and or comprehensible that the circumstances follow the time and temperature, while the later obeys on what the circumstances has had to offer and this reflects the nature of Quintessence; Fairly, elements undergoes test and Quintessence carried out to every entity. And it is amazing that the **(whole)** transmutation's process produce and cause the elements to exist, or obtain or procreates life and or matter in the universe as a product or as a consequence; one can consider this event as either purely circumstantial or circumspect, or can conceive as a miracle or usual occurrence, or an extraordinary or common phenomenon taking place (**As Heraclitus take His cue on this matter saying; "everything's change and even sleepers are workers and collaborators on what goes on in the universe" – Perhaps this is one reason, nay, don't be surprised if you find a number of men struggling to make ends meet, mainly because they had misconstrued Heraclitus idea, and that they opted for a not so lucrative career and that is to be a collaborators of this [sluggish] world. Blame this phenomenon to Heraclitus, one can say. It is funny but sometimes it is true you can find event or something in a (house) Chamber really slumber; I wish to soothe this urge by coming in to Las Vegas to watch Manny Pacquiao fights. I mean, I'm curious but I'm not quite sure if I'll pursue this one or the career, if you ask me, I'm slumberous**) and that carried out the task in a "discreet or calibrated manner" yet in a quantum degree of its intensity,* amount of an attribute, quality and accuracy by which unit is measured or justified of it's coming and going by circumstances thru time and temperature.

Quintessence is not that complicated as other may think so. Simply its duty is to work out in settling the disparity in temperature, a human for instance perspire, burp, yawn, sneeze among other, while when the atmospheric pressure increase, water evaporates, condenses and rain, abrupt or instant condition creates lightning and thunders in other cases. This writing understand that one consider these things as non, but a natural phenomenon, nevertheless, the central idea is more than this because it denotes the natural balance or equilibrium, and that maintain a state of stability resulting from the cancellation of all forces by equal opposing forces and that to prevent "rude or ruling" elements to take preponderance of the system resulting to a stable state or a harmonious, satisfying arrangement or proportion of parts and elements (balance), is therefore what this philosophy is trying to prove. In other words, **Quintessence is the sensible universal entity, overseeing the universal affair of all the entity, abstract or tangible including itself, wherein, itself is a product of the universal event and or contrivance, therefore the Methodology of Existence; The Fundamentals; The law; The Theory; The Creator; The Destroyer; The Ruler; The Peacemaker; The Regulator and a Pendulous Equilibrator providing or setting up the universe with the natural balance and that prevented a possible collapse scenario, is the chief reason of what causes us to exist in a material world. In other words, quintessence's a life giver.** It is notable however, and that spiritual concern might need more than this as applicable; this mean that as far as the comfort zone of one's soul is concern, the Noble deed's one way, and that's free will is restricted to oneself. In other words, rather, we can conclude that the fifth element or the Quintessence has a value of an "elevated" person's character or "noble spirit" and that the duo had an inclination to each other therefore can coexist at the summit or atop of all things.

In addition, rather, according to Gottfried Wilhelm Leibniz 1646-1716, a German mathematician and philosopher, it is God or the Monads that wills the pre-established harmony.

At this point however, it is notable that since Jesus of Nazarene challenged the idea or concept of His Great Ancestors doctrine and belief, the irony, rather, the big and yet only difference was that the notion that God lived alongside or interact with the patriarch, and that speaks of literal vision of God, wherein the former instituted refusal written from the Letter of John 4:12, saying **God is Love; No one has ever seen God, but if we love one another, God lives in union with us, and His love is made perfect in us.** And Jesus has once said that He come not to abolish the law (of Moses) rather to fulfill it. Base on this concept, the idea of Quintessence is to serve as an intermediary between the past and present or future, and that to harmonize the ancestral law or belief into the current legal system or legislation or technical and scientific knowledge in order to save the Earth as the purpose on its summit. We have to note however that religion is the basic, nevertheless the fundamental law of the land, but the law on today is the best rule or the most beautiful law has ever written of mankind so far **(In saying this is that backwardness [or conscientious ignorance due to self-interest] is really a great factor to radical view that breeds terrorism. And terrorism that was emerged or "cracked" upon religion [for different reason such as hatred, insecurity, frustrations and the like], is the monstrous atrocity the human had witnessed and experiencing nowadays)**. A prophet then could be a lawyer or legislator on today. In the year 4000, imagine a Cambridge or Harvard educated prophet. And one's not satisfied due to inequality, like Jesus of Nazarene also called as Christ, initiated reform. And the list of the reformist will fit not to write into this page. In this case rather, in support of John the Beloved, and that consider and take love or loving or thoughtfulness, as the most beautiful things as Neutralizer and the value of Quintessence is in yours. A must see Book 1 for additional input – The {Love's} Link between Science and Religion.

INTRODUCTION 8

The Shrewd

I'm trying to believe, nay, I don't mean to brag, but it is such an honor to compare or at least to correlate this writing to the works of the finest and of great mind, and that its gist shares the principle of the German wizard's named Gottfried Wilhelm Leibniz, and that His notable works include the theory on "Monads." It compared with the corpuscles of the Mechanical Philosophy of Rene Descartes 1596-1650 the "Jack of all trades" famous for his line "cogito ergo sum" or "I am thinking therefore I exist" and *others *as this was mentioned above and or on the following, nevertheless, encouragement was from Francisco Sanches a French-Portuguese physician and philosopher, 1550-1623 [author: That Nothing is Known] as He said; "you need to read books and compare it with the facts until the very end of your life."

We have to note however, that interpreting someone's work is not just sharing the central theme but in doubt, one should or has to make an investigation, or it is an essence to know or prove an idea on how it arrived into such conclusion.

Monads as Leibniz declared, are elementary particles with blurred perception of each other. They are the ultimate elements of the universe. The monads are substantial forms of being with the following properties: they are eternal, indecomposable, individual, subject to their own laws, un-interacting, and each reflecting the entire universe in a pre-established harmony. In addition, Monads are centers of force; substance is force, while space, matter, and motion are merely phenomenal. In addition, it said that by virtue of the principle of pre-established harmony, each Monad follows a preprogrammed set of instructions peculiar to itself so that a Monad knows what to do at each moment; e.g. each human being constitutes a Monad, in which case free will is problematic. God, too, is a Monad, and the existence of God can be inferred from the harmony prevailing among all other monads; God wills the pre-established harmony **(source – Wikipedia, the free encyclopedia)**. *Nevertheless, in reminiscence of the ancient Greek philosophy, it was said that all matter was made up of Water from which everything proceed and resolve, this, according to Thales 624-546 BC, one of the seven wise men in Greek and the founder of geometry and abstract astronomy. Unexplained, He left a peculiar quote and that He said: "All things are full of Gods."*

On the other hand, a little late of His predecessor named *Anaximander of Miletus 610 BC – 546 BC **(*Held the notion that the earth is aloft, not supported by anything, and this from the assumption that the heavenly bodies described full circles around the earth, from which He said that it stays in that position and does not move in any particular direction due to equal distances from all other heavenly bodies – source: thebigview. com/greeks/anaximander.html)**.

In another case, a Greek Philosopher named Anaximenes 600 BC - 528 BC, believed that the air is the primordial substance. He postulated that one time everything was an Air and it is the source of all things. And while He ascribed to "Air" divine attributes **(In this assumption, we have to note however, that the Aztec, or the people of the central Mexico [Latin America] and the ancient Egypt believes in the divinity of Sun, while John the Beloved of his first letter 1:5 and 4:8 of the Christian or Catholic bible mentioned that God is "love" and God is "light" in which the Book 1 correlates to an attraction or gravitational theory of Isaac Newton which is literally true to an operation of a heavenly body like the sun and or a galaxy that is literally a gas/light element; additional citation or a must see input in Book 1)**, *He laid a concrete or quality account of the fundamentals of aggregates and that He said; Air differs in essence in accordance with its rarity* **(correlated with heat)** *or density* **(with coldness)**. *Specifically,* *when it is thinned it becomes fire, while when it is condensed it becomes wind, then cloud, when it is more condensed it becomes water, then earth, then stones **(source-http://www.iep.utm.edu/anaximen/)**. In addition, His account that "the sun does not travel under the earth but circles around it," could had been misconstrued or carelessly interpreted or mishandled the literal concept of this passages and that regarded as **geocentric theory** or earth in the center of the universe; that was adapted later by the Greek – Roman citizen of Egypt; He was a mathematician, astronomer, geographer, astrologer and poet. Author of several scientific treatises such as Almagest **[astronomy]**, Geography and the "Four Books" that deals of astrology, His named was Claudius Ptolemy c. AD 90 – c. AD 168 **[source: the Wikipedia]**.*

*And on present era, according to, rather claimed by the Catholic church, 100 AD was the composition of the New Testament bible, particularly that of the book of John's that includes the book of Revelation. Regrettably, if it is the right word, the geocentric model was considered by the Catholic Church, and though draw support from the like of Danish astronomer named Tycho Brahe 1546 – 1601, however, brought out discomfort, dodge to avoid harassment or persecution, to say the least to some of renaissance thinker or polymath such as, rather, especially of the like of Nicolaus Copernicus, Polish 1473 – 1543, if not one, were the greatest among his contemporaries, was then a mathematician, astronomer, jurist with a doctorate in law, physician, quadri-lingual polyglot, classic scholar, translator, artist, Catholic cleric, governor, diplomat and economist; Though he was not the first to propose, Copernicus designed the **heliocentric model**, or the sun at the center of the universe in refutation of geocentric system; In this case, rather in here, or to support the idea of global warming fact, the essence of Heliocentric Theory is undeniable, or in really great significance mainly because it laid down the very foundation of the solar system functions and operation in general aspect.*

*In addition, nay, interestingly on this book uncover the idea of the moon quadruple motions **[see also Book 1- Moon's quadruple motion]**, that tells contrary to scientist's faith that an earthquake and tsunami are in fact completely unpredictable phenomenon, is wrong, this treatise could argue. In relation with the Earth celestial motion in particular, and this may cover the entire field of* major event or operation that chip in from, or a pre-indicative of the end of life and or biodiversity's theory or assumption, and that might be, or may take place soon, if we do contend not or upend the global warming phenomenon in the planet. It goes down to modifying and or wish to supersedes earth's essential hydrological and geological function, and that designed the formula on predetermining tsunami and earthquake, or specifically predetermining on when and where great upheavals like these would actually takes place.

With this idea, to say that the earthquakes and tsunamis are unpredictable nature's upheaval is a thing of the past. The concept include, nay, uncover the real theory behind the Tides (**low and high tide that scientist claim causes by the moon's circumnavigation around the earth is definitely false**) that it is merely the *revolution of the earth propelled by the sun (*****that creates ocean current; current under the ocean, has a significant factor or essential and specific duty and that is to cool the earth, as the radiator of a car cools its engine thus eluded a possible breakdown due to friction or heat; and overcoming resistance that leads to overheating and fusion that causes engine to malfunctions, is the essential knowledge this writing wanted to say in order for, the engine or earth as an entity, to save from global warming**), therefore water shifts from top to bottom (**falling down**) of the earth, thus, creates wave and tide, and or tides and waves creates the wind as a result.

This principle is in contrast with the **existing theory (****geocentric system; originally mentioned in Ptolemy's Tetrabiblos, perhaps the idea was from Anaximander of Miletus, 610-546 BC or on The Book of Joshua 10:12; except Copernicus and Galileo's [idea] which is unfortunately unsupported [by this theory], most of the medieval and brilliant physicist and or cotemporaries are erroneous, and some of them, only because, as this writing see it, besides the absence of the fundamental theory, is the inappropriate illustration of earth in respect with the core and operation of sun that leads to wrong assumption and application of the current data**), specifically, that the tide is the gravitational action of the moon upon the earth, and or the wave was created by the wind, are gross assumption, and that in totality are indeed wrong. In other words, operation of the body of *water which is vulnerable or susceptible to speed, is simple as the fan at rest, produce no wind, and so the water that is calm [**water positioned leveled on top of the earth and dormant or inactive for a certain time]; Due to** Earth revolution wherein its speed and diameter are in proportion with time, the moment that the angle of the earth shifted, the water starts to move or fall and refills with the one from the off-shore and that the gushing of incoming and falling water's interaction creates wave, and fanning [racing of water towards the shoreline] begets wind and shifting of water makes the tide or tidal activity **(see Book 1 for the complete version of the theory or Wikipedia's history of the tidal physics for additional input or references).***

And in addition to this, the concept for the advance meteorology or comprehensive and accurate weather forecasting and season's analysis are given emphasis. And moreover, rather, the total account may paved the way to the universal operation, the fulfillment of the theory of Universal Gravitation in particular postulated by Isaac Newton; English physicist 1642-1727, as well as on those Copernicus heliocentric model and Galileo's most anticipated compliment and or support so as to evade him of incarceration or house arrest. It goes well to Coriolis force and effect from French scientist Gaspard-Gustave Coriolis, 1792-1843 and the Special Relativity Theory advanced by Albert Einstein, German born theoretical physicist 1879 -1955. In addition to these, is the elucidation of the Big Bang theory originated from Monsignor Georges Lemaitre, a Belgian physicist and a Roman Catholic priest and developed by the Russian physicist and cosmologist named George Gamow 1904-1968, as well as the Steady State Theory elaborated by Hoyle, Bondi and Gold, and the clarification of the Black Hole Theory where in revisited by the English theoretical physicist Stephen Hawking 1942, and all the way to the origin of the universe and or its metaphysical attributes.

*With all of this, nay, with all of the wonder, one can say, as far as the author is concern, and this in reference to the denials of "heliocentric idea" postulated by Copernicus, what might be the deplorable idea is nothing [**may sound overly harsh**], rather disappointing about *Heliocentric theory [***citation on later part**], **is** only the way it's pronounced or that its pronunciation only sounds, or overtones may not suit well to everyone hears and thought; **hell-yu-centric**:*

I don't know if I should blame the Greek where the word originated from, or Sir Joseph Norman Lockyer, 1836-1920, an English astronomer for discovering Helium gas out of the sun's spectrum, and that, I suspected, nay, if it is the only concern **[deny, contradict or refuse to believe]** *of religious fervor to totally adapt or harmonize its teaching of truth with the fact of science, I suggest and or offer this writing as* **Helli-outbound One model** *theory, also called as the thwarting of global warming, or simply means as cooling the earth for its existence. Perhaps it is a great relief, for I understand, rather, believed that no one will love to accept "hell-yu-centric" knowledge, especially if you are an advocate or preaching and or learning moral philosophy.*

And in addition, Galileo Galilei, 1564-1642 an Italian physicist, mathematician, astronomer, and philosopher who played a major role in the Scientific revolution supporting Copernican principle, thus, tried by the Inquisition, found "vehemently suspect of heresy", forced to recant, and spent the rest of his life under house arrest **[source: Wikipedia]**, *as well as those reformists philosophers and or theologian like of Desiderius Erasmus of Rotterdam 1466-1536, Francisco Sanches, French-Portuguese 1550-1623, and or Baruch Spinoza a Dutch national 1632-1677. Furthermore, since educated from European philosophers in general, or from one of the entity above in particular, this treatise believed that the same fate had happened to Philippines' National Hero named Jose Rizal 1861-1896, a brilliant and young reformist, clashed with the current course of Philippines politics and society, thus exiled, charged with sedition and executed by firing squad, this, to name a few of the renaissance Inquisition. Inquisition however is a thing of the past and the Church express regret and sorrow on this, but this humble treatise ask a little more importance that have to do with the plight of the people of the reality of natural sciences, especially when it concern or comes with the natural event or disaster* **[see also the Book 1 or All But the World is Loving ISBN 9781434983824 available on Google, Amazon, Barnes and Noble, Rosedog or Dorrance Publishing and other ebook store; and that I ask for pardon for other retailer that may not be able or yet to mentioned here such as thebookcheckout.com that possibly available {but correction must be made on the information on this site and that the genre of these books is non-fiction instead of the fiction entry that** *they've made before any correction}, for additional input regarding on today's true concept of the church, and that with regards to this topic, John the Beloved, wherein Jesus of Nazareth instituted His church, thus considered in here the true Vicar of Christ {on this era} and Saint Peter, the chief of the Apostle and regarded as the first Bishop of Rome, and His successors, as the Church guardian].* For this reasons, made a great, significant or unprecedented impact as far as the religion and natural science oneness or holism approach or the compatibility or harmony of belief is concern. And that, devious or deviating from the fact of a natural science which is indeed, if not highly probable, one way or another, one can, rather, might lead to inappropriate application of method or law which may induce confusion at least, and tragedy out of natural cataclysm at most **(In 2013, Philippines suffered earthquake and the world's strongest typhoon so far)**, which is in fact the utmost concern of this writing. And the interest, as far as relating with the solution is involve, specifically, with regards to the human trend or its earth activity in relation to the impact of global warming and earth surviving method of existence, is providing the future generation of a safe and healthy environment.

Furthermore, Heraclitus of *Ephesus – *a city of Greek Asia Minor or present day western Turkey, who lived around 525 BC – 475 BC, famous for His perpetual flux theory, promulgated that all things are flowing and that nothing is permanent. He said that Fire is the origin of all matter; through it, or purification of a certain element were carried out by fire, which is cheaply understood in here as heat, nevertheless considered as co-equal, essential or an integral part of the significance of the "Theory of Everything," wherein, it had been preserved or safeguarded from the following concern. In this case, nay, in a certain degree, since commentator considered Heraclitus as pantheist, it says that "drawing unsupported conclusions from the fact of perpetual motion may be dangerous; but the fact of perpetual motion itself is no threat to human existence, epistemology or theories of truth" **(by John Scott – Individualism/ courtesy- Bertrand Russell)**. This was true according to account that Heraclitus produced a book that His followers said was hard to read or difficult to decipher and legend has it that a certain *Euripides gave Socrates a copy and ask Him what He thought of it. He replied: What I understand is splendid; and

*I what I don't is so too – but it would take a Delian diver to get to the bottom of it (***citation: Diogenes Laertius, Lives of Philosophers, II, 22**)."*

*Almost if not entirely, *Heraclitus sets the fundamental of the origin of the universe in one hand, and on the other as this writing see it, Heraclitus ideas specifically those He called "Logos" or the fundamental order of the cosmos that brought out the notion's "All is One or from all things one and from one all things" (**Its vague but the author see the same proposition when Jesus of Nazarene said that "I and the Father is One" or perhaps the singularity that Hawking is talking about**), sets the tone for the universe's mechanical operation, and coincidentally the idea on this writing concurred in His proposition and that said; "This world, which is the same for all, no one of gods or men has made; but it was ever, is now, and ever shall be eternal fire", carried out the anatomy or teleology of the origin of matter. In other words, fire (**heat or the time or degree of temperature**) govern the eternal transmutation of forms or entities such as the four elements' water, air, fire and earth or its atomic attributes, wherein cosmic balance [**the quintessence or void or the neutral point**] on their struggle, or the other way which is cosmic struggle on their balance leads to no one gains preponderance. In other words, after a certain degree of process such as disintegration, purification or rarefication, sifting, felting to name a few, express on Time and Temperature, again the elements recombined (**cosmic cycle**). In short, perpetual process or operation of the universe considered as "painful" most especially to radical faith and on a certain view and belief also applies on science as well as religion credence, if this subject matter differs from metaphysics in particular, or philosophy in general. But on the entire materialistic world, as we have seen, however, that we should be humble by the fact that nothing can refute what is the Truth of the matter. And this concept somehow found a little help or comfort from Empedocles of Acragas, 490 BC – 430 BC of His notion for the Love and Strife model, which possess similarity with the Yin and Yang of ancient China and or the Trimurti of Hinduism, while the Genesis creation theory of the Bible's old testament resembled at least the genre of writings. And Empedocles book "On Nature", and that explained and might lead to Darwin's theory of evolution more than two thousand years after Jesus of Nazarene. And the long list goes on for the prominent ancient Greek philosophers such as Pythagoras, Parmenides* and Zeno, Socrates, Democritus, Plato and to one most notable Aristotle among others. And this, with all the best the idea *[experience, wit and courage or guts, fortitude and effort]* this tenet can offer, is to laid down the thought, and that we human, has to protect the environment on what we are capable of doing here in the earth, such as reversing the trend the way we treated, or specifically mishandling of its natural resources, to the point that we can consider activity as abuse, thus, taken for granted the essence of survival and existence or the one we can call as the natural order of protection. Failed to counter the *global warming inclination, and that shall "hyper" the usual activity of the earth. And as we can see it may facilitate or expedite its process upon submission to the sun, therefore induces more powerful earthquake, pungent air upheavals, crushing tsunami, and shifted in between overwhelming flood and intense heat and drought, therefore will cost us the planet and our very own existence soon (*citation on the following part or in Book 1- All But the World is Loving; specifically the articles on Global Warming and on The Origin of the Universe).

THE THEORY OF EVERYTHING

On a modern physics, a theory of everything *[refer to in here as ToE]* would constitute or unify of what the scientist or physicist called "all the fundamentals interactions of nature" stated as the gravitation, electronuclear force, the interactions; weak and strong and electromagnetism. In this case, a person that should be knowledgeable of the theory of everything basically, a person that needs to know everything and that include a modern day problem unknown in earlier times. And meant not to brag, but that means is to include and divulge the deepest religious aspect of the community or of the world, that this writing considered as science or scientific field of the ancestral time, but was or could had been misconstrued at the present time? Anything unknown to others, might be taken away by someone else, something that has left unfounded, someone else might takes it place. Straight forward, Assumption is an assumption and a Truth is a truth and that One must live in accord of accuracy, or integrity or honesty or with the verisimilitude of matter. Feign or abstraction to govern people especially the intelligible youth of today could be a hardy thing. Religion *then in the absence of science, or science in the absence of religion, and this require a moderator. Someone needs to say these things.*

The long list of attempt by the physicists, scientists and philosophers [refer to in here as PSP] to discover the Theory of Everything, was noted as early as the Greek ancient philosopher's era which was widely known as the metaphysical view. While their renaissance counterpart, specifically, Copernicus' Heliocentric Model, Galileo's Astronomical Observations, Hubble Expanding Universe, Kepler's Planetary Motions, Newton's Gravitation, Leibniz's Monads, Descartes Dualism, and or Spinoza's Monism up to Dalton's Atomism theory and that really found their respective places in their respective field of expertise. Likewise, Einstein's Special or General Relativity, though found out not so perfect model, yet, comfortably sits inside the arena, was the framework of Hawking's Singularities and Black Hole Radiation to Milgrom's Modified Newtonian Dynamics [MOND] and Bekenstein TEVES and black hole entropy. Indeed on his authored books and or movie, Hawking had the most intense or jaw-dropping desire to develop the Theory of Everything, or at least to design an equation that simply describes the origin and operation of the universe. However, Fundamentals is the essence of the thing (that defeat skepticism) in order to come out with the idea that those great thinker had misses from the past and for a long a time (that could have alter the course of education or knowledge leading to a pragmatic approach of preserving life and or nature) and fortunately inscribed in here. Looking for the theory of everything or of the general equation, rather, this writing specifically, is like one of those who earn a living from digging in a file of debris hoping to come across from a previously missed precious stone.

Identifying theories in the field one after the other, is like using an iron pole or sickle looking for a clam scratching throughout a marshland or in the expanse of the shoreline. In order for one to have a good enough meal, should possess the virtue of determination, or must focus and brave the wind and cold and crooks. Putting them together all in here, seems more than that of cliché if not someone would accuse this writing for plagiarism anew. Nevertheless, this writing admire every man breaking their back for us to learn and or trying to give their best to subdued ignorance, whatever the method of education, whether it is work of science and religion, and that, with all honesty, since I've never been, yet longing to enter a university, this work's wholly credited from them. In fact, nay, compare to their work, while one can consider this writing as guy on the sidewalk, with their [PSP] great contribution in the educational institutions and industry, is like a flamboyant and indeed a beautiful woman to me, talking to her cell phone in one hand, and holding a Kalashnikov on the other and that behind the wheel of a sports car; a Ferrari, Volkswagen, Peugeot, Ford or Rover, Toyota and you named it, and really shine them with Greek-Polish's work. And that, accelerating with the speed of sound, the guy tries to run after the woman, only to tell her that she forgot to have her seatbelt on [adlib; To invite or not to invite for a ride is another story, or perhaps David Hilbert another problem].

Anyway, taking a peek on the different data, such as Ryle's super dense or Big Bang theory, advanced by Hoyle, Bondi and Gold, the Steady State or Continuous Creation theory, the Nebular theory postulated by Kant and Laplace, the planetesimal hypothesis of Chamberlain and Moulton, the Tidal theory of Jeans, the Twin sun theory explain by Hoyle, while more other or advance theories such as Lemaitre's Big Bang, Hubble's expansion of Space, variant or series of String Theories, M-Theory, Quantum theory, and the Uncertainty Principle and The Big Crunch among others that might "encompasses" them all, proved this writing right that men quest to find the theory of everything is an elusive thing. It is like the game of the wit and the brave heart and the thirst for the unification of the theory of everything, as this writing saw it, is unquenched so far, mainly because in the lack of, rather, in the *absence of the Fundamental (*incomplete or unjustifiable theory paves the way for Religion in trying to gain the upper hand; nevertheless, this writing believes the significant of theological science wherein in fact the idea of Jesus of Nazarene in redeeming his people from a possible flawed belief, wherein opposing this "faith", and that pride that manifest, rather, among his people to concede, considered or in a way as apostasy and that could means death; As far as religion is concern, The Theory of Everything is the most forbidden knowledge [pro-reformist: Socrates, Jesus Christ etc. a pantheism, agnosticism to an atheistic viewpoint], and that in a certain aspect, may surmount or supersedes the fundamental teaching of the congregation. Nevertheless, could be the great idea of Jesus of Nazarene when he talked about the "kingdom of heaven" or the "hidden treasure" [Matthew 13:44-52], and perhaps one, if not the main reason he was denied in Nazareth, his hometown. Great evocation, but one can correlate things with the passion of Stephen Hawking to find this "treasure" or knowledge as he consider the Grand Unified Theory or equation that generally described the operation and existence of the universe [Singularity] as "the thing" or "the one" "worship" by cosmologist [on the movie *The Theory of Everything*, when asked by his girlfriend then if what is the equation, he answered that it is the question]. And at this point of scientific era, it's not surprising to sense scruple or subreption or the cover up of a certain congregation in order to ignore the truth or theory of everything that they thought may negatively affect their business or congregation; the quality of life over the essence of nature, rule of law and truth of the matter and that may save the planet and us inhabitant, from extinction. The great question is that is it morally right to believe or feign on something that doesn't exist in order to govern people which has intellect and civilized manner? In a sense, or some say, somehow it is better to believe. Indeed the promise of the afterlife, to be born again, to reincarnate or everlasting life is a supreme purpose that the so called faithful [intellectual persons] would like to attain and that should yield a sublime trait or characteristic of human being to comfort the soul in the demise of life. Jesus of Nazarene and John the Beloved [considered in here as the real vicar of Jesus Christ, and was told on Revelation 10:11 and that "Once again you must proclaim God's message about many nations, races, languages, and kings."], concluded, and that God is a Spirit and by the Spirit [only] we can worship Him and that is thru faithfulness or intellectuality. And if the afterlife may take place somewhere else's, or say the paradise is nowhere in this planet to be found, mitigating global warming is in fact unselfish deed and that at least we preserve, or save our future generation's home from burning by its own creator, the Sun, anytime soon. Basically, the Sun absorbed the planets inward, or towards its core. The veracity of this notion, rather, any idea that may counter this reality must come forward, otherwise we have to settle global warming by whatever the *human being is able to do, whatever it may take or however the degree it matters; the tendency to work effectively and succeed. And this writing believed that some of these practical or efficacious remedy are vigorously planting trees or the massive reforestation, daunting [illegal] logging or deforestation, minimized or controlled, and ceases on gas and oil production eventually, wherein these remedies totally offset the green house emission only that scientist pointing at as the [main] source of global warming. This writing doesn't mean to brag and or scorn any individual, but assessment on this matter [global warming] seems to be vague considering the general aspect of the operation and existence of the planet, and or poorly evaluated if not just simply under estimated without assurance that limiting greenhouse gasses will in fact works against global warming. Compared to the value, richness, versatility and or universal applicability of the idea expresses on this tenet, it tells us that we are indeed running out of time. We must beat Nostradamus' prophecy that the end of the world is on the year 3797, wow, 17 hundred years more to live, that's pretty close. Accurate or not, the good thing is that he warned us. Whatever the method he used to tell us this idea, and fine if he carried out mathematical calculation, but a divination like this is an epitome of unselfish act. Sure he has the lead to arrive in such daring conclusion and this writing believed that this might take place, at this particular or given time, and that if we do less, or nothing at all to counter such prediction. Say using horses for transportation and relatively small population then, this writing's trying to say is that if he overlooked to consider the manifestation and effect of global warming in general aspect, the bad thing of this revelation is that it may come ahead of time, and this should remind us that every seconds count in this case. One way or the other way around, and that the truth of the manifestation of the afterlife will take place on the very same planet we live in, I believe everyone would agree, and that no one would love to live in the future on a burning planet, as we know it's hell.);*

Item number six, stated as to "Axiomatize" all of Physics from David Hilbert's 1862- 1943, a German mathematician's 1900's sixth problem, wherein physicists consider on today as the theory of everything. Knowing that after they dug enough for the principle, or the "treasure" they are longing for, barely indeed, specifically as thin as the Victoria Secret's underwear, they just missed it. It is almost there for what we consider great men is looking or longing for, and it is interesting in one point and exciting on the other, I mean the hunting for the Theory of Everything. The Greeks started it hot by laying the metaphysical foundation by instituting the origin of the matter; the water and earth and love and strife from Thales and Empedocles, especially the air and fire from Anaximenes and Heraclitus. After the atom's concept by Leucippus, then the English takes charge sizzling of the Newton's gravitation, or love theory's counterpart on religion before they arrive on Dalton's formulation and the French guy Coriolis force or effect theory which is in fact the fundamentals of *inflationary gravitation (***e.g. galaxy, sun; Coriolis theory is synonymous and or work side by side with Newton's Universal Gravitation and that its principle is not just essential to metrological advancement but work as well in aviation industry, marine and most of power generating and reproduction unit)**, *the Lemaitre's Big Bangs and Hubble's Expansion of the Universe to the idea of the Boson's particle accelerator. With all of this, rather, with the chronological order of event and its overtones, I understand, and that's poignant or unfortunate that not everyone could grasp the idea on the creation theory on Genesis and that this writing consider science on that era, nevertheless counter by Jesus and sure it does fall or come short of word and appropriate terminologies to reach his objective, and that to totally divert or reversed their believing therefore submit himself to death to prove the veracity of his claim and so I believe this tenet to the best of the author ability. As a result, they agree in one, they disagree from or for the other thus, none of these attempts were successful. And to make it short, this writing hope is to compliment the work of Jesus and the like of him who break their back for the welfare of the planet, biodiversity and of the common good and thus it is the author's turn to take on the wheel (and be with the woman on the sports car and have fun and explore the world of astronomy and science).*

The Universal Gravitation

The subject, postulated by one or the greatest of the scientist named Isaac Newton, described it as the pulling of an object towards the earth. Albert

Einstein nevertheless, considers it the force warping of the very fabric of the universe. One can come up with the definition of the term the simple way for the commoner to comprehend, and the complex or complicated one for the erudite and scholars to foster (please note that the rest of the idea is in support, direct or indirect explanations for any question that may arise from this subject). Simple equation that unifies all the theories must learn the fundamentals or the very origin and operation of the universe. As an essence, rather without this, the theory of everything in here is just another missed or failed attempt definition.

To come up with its operation in particular, **Universal Gravitation should be define as the capacity of the body to draw an element (or gasses specifically) towards its core (of production). Its main purpose is to fuel itself for combustion or nuclear fusion and production (of heat) known as compression (of gasses) in order for the body to stay afloat, diversify and exist in the firmament.** *Out of this principle, we have to perceive the basic knowledge, and that a balloon filled with gas stays afloat in space. Dark matter (or space) though universal and encompassing, however, is lighter and or vulnerable element, therefore give way in the creation or in the presence and existence of a much more heavier or strong or sturdy element such as light (or fire such as galaxy and sun), planets and asteroids. It's like an object or ship on the body of water therefore displaces or sanctions a certain space. In this case, to push or set aside or to defeat [temporarily or in unspecified time] the dark element or matter in order for a body to exist, is the name of the game* **(Darwin's Evolution says that able or stronger cell has more capability to survive or should we say that God favor only the strong?).** *Serves as the partition wall in space, and that whatever the causes of the disintegration of a certain body, the dark matter (gasses/space) in which, nay, in strict sense can consider as *elastic or a flexible entity is therefore shall regroup, solidify or mend itself once again (or level back from a temporary displacement or dissolution or disposition). In other words, rather specifically, in the demise of matter, the light or body such as galaxy, the Dark Matter or Space and or Gasses (characterized as omnipresent, omnipotent and omniscient; see also the theory of Quintessence for additional input) regain its "Loaned Post or Property". Or as the object in the body of water has been removed [lifted up sanction], therefore the level or element of water regroup or reinstated*

(*whatever the degree of mass or weight of the matter, the space or gasses [liquid or water] as vulnerable element, and elastic, expand or regenerate [by compression] thus provides gasses and or space. In other words, space or gasses, and that as generous as it was and it can be, give way for every "stubborn or sturdy" entity; if you will, one can cogitate, recollect or correlates this idea to the ancient thought [of scholars of most probably a science subject then, or scientific thought of ancient scholar] of what we can consider, or as the author see it, is what we known as the religion of the present time. In fact, nay specifically, the "Love" word of religion (then) could be the counterpart of the word "gravitation" invented or popularized by Isaac Newton on the later era, wherein both vocabulary, literally signify "attraction". Therefore as far as the comparison, analogy or availability or the use of the word in different era or occasion is concern, this treatise conclude that the subject matter, are in fact the same thing or having similar connotation, therefore consider in here as "One". In other words, significant, nay, essential, the "quality" relationship between these words is in fact, rather, as the author see it, is the link between science and religion. Should we say Religion in the absence of Science, or Science in the absence of Religion? Adlib: Mr. John Templeton, philanthropy, put a great price for us to discover and to learn on this thing. In the absence of reliable information, or of undependable and or unconvincing notions, individual or a community is tending to find a place left unfounded. Anyway, we have to work hard, find and unleashed the Truth, because Truth is not a threat to human existence; the truth of the matter is in fact what really matter in this world of existence, of human existence. Let's prove the veracity of every claim, and make sense out of change).

Deriving, rather a formulation of a simple equation that may unify all theories in the field of Physics is possible, but as the physicist contend and that is as long as it can answer all the questions that will be put forward. And it's not an easy task to defend a great idea. Fortunately, uncovering the fundamental that support the theory of everything could be a good try, though we have to note that the full potential of the equation, or the specific application, this writing doubt, will satisfy or please the perception of the great mind of skeptics mainly because, rather, since a body like galaxy is dynamic and vibrant substitution could be problematic. However if a body reaches its full potential (Chandrasekhar Limit) or the culminating point of the body that is large enough to diversify, is only the point we can derive conclusion wherein, in human aspect is improbable (it is impossible to determine that a body is fully grown up or reaches maturity). Like in human being, different body has different metabolism. Nevertheless for the sake of Stephen Hawking, of his wit, desire and determination, and sure a laudable effort to contribute in this field of academic, the origin, operation **[one way cycle of operation from repose to reproduction and reposition; element of gas to liquid to solid to liquid to gas]** *and perpetual cycle and existence of the universe, this treatise consider as the most simple equation in the world but powerful enough to consider the history of the universe and mankind.* **C=T/t. or C=T.t Circumstances or Condition with the factor of Temperature and time. Or Circumstances that is equal to Temperature in proportion (or complimented) with Time C=T~t.**

Temperature complimented with Time, on its fundamental and main factor of the operation. It can be express as Temperature power by Time or Temperature over with time factor. $C=T~t$ *or* T^t *or* T/t, $(T.t/t)$. *Considering the relationship between temperature and time factors, in strict sense, we have to consider that each of them differ in circumstances. Specifically, picking up the degree of temperature can be consider acceleration with time, and reaching the temperature peak point could slow it down, and that may be true the other way around. In this case, the theory on the summit is that the Circumstances is in fact the actual modifying factor; a condition that determines or signify the course of action or execution (say, in a military drill, the word "forward" in a "forward march" command, is the factor[s], and "march" as the execution order). In other words, the real authority who order or decides on one's fate is the Circumstances, and that if the circumstances permitted, thus commence (the manifestation), and when the circumstances satisfied, therefore execute. And this conclude that at any given point of temperature or time [mutually, reciprocally, collectively or simultaneously], or condition in general aspect, the Circumstances works at will on what it will on its will.* **Circumstances is the manifestation of Chance, that is, albeit of the satisfaction, is in fact the dereliction of contributing factors; a certain procedure using an alternative channel,** *passage or route, a detour in a certain case. In human aspect, the unknown, uncontrollable or unexpected. In strict sense, however, can be consider an element that is predictable and controllable by its own virtue of circumstances. In one hand, complex things or event can be consider happening by chance and that things miraculously coincide, or plainly, a normal circumspect in the other.*

Temperature [commonly] known as the degree of hotness and coldness, and in here, define as the Sensitivity of the whole entity and or all of the things that matter. It is, but not limited to the intensity of radioactive or nuclear force, molecular activity and or chemical reaction. In its basic or simplest form of function, equation's define as T~t=EMP(t/t). The temperature that works in Circumstances or on its operation is simply or equal as the electromagnetic (EMP) pulling forces complimented by time or by the timing that lay on circumstances. And on cryogenic time, it's the purification process by contraction base on the degree of temperature and that separates the pure gasses or element from *hydrocarbon (*water plus carbon equal to dried ice) and this element become the potent cell for big bang that creates the galaxy.

Temperature is innate and latent to all entity or things; a one-way [toward the prevailing or ruling forces or circumstances, or factors of temperature and time] stream of forces originate as the result, rather, an outcome of the thermo dynamic activity of matter and space. In an elevated form of matter, it expresses as T=EMP(t/t)+emp(t/t) which is the electromagnetic pull of temperature in the space with the electromagnetic discharge (push) from a body. It's the conduction and or reaction, or an interaction between forces such as friction, attraction or tension, a transmutation's process. It is the driving force behind the dynamic universe that circulates between the expanse of coldness/ darkness with, and or against the heat/light body in the firmament. Temperature [complimented or in proportion with time] dictates or satisfy the reason of existence, de-existence and re-existence. With the attributed nature of Circumstances, [ruling] Temperature's aim is to conquer and subjugate and prevail and destroy and create and recycle; the whole process (pull and discharge of forces - electromagnetic conduction serve as the transformation or transmitting power) is in fact produces or the Creator of a perpetual cycle universe.

Dark Matter or space, or gasses in space below or in absolute zero temperature is the transformation or transient point by contraction, the homogeneous way, as fire or heat (The scientific or technical term could be consider as the one way "electromagnetic pull [or attraction or conduction" of an element with the same value or characteristic] towards the {core} point of {cell} production that denotes a prevailing [influence of greater] Temperature). It's the purification process of the space; the gas's element itself in it, and that pave or leads the way to the construction of carbon gasses or dried ice (And that in strict sense, the [should be] refused element/matter, is in fact the viable cell (potential energy) or essential component responsible in producing [another] body, the origin[nal] way, and or offspring through the synthesis [sexual reproduction] by way of powerful concussion or collision and revolution, as the method present in existing or latest reproduction/ evolution theory. However we cannot discount the possibility that classical method of production takes place in most remote places of the firmament and or perhaps to the far end of the suction chamber of the Galaxy [while on the Sun's aspect, it's the creation of planetary and satellite body]. It's the Temperature [and the Time however true and work alongside, but act considerably as secondary factor, because in strict sense, rather in a certain application, however innate, the essence of degree of Temperature is required more than that of the Time aspect, specifically the later application depends on the former characteristic or trait, and or varies with the Temperature has had to offer] that is mainly responsible for the evolution of a certain organism or species, to commend or cease, its production [See the following theory on Big bang, Galaxy and the creation of Sun] which is absolutely and precisely true in the case of human being reproduction method. We have to note that the quality of sifting and purification, or separation of the compounded gasses depends on the capability of Temperature; the extreme the case is, the purified the gas more, and the harder the refuse element or dried ice, that is an epitome of a great potential energy that is like a ball on top of a table in a simple analogy). The great factors on shaping this gigantic element is the Temperature [that exerted the full potential or its essential or the ability of contracting force to form a body of dried ice], and the element of "Time" can be consider if not working alongside as skeptics [or Scarlett Johansson - the movie titled Lucy] may argue, on construction process, wherein the mass or volume [of sperm as the gigantic dried ice] will satisfy to set off as the monstrous object that detached from the main frame or the whole element itself that is capable [fertile] enough to ensued a successful production of body like Galaxy through a certain process called the Big Bang or the collision of the paternal cell with its maternal [female/egg cell] counterpart.

From a dual stage of creation (*conventional way or old fashion or the cold/ cryogenic time and **mass production of a body by heat/friction as the latest method manifesting on a body of galaxy), a complex or elevated method of functional universe, considering its specific task, **Temperature** *is propagated or power with* **Time***, as the* **Electromagnetic pull** *(*as first stage) over the space known as* **Dark Matter***.* **Big Bang** *event is over the* **Volume** *and* **Mass** *of a Body (carbon dioxide or dried ice) over its* **Hardness** *over the* **Speed of Travel** *over* **Resistance** *multiplied by* **Friction** *over the* **Point of Contact***. And or over by* **Universal Gravitation [**as the second stage]** *as the rate of Body's* **Speed of Revolution** *over* **electromagnetic force (as push)** *over* **Resistance (Purification, Compression and or Nuclear Fusion and Nuclear Fission or Gas Discharge).**

T = (EMP$^{(-c)}$)(emp$^{[c]}$)~t -- actual event or creationism on initial stage simply express as

C = T/EMP+P[~t]

wherein:

T= Temperature EMP= electromagnetic pull -C= degree Celsius in negative aspect/ cryogen time emp = electromagnetic force C = degree Celsius positive aspect t= time [~]= equal to or in proportion or complimented with P= Purging

$$G_u = (EMP.B_{b/[V+M/H/}\{S_{t/[R(F)]}\}/P_c)(emf.R_{s/}[R/F\{P+C_m+N_f+N_d\})(t)$$

or Universal Gravitation can be simplified and express as $T= {}_{Rs/Nf\,(Nd)/Y[-t]}$

or Gu= Rs/EMP+P+Cm+Nf(Nd)/Y[-t]

wherein:

G_u = *Universal Gravitation Rs= Speed of revolution EMP= electromagnetic pull (negative aspect)* B_b= *Big Bang V= Volume M= Mass H= Hardness* S_t= *Speed of Travel R/[F]=Resistance/Friction* P_c = *Contact Point* $_{emf}$= *electromagnetic force (push/positive aspect [from the operational body/ galaxy]) P= Purging/Purification* C_m=*Compression* N_f=*Nuclear Fusion* N_d=*Nuclear Discharge (fission) Y= Growth t= time [~]=equal to or in proportion or complimented with*

We have to note that any mathematical operations, comparison or substitution can be consider complex and or can complicate the system (like the "essence" of time, in philosophy, number is a mere assumption adlib: please don't ask me if "mathematics" has something to do with a person who opted or prefer philosophy in the first place; the best thing to learn in life, is the [moral] philosophy, they said). Anyway, depending on a person academic background or skepticism, approach however variable and or complex, but to achieve a balance state or an **Equilibrium,** *the fundamental of existence, method can be reduce or simplify to the simplex form of equation, or the idea require the simplicity of the method of operation. Like a snow that fall softly into the ground and a sharp double edge sword, the essence of knowledge of the theory of everything should come naturally and penetrate with ease. And without burden, should sit comfortably as the fundamental [concept] of learning.*

The first stage of the creation is to build up the cell responsible for the Big Bang that creates the body of Galaxy. The second stage is the operation of the Galaxy wherein the duty of speed of revolution's and electromagnetic pull is set for self-correction or body's stability. Its primary aim is to build up pressure, heat or gasses to stay afloat in the firmament. To balance the system, the kind of unrestricted operational body is inflationary - suction gasses into black hole or port, compression, absorbed and diversifies, and excess of element went out through the equilateral point (edge) by centrifugal force or action. In case of dissolution, and whatever the cause of the death of a body like galaxy (more likely of choking or partiality in production), is that, dark matter will reemerge, occupy space and preponderate and that is to go back to the first stage once again and create a perpetual cycle.

The Cryogenic Time

Cryogenic term is related to cold or low or to extremely low temperature that is capable of burning. It defines by the academics as the branch of chemistry and engineering that involve the study of the very low temperatures, how to produce them, and how materials behave at that temperature. *But first and foremost, this writing note, that one, or chemist specifically must be aware of the logical pitfall observing this phenomena. Say in a closed or limited container that depict a literal observation of an experiment (**water or liquid in a plastic container that turn into ice; by contracting force, container bulges because gasses is forcefully attracted by or in response to the temperature of the refrigerant), but could yield a wrong conclusion or hypothesis against the fact in an actual circumstances, specifically, in an open space like the firmament (**unconfined element in a firmament undergoes contraction), in which define the real nature or full potential of the subject matter (natural and unsupported), thus, theory and the actual circumstances define in here, is in contrast with one another [*citation's shortly on the following].

To think or to consider the era of cryogenic as the beginning, or halfway after the beginning, all the way through the creation of the universe specifically the Galaxy as the foremost creation as inflationary body (and to think that a "dark matter" is in fact the counterpart, and or space that exist in the absence of "light element"), which is against the "dark matter or energy" consider as the pull of cold's contracting force, can be a good start. Nevertheless, the most essential aspect of the theory is to think that the Temperature and *Time (*could be consider as secondary factor because it was only invented by human, perhaps by observing the variant in Temperature) is the *supreme authority that command or trigger the transformation process of every entity in *the universe* **(Element or Matter in the universe sense and obey only the essence of Temperature for its existence. Human or being with thinking, had control over their lives, but in strict sense, the Temperature dictates longevity therefore exist or desist. And Time, though offer the method of organized comparisons or measurement, but when it comes to vagueness of space or the firmament, is immeasurable, and that in strict sense, deemed unnecessary).** *Temperature initiates the actions or the struggles in between the elements of their provisional or impermanent destiny (*the veracity of this claim somehow may hurt those who believe in something that pleases them, nevertheless, denying the truth or the significance of the idea shall compromise safety and or existence of human being, inhabitant, biodiversity, and the planet itself. However noble teaching and works adds beauty in human's life and existence, and for the faithful, the comfort of the soul in the demise of flesh. Anyway, we have to note that gas or variant of gases, is a synthesis of the elements. And to achieve the purest of the element [in which associated with the Temperature] is to come out with the "God" particle or the Neutral aspect of the element, and that everything had been originated. In other words, or as a compliment on this idea, is that gasses on the space is like water in the oceans, however it was dense, you can reach the bottom that holds or support the water in place. Literally, from the solid structure of the ocean we can have or go through various element or component until we reach the core of the planet. And from this layer/structure or innermost point, since the planet is round and floating in space, we can go through the same element until we get back to the structure on the other side that supports the water in the ocean in place. And so the gasses on the space are, and that however it was dense, one can penetrate and get through its stages through the application of "varying" temperature has had to offer, and that means, one can think that is in fact impenetrable because of thermal limitation the nature or technology can provide. The pure element is the element's pure and is the banking point or core or central point that holds the space on its own, or in place).*

*And one of a million dollar worth of question is how do these elements, the light and dark matter specifically, exist, and since in strict sense they are an opposite energy or contradicting forces, what does it takes, or the fundamental of operation of existence, for them to co-exist? [**The theory that holds on to** *"push on heat" and "pull on cold" is in fact, the one-way stream of energy, or the supreme power that no entity can stand against. And that in ancient time, knowing that it was interpreted or assumed the work of God, and that anyone who works against a prevailing and one way force [of noble deed], is a sin and means death actually, is a great and a crude statement]* How does an equilibrium, a neutral point or a partition wall work in the system? *In strict sense, rather, we have to note early on this thing that the pushing and pulling forces or pressure of light or heat and cold or dark element is in fact a "One way" or "Mono" operational principle of the matter. In other words, depending on, or whatever the circumstances has had to offer, Force or forces are must be re-generative or renewable, otherwise non-operational universe as we know would exist, or would exist not at all. When dark matter or coldness preponderates, it creates heat or fire, and when the later dominates, it annihilates each other and creates space. And this is the fact, that no one has a total control over circumstances, and that even the supreme authority of Temperature has no control over itself from taking its course, otherwise the Nature grand design of Regeneration or God's perpetual, elegant fashion of [moral] reformation? So as the faithful said and that God is forgiving? Locally, nay, planetary concern, this is the very principle of laying out the fundamentals on emphasizing the essence of planet's existence; to mitigate global warming by inducing renewable energy and deferring activity that compromise its element, the whole assembly and inhabitant of the earth).*

However worth notable it is, and that a perfect model of the universe or the true theory of everything can proceeds either from starting halfway to the summit, or halfway going back to the origin or the fundamentals, and for those who may have the "ladder" can carried out proceedings starting from the very beginning all the way to the summit. And if its "faithful" with the Truth, or the theory that is true to the Fact, is therefore corroborative, one way, or the other way around, and that is from the fundamental to the summit, working back to its novice. Stephen Hawking's idea of Singularity however may work, but without the knowledge beyond the big bang or fundamental theory in general aspect, unfortunately their idea cannot stand alone in this case. And the catch's, Truth works on theories like a sieve on the field; it goes and unites with those of dependable, honest and factual, and it invalidates and disregard otherwise.

It is notable that hard science theory or hard concept on religion is therefore a hard thing; Sure, nay, as a result, one must understand that not everyone can comprehend on a tenet that is not supported by at least logical reason corroborative with the fact or *tangible things, to say the most or *hyper, as other may consider as overly stated. Nevertheless, complimenting or proving this thing with a concrete evidence or specific comparison where in the theory is consensus, is much better than an assumed truth or feign or conjecture that is highly improbable; In this concept, this writing hope for this younger generation to perceived things or presages in ingenious manner at most, if not to learn to "read the writings on the wall" at least, where in, we, or our predecessor's in a certain field and point of time, could have been failed miserably, however, given the difference between circumstances, we should understand the learning process that may take time. In other words, balance approach, the stable mental or psychological and emotional state and a harmonious or satisfying arrangement or proportion or parts and elements to produce an Equilibrium that has the power or means to decide, is the success or the triumph of logic of reason [a must see Black Hole theory on Book 1 for additional input].

Literally, the fact that in the absence of light [or heat], it is the darkness [or cold] that shall exist is basic and comprehensible. If the later take preponderance, it must be a cold or Cryogen state. In this case, if the firmament or the space which is composed or made up of different [degree of] gases, is under the rule of cryogen, therefore elements is subject for transformation to what the cryogenics [degree of temperature] has had to offer. Specifically, elements or gases went through extreme purification process by Contraction [In this case, this writing's give the credit to Greek philosopher named Anaximander for his concept that the universe arose out of the separation of opposite qualities from one primordial substance]. As a result, the lighter, or could be the hydrogen gas in particular, separates from the refuse or denser one and that is the carbon dioxide or dried ice. The dried ice clamped together and *again, on what the cold circumstances has had to offer, went through cryogenic hardening. It is notable that object undergoes hardening by cryogenic method is much better than heating process especially on the firmament wherein its full potential, the time and temperature is fully expresses. Element's *shrink and more compacted [*The reason this writing pre-noted to beware of the trouble in the observance of cryogen experimentation; In a very low temperature, the carbon dioxide or dried ice, that is the refuse material, should not expand but compacted; However, if the matter is confined, since it may depicts bulges on a container {plastic} the observation however is correct, where in the suction or contraction force or process pulls the purified gas or the element that depicts the same thing with [and that means coexist] that of the ruling temperature through the element of the refuse or denser substance itself, therefore bulged as a result. The scenario is like extracting a seed from the core of a fruit or by pulling a fish bone out from the flesh itself by force therefore bulges] thus, contraction depending the degree of process (time) and temperature could yield the hardest material one could ever make or fabricated, thus, dried ice could become hard or it is the process to create another element like diamond.*

After millions or a billion of years in a sole and yet, constant suction or contracting process, we expect the microscopic element (dried ice) is now relatively monstrous and gigantic in size [see also Book 1 for additional input]. We have to note that this view described the initial state only or on primordial phase of universe's creation process and that for sure differs from what we observe nowadays. Specifically, the steady state creation process or the body's ability to procreate itself and that the greatness of dark matter which is extremely cold in temperature leads into friction that creates fire as the Galaxy we have observe today. While it is not discounted that the creation of a certain body like the Sun undergoes the same process as the Galaxy has been originated, nevertheless, it is consider in here that the former is in fact the offspring of the later [This is the notion wherein this treatise believed to be in harmony or correlates with the Old Testament creation theory, when they said in Genesis 1:26 and that; "Let Us make man in our image, in our likeness…," and this proposition consider as crude if not concise, against on today's scientific, detailed or well explained concept on anthropology and or biology or the evolution theory of human being and that originated from a universal common ancestor. And thought to be great, rather in strict sense, as a consequence from the process out of a Neutral cell or simply the virtue of the Quintessence; The problem of the ancient time is that they thought that sex as the Original Sin, and that was the cause of death, and they burned incense and offering for the atonement of "Sin". Jesus of Nazarene also called as Christ, however, born of a virgin, put foot down and proved that the greatest of the sin is the defilement of one's thought and that leads in putting away of what he called the Holy Spirit {the actual noble deed} and his faithfulness conquer death and that put things together].

The Big Bang

The Big Bang theory is the prevailing cosmological model that described the early development of the universe. It said that the universe was once in an extremely hot and dense state which expanded rapidly. This rapid expansion caused the universe to cool and resulted in its present continuously expanding state. After its initial expansion from a singularity, the Universe cooled sufficiently to allow energy to be converted into various subatomic particles, including protons, neutrons, and electrons **[source: Wikipedia]**. Concise or crude, but this idea might be considered correct, only if a person knows the fundamentals of operation. Nevertheless, logical pitfall is the common concern and confusion is one of those.

To those who had not been to the Book 1 or All But the World is Loving, the great challenge on this notion, is on how the Big Bang takes place and how a galaxy is was created. In here, the cryogen concept that explain the initial process regrouping a certain element or a refused material from contraction's purification process, which is what we known the carbon gases or dried ice, into a denser and or massive state or matter million or perhaps billion times the size of the earth, and floating in the space.

Without the fundamental, or in the primordial state that has no concept of the gravitational process, yet **[we have to note that true in every aspect and or all places, development of body's structure's one way or a mono procedural and homologous process – corresponding or similar in position, value, structure, sequence or function and or criteria in general term]**, *a massive and denser body, consider at this point as the Patriarch, which this writing described as "Gigantus Quantitativus" or a very large object, is tend to *drop and hurled, and that once the momentum takes place* **[*drop and momentum can be a detachment of a portion of the dried ice from the main frame or of the whole cell assembly itself; see also Book 1 for the theory of virgin conception or natural outgrowth or the self-ignition course of action and brought Galaxy into existence, deemed as one of a million chances]**, *hurried and or catapulted in space, with the virtue, or thanks to its own weight.*

And this, the theory become apparent when someone think that in all the expanse of the universe, the cryogenic procedure commenced simultaneously or all throughout the firmament, thus, the great [sperm] cell or matter in great shape **(consider in here as the patriarch and the egg cell is the would be [stationary] counterpart)** *and moving with tremendous force and speed and travels billion of kilometer, and that depend on a body's capability to last, circumstances, or its mechanical structure against resistance or friction on space. Along the way, with no particular or specific target, could have met or hit His counterpart by fortuitous* **[in the creation or on the beginning of the universe the patriarch's definitely promiscuous, while in human aspect, it is very fortunate that men and women have plenty of choices, and by the latest technology, meeting the love one online is easy now a days; however in this instance, if the uncertainty principle of German Physicist named Werner Heisenberg, applies particularly in quantum mechanics in which states that it is impossible to correctly determine the position and speed of a subatomic particle, this idea precisely applies on creation of the galaxy, its gigantic counterpart]**, *and that ensued collision that we can called the* **Big Bang**. *Big bang is the heavy blow between a violent, rugged and strong densely pack carbon dioxide* **(dried ice** *or group of ices)* in a single or in a series of collision and cannot imagine sounding loud and dull. It is like striking a match into a counterpart thus ignites. And with the presence of hydrogen gas in space extracted or existed from purification or contraction process in the cryogen stage, and that help ignited the union of the two bodies that created the Galaxy as result (Vector). A galaxy rotates one way **(centrifugal force's momentum taken from the collision)** and it contracted gases from the space and feed to its port **(through the black hole)** and leads to the chamber or core for nuclear fusion for its survival, therefore ever diversified **(until it may come to its [Chandrasekhar] Limit)**, floats and existed in the firmament. And the Universal Gravitation applied on this body working like of a centrifugal pump, is a multiple process sum up as Revolution, Suction (gravitation/ attraction), Purification (Tensor), Nuclear Fusion and the Nuclear Fission of gases through the equilateral area or edge to balance the system (Scalar). The body like Galaxy, or Sun consider in here as progeny, sucks and feed gases into the opposite ports collides and increase the velocity and magnitude or power and heat and with the help of centrifugal force acting on its body, discharge gases to balance the system. And the manner that this body doesn't collapse or discharge all at once, mainly because of the strong gravitational attraction or attachment on its body **(consider in here as *Post Positive Area; a must see Book 1 for additional or comprehensive input)** that serves as the *Casing of that gigantic gas pump known as Galaxy. And this simple or basic procedure that is repeated again and again, day after day or night after night becomes a cycle that we can consider now a Steady State methodology of creation wherein the sun consider as galaxy's offspring. In other words, through the powerful centrifugal force acting on the body of Galaxy, it creates the Sun, or regenerate itself through its own spiral arms **(see the Book 1 for images and additional and comprehensive input regarding this idea)**, and the catch is the evolution of creating a galaxy the original way (big bang) could had been ceased or altered by the virtue of the circumstances within. Wasn't correct the author of Genesis of the Old Testament when he/she said that a woman was made out of the flesh of a man? Does it consolidate that the theory of religion and science is nothing but one?

And the question preceding the next stages is that; how could a certain body or Galaxy survive and operate in particular, or what is the method of its existence in general? And considered the Sun as its offspring, how could a body like Galaxy procreates another body from within?

The Galaxy and the Universal Gravitation, Operation and Existence

*Besides the metaphysical theory of the four elements namely air, fire, water and earth, and with Greek's Heraclitus' Fire and Flux theory and Empedocles' Love and Strife, the Universal Gravitation idea postulated by the English Physicist named Isaac Newton, is one if not the greatest contribution on the field, this treatise could claim **[by this article a must see Book 1 for the theory of the link between science and religion – The Love and Gravitation].** The fact that the essence of Gravitation signifies the existence of a certain body, specifically, a Galaxy, and that signifies heat and the procreations, and that tells about its offspring, the Sun in particular, and this body creates the planet like the Earth, and push on the creation of human being on its permissible or allotted time of biodiversity.*

*In one point, it's hard to believe if not really unbelievable that the huge body of fire and immense heat that manifest on a body of Galaxy [with the billions of sun or star in it], originated or brought out from the huge volume of dried ice, a refuse element from rarifying gases. Amazing indeed, and might require a tangible proof to prove the notion. Based on this idea, European scientist could tell if the Large Hadron Collider is in fact useful in this case or could have the ability to mimic or simulate the big bang. If that so they must ceased it from operation neither try because they might creating a monstrous machine. Anyway, the idea of universal gravitation might be consider as the fundamentals of the theory of everything, but unfortunately the author (Isaac Newton) were unsuccessful or misses to provide then, the most important aspect of the concept, that any notions in a subject that matter is required, and that is the Principle of the matter's origin and existence **(And legend that it has, when someone ask Newton what is the cause of Gravitation, he loftily declared that it is enough for him to know that gravitation exist, is like a pinched on or a thrust on a gas filled balloon, and this writing hope not to sound***

conceited, but in this treatise believe that it cover up and fulfilled or consolidate the essence, rather, preserve the significance of the idea). *And in this regard, in the absence of the foundation or central structure, this writing observed that the general concept of Big Bang, Galaxy formation and operations, the Black Hole and or Dark Matter, and the String Theory among others, was wildly amiss. I'm no Physicist, yet this treatise afraid that the concern body working on these things would arrive on the real objective since working on the great elements to *unify the nature interactions [****citations on the following***] were likely to fail mainly because banking or being dependent on the sophisticated or scholarly idea, may not suit or work well in this case, as it was proven by the different attempts on different era. The mechanics on thinking of the big one's may require a different approach in this case. In other words, this treatise believed that [**if**] we cannot "tame the bull by the horn" [**and not**] all the time, and especially if it is a cow, as I have witnessed, someone have to try from behind, and it may works, and that is the gambit of instinctive, natural or conventional or literal method of measurement and or comparison by "experience". We have to wary that the fact in this case left unexplained, could had been "exploited", and the time that the truth of the matter uncovered, could had been "abuse". And this is the serious concern of John the Beloved, author of the book of Revelation; yet, skeptical (figurative language and he dodged the authority from Jerusalem and migrated to Turkey; while Nostradamus in a certain aspect, Copernicus a medieval thinker posthumously publish his idea, as he seen Galileo condemned of his writings. And a little earlier, the same fate was true with Aristotle as he said "I don't want Athenians to sin *twice against philosophy" and thus left Athens [*initially with Socrates]), nevertheless, John opted to tell the Truth, an introduction to scientific revolution, or in strict sense, a pantheism view, for the sake of mankind.*

When the Big Bang ensued, or bodies with great magnitude with the capacity of hundred million atomic bombs, smashing to each other is really great. Collision or struggle alone between bodies to create or transform into another body might even take a hundred thousand or even a million of years. That was long in human aspect but could be true in a huge or immense cell. And it is notable, and literally, the point of contact itself is important as the vital aspect of the theory. Mainly because it would determines the body's manner of operation or upbringing. In other words, nay, specifically, if the point of contact or hitting from the patriarch goes well right in the middle portion of the matriarch, thus splitting them into two, able body's, would create at least two gigantic bodies, or a twin galaxy as a result. While in a certain case, if the point of contact shifted or had an inclination on either left or right side of the body, depicts a clockwise or counter clockwise revolution of the merged bodies **(patriarch and its counterpart-matriarch)** which will become now one of the star or galaxy we have witness in the sky **[a must see Book 1 for additional input].**

And with the acceptable or corroborative circumstances, and that for a galaxy revolution or rotation to commence, required the above, or the following procedure. Specifically, the point of contact between the two bodies smashing together created the sparks and fired up, thanks to highly combustible hydrogen gases that present in the surrounding. And the momentum of the patriarch in line with the point of contact, must developed a circular force commonly known as the Centrifugal Force. The centrifugal force is responsible to rotate and coiled thus compress the merged body one way and of elliptical manner. As a result, it developed a Suction Power or Vacuum Energy that causes to drawn in a proportional amount of the highly treated gases from the firmament in the cryogen stage, the Helium/Hydrogen gas in particular. And into the suction ports of the Galaxy, it will be purified once again. Heat treatment converted *Helium gasses into Hydrogen [***different atomic weight and property or the element's nature; the cold gases that passes to the black hole that serve as heat exchanger in this case, therefore elements were purified]** or much purer gases, perhaps the so called "Boson" particle from within the Whirlpool or Event Horizon of the Galaxy, before it feeds into the chamber or core for nuclear fusion, is a self- fueling process. The porch, or port of entry of hydrogen gas is on both sides of the body, the north and south portion **[and if the condition satisfied, say, the body's size or diameter that big enough to depict a space, and that will creates the Black Hole wherein in feeding hydrogen gas's main purpose is literally to fuel, and add pressure and ignition for combustion, and that works like a piston rod but gas's non-reciprocating, or one way operation, and this help to prevent Choking; citations on the following or must see Book 1 for its theory]** that serve as the *"Piston" that operates under the Suction pressure, and that help to build pressure or compression to facilitate a successful nuclear fusion. By the centrifugal force acting on the body, the fused gases, that can be consider literally as light, or the energy in this case, cleansed to the optimum of the impurities the body has had to offer, spread out* (**nuclear fission**) *or discharge back and or directed and dissipate into the space through the center axis (blade or edge) that serve as the exhaust chamber and that depicts an elliptical water sprinkler but the operation of a circular milling machine. And that works like or the fundamental of a muffler of an automotive machine works. And in addition, the *Post Positive Area, as one of the most important aspect of the theory of the body existence, wherein it serve as the Casing of the body or the "Pump - Impeller" assembly; With dual suction port, a galaxy or sun is in fact works in elliptical manner like a giant centrifugal pump works [****flesh and muscle and skin in human aspect that absorbed nourishment and facilitate growth and protection of the more "fluid or susceptible" internal tissue or element; see also Book 1 for additional input***]. And that play a great and significant role, where in its highly strong gravitation or heat, provides room for the growth of galaxy as it* [**discharge and at the same time**] *absorbed some of the gases or nourishment to diversify or expand, or for the galaxy as a whole, its main purpose is not to "bleed" or to prevent gases to spread all at once therefore exist in the firmament.*

*It is notable that without the brain, human body and or galaxy's natural instinct, or interactions works, provided, or by means of sensing Temperature alone. In other words, the operation of a galaxy and its existence is simply correlates with the human aspect; the digestive system and the method or skills of surviving. It is notable that reaching up matured stage, or the body's growth saturation point, also or scientifically called as *Chandrasekhar's Limit [****1930's theory attributed to Indian-American astrophysicist Subrahmanyan Chandrasekhar; though found his concept of star's i.e. galaxy or sun, radiating or expanding limit, conform or in accordance with the nature of a body, nevertheless, nay, on the contrary, arose controversy of his notion of the body's contraction and demise, which this treatise claimed as exaggerated if not a superfluous one***], may maintain the body or live up to its surviving skills or existence, unless or otherwise another "able" body* *or circumstances disrupt the system, and that against the very principle of the operation or of the gravitational process, specifically the feeding of unequal mass of gases on either of the port by the suction process; aside from choking or blocking of any of the suction ports or of both. And though highly unlikely, but cannot discount the possibility that blocking the air exhaust chamber or the "energy" discharge port [or rectum or anus in human anatomy; while excreting gases on this point of a galaxy and that one can consider energy, is actually a refuse element], will create immense pressure on the body and that the so called post-positive area or the skin, that wouldn't be able to handle the situation or affair (old and great), thus, commence or lead to self- destructing process, and in so doing, rather in that case, therefore collapse and or death of a body is imminent [a must see theory, illustrations and additional input in Book 1].*

In this regard, the Creation theory on Genesis of the Old Testament, and that God said, "There will be light".... "Let us make man in our image and likeness...," can correlate closely or highly regarded on this concept (depict more likely as a reproduction method - galaxy produces progeny from within itself and so on the human aspect and that in a certain way, cedes the production of the body the conventional method or through evolution method, wherein, each or the entire aspect were dictated wholly by the circumstances or power of the Temperature has had to offer; while to procreate the conventional way is a lengthy process, mass reproduction takes off in a perfect circumstances like the operation of galaxy and ideal human condition through sexual reproduction), like the ancient Greek prominent philosophers, as Crude, and yet very promising scientific idea of the fundamental order of the Cosmos.

Anyway, to summarize the galaxy's operation, is that, it rotates, sucks and purifies and coiled gases, feeds in the opposite ports of the body leading into the chamber for nuclear fusion, and the nuclear fission is energy's discharge back and dissipates into the space carried out by the centrifugal pumping force through the body's equilateral zone in proportion. At this point, it is apparent that a galaxy in normal operation, in every second's constantly feeding and oozing gases, growing or expanding and gaining strength; the temperature, power, energy *and or force. In addition, as the circumstances satisfied, it is viable, or able to procreates another body or specifically the sun as its *offspring [citation on the following] until it reaches its limit [old or matured stage] or the inability to expand or handle the situation due to excess load or heavy masses of gas. It is notable however, that as long as the body possessed a healthy lifestyle or sound gravitational process, or specifically can handle the state of affair, arriving on the limit prescribed is not the end but able body can exist or last in almost perpetuity, and that optimizing equilibrium state and or under the rule of the fifth element which is the* **Quintessence.**

The galaxy operational process, say, the vacuuming or suctioning, looks and sounds like draining a fluid in a sink, and discharging gases oozing like an elliptical water sprinkler does, and if someone deprived or poor of the faculty of sight, the Galaxy sounds like a honing giant fan or perhaps the dropping of waterfalls that could be heard from a distance. And the body's multiple or general operation in what we call the Universal Gravitation, and this, we could be proud in fulfillment and honor of one of the great or the greatest English physicist named Isaac Newton [a must see Book 1 for additional input].

Taking the cue, nay, the catch's from the vantage view of this case, is that in one hand, we can established the foundation that can or will unify different theories in the field, and that however conformed with the fact or depicts the real nature of the elements and of the universe as a whole, while on the other, is to disregard or eliminate those theories that will be consider as out of order or in contrast with the law of operation of the universe, particularly against the operation of a body like galaxy.

To be specific, the firmament is filled of element constantly on the move, and that besides the transmutation process, due or mainly because of the very nature of the circumstances, and that everyone is floating in the space. And movement of a certain body lead in producing or developing frequency dependent on what the body has had to offer; the larger the body like galaxy is, therefore a great wave can be created and that more than any other body in the firmament could do. Interactions of nature and the element within, deemed or read by the astrophysicist spectroscope's Frequency, nay, specifically, uncovering the real nature of String theories, the Weak and Strong Forces among others, most likely to be coming from the Galaxy and that depending on the point of measurement, the Strong Force or great wave in String theory in one hand, is the frequency closer to the body or source. In the other, the weak force and or feeble wave, indicates of the frequency away from the source in contrast. Likewise, rather it is true with the suction frequency of the black hole or ports in the galaxy and that depicted a high velocity on element closer to the body, and it is true the other way around. And this claim supported the observation made by Johannes Kepler 1571-1630, a German astronomer that said planets moved around the sun in ellipses and not in circles and that they move faster as they come closer to the sun is indeed correct in this case.

Furthermore, it is notable, rather, from this writing's view, and that mathematical equation derive from this phenomenon, is not really problematic, however not ideal either, this writing could claim. Or pardon this word but in an immense body like Galaxy, mathematical application or substitution is a mere assumption; it is impractical in a way, or inapplicable to say the least. But this treatise mean it, that it is more likely to fail due to the following argument or an application of Werner Heisenberg's uncertainty principle that states; it is impossible to correctly determine the position and speed of subatomic particle like the electron:

The galaxy in fact is a vibrant, cumulative but it is not really perpetual or ever expanding body, however as long as able to expand, it goes, and that getting bigger and bigger overtime. For this reason, give the hard time or uncertainty, as well as the assurance to determine the limit of the expansion of the body, thus arriving on the perfect mathematical equation for that particular body could be gloomy for the aspiring one, thus any measured frequency before someone end up from talking, could had been change, therefore, inconsistency of reading might or sure yield different result thus, comparison could be futile. This notion nevertheless complimented Heraclitus idea and that He said "all things are flowing and or no one could steps into the same river twice"

Anyway, the concept in here, is not to undermine the significance of the idea of the entities, instead to compliment the Raman spectroscopy's observation and that detecting low-frequency mode, like the sun frequency in relation with the earth operation, is an essential tool to identify activity such as *earthquake *and or tsunami, where in this idea found to be bind with this phenomenon, the frequency in particular, and that in fact destruction cause by the natural phenomena is identifiable before it could actually hit the ground and or takes place. And this, is in addition to the formula, indications or circumstances that precedes these phenomena [*citation on the earth article or must see Book1 for additional input].*

The Black Hole Theory

The total concept of the nature of Black Hole described in here was totally independent from any other theories in the science or astrophysicist field. Neither brilliant personalities from medieval or renaissance era, as this writing knows it, that current proposition regarding the subject matter were wildly distinctive or perhaps at least a considerable similarities in some specific or common point. In other words, nay, a would be consequence is that should the governing body found the author's black hole theory described in here is correct, shall supersedes and or set aside those existing theories in the field deemed to be superfluous or unnecessary. The primary and only concern, rather, aim of this idea is to impart knowledge the best the ability the theory can offer in the field. And in this case, whatever the outcome might be, as we are all looking for the truth of the matter, we'll therefore proceed on the comparison.

Without further ado, the Black Hole appear to be black in color mainly because it's a huge space that manifest on the suction port or chamber out of the operation of the body. Specifically, the Galaxy's speed of revolution that has the centrifugal force applied on, and that stretched out the light or gas property therefore creating a hollow area in this particular point. Besides the extreme pressure on it, Black Hole in this case is considerably hot in temperature mainly because it is a "stone throw away" from the event horizon of the Galaxy. It appears black in color due to properties involve; the area and depth, or downward degree of gases. In fact, if a galaxy for any reason collapsed, the black hole will then again mend or solidify with the space or firmament which is its nature and or its own habitat. In other words, a light or galaxy or sun is a partition wall in, or of space which is dark. We have to note that since the galaxy is gas in definitive property, the gas or light will tend to yield whenever the forces is applied, as the centrifugal force is acting on. It is like a birthday celebrant blowing a candle light, but on this time, in a circular manner and that would depict a vortex point that represents the origin or where the force of the body is obtained.

The vortex point of a Galaxy, the black hole that signifies the space, is a spiral current downward **(downdraft {[in a vertical point of view]; we have to note to be aware of the essence of heavenly bodies correct or appropriate illustration as it play a very crucial or significant role in perceiving the idea of the operation of the universe wherein local application include the idea on why we must contend or mitigates global warming without delay is one of those. "Without delay", as far as the global warming is concern, is a concise word of a very serious concern} of hydrogen gas leading to the chamber)**, is in fact a sink hole in common term. Or technical terminologies could be that of the "carburetor" in an automotive system that the gas is being feed or fuel for combustion in order to keep the engine running. In addition, the proposition in one hand that said the Black Hole is extremely hot and or pressurize is correct, this writing can attest, however, the notion on the other that said its extreme pressure or gravitational action is so powerful that even light cannot escape from it, is gross, this idea can contend (see Book 1 for additional and comprehensive idea and or comparison).

Well, first and foremost, we have to note that gross assumption might lead us into another gross assumption such as getting into the Black hole may lead us into another dimension [of space], and knowing the veracity of the subject matter consider absurdity. In a simple method of comparison, since they depicted the same principle of operation, we should not be confused of a black hole from a vortex, maelstrom or whirlpool. It's a quagmire of gases easily perceptible in spinning machineries such as blender, dryer and this writing doesn't mean to brag, but palpable by way or over a circular motion mixing a cup of coffee and a creamier. Whether the case involve in a twist is in a form of a solid, semi-solid, liquid or gas entities, as long as it satisfy the condition, which is the keeping of struggling equal and opposing forces, or at least a current against the same property that rest on, or fortified by a bank, and as the current turns back, may create twisting motion as a result. And though *unlikely, we cannot discount the possibility that in a massive body like galaxy, forces pulling away in an opposite direction whether from the same point or different source of power, will then create a twist in a certain point of space [**like of manually cranking an engine using a snap rope; absolutely this principle applies precisely and foremost to the operation of the galaxy, on the origin and or creation of the sun, planets and satellites such as moon, not discounting the making of a cotton candy or green cheese; see Coriolis effect/force theory**]. And as the circumstances satisfied, it will occur in any field or ground or space, especially places where fluid, air or gas's involve; the angular velocity and momentum, specifically the angular contact or *deviating point and that will yield a spiral motion as a result and usually could aggravated the situation owed, or by the virtue, or provided by a "space or outlet" or arena or ground to "play" with, and proved "masculinity" or prowess in between opposing forces that can be view in a vantage point [like a black hole in a galaxy, and the very circumstances or the plight of the planet upon the sun; in this case we can't depict black hole from the sun mainly because, rather in fact, we are inside the black hole itself therefore must mitigate global warming in order to delay the suction process instigated to our planet by the sun prowess] and or consider a current magnetic or downward pull in a literal aspect [***a must see Book 1 for the theory of the black hole and the manifestation of air upheavals for additional input**].*

Black hole particularly, in a common, yet, easily perceptible and unmistakable similarities or equivalent as in comparison, is a gas refilling point or port in one's car leading to its engine to fuel it. Consider vibrant, black hole in a galaxy is the vortex point. In this regard, the "space" that constituted the hole, or size of the inside diameter of the pipe car's gas port, where in, in a galaxy that is wide and immense in appearance, is big enough to depict it. *While in the case of sun or our own solar system, planets are already struggling inside the [spiral yet in a horizontal position] cone shape cavity and working up against the magnetic pull of a black hole, but in this case, rather, as we see the Sun itself is the entry point leading to the combustion chamber. Inside the horizontal funnel or cone shape chamber, visualized planets and their satellites in sequence and this precisely depicts the scientific data of all the circumstances, especially of its individual operation. We have to note somehow, rather a kind of relief to any *"anxiousness" that said all of the sun's creation will submit back to this life giving body, which is indeed correct in this case. Nevertheless, horizontal perspective or positioning of the planet and its mass coupled with the cold environment, is in fact helping on delaying the planet's sun suction process and this give us a chance or a room to maneuver and or recover. In this case, once again let me take this opportunity to remind everyone that we must mitigate *global warming* **(*cause by deforestation, oil and gas production and consumption)** *mainly because the more hotter the planet is, the more likely to be attracted by the sun* **(Newton's universal gravitation)**; *the more we are closer to the sun, the violent the storm were going to deal with* **(Kepler with Coriolis effect theory),** *the extreme hot and [somehow] cold temperature we are dealing with, the more it induces water [rain and ice thaw precipitation] therefore floods* **(Dalton theory),** *and the awkward movement of moon and earth will give us the trouble of violent and frequent earthquakes, as well as tsunami. And in due time, rather in worst case scenario, specifically the greatest of the storm, might cause, or cost us of the earth and moon to part ways* **[the scene is like a couple of spinning billiard ball and of great orbital motion's speed, forced into a *cone shape spiral pocket [*black hole or port]. And that if this writing is correct, like the Mercury and Venus, wherein this writing considers the former as moon to the later, could have been together for a period of time and part ways eventually; citations on the following earth and moon article].**

The black hole is a point or the port of entry (the mouth in human aspect) in the central region where the hydrogen gases passes or went through to fuel a body like galaxy or sun. These porch, as explain on the previous article, is a dual suction port located each on its side, thus, depict a black hole, each on every port **[a must see theory on Book 1 for additional input].** *Besides depicting as the gas's port or point of entry, the Black Hole as the hydrogen gas itself, helps to stabilize the operation of a certain body, particularly, the Galaxy, mainly because the pressure ascribing to it, serve as the gas's, yet, formidable shafting. The shaft in any rotating entity whether it is a wheel, a bobbin or a disk to name a few, help to prevent friction upon operation, hold the matter in place or stabilized its position are some but definitive function. In addition, the suction or under the influence of gravitation, thus, pressurized element, the* *hydrogen gas to be specific, help to an efficient and successful nuclear fusion in the chamber. It serves like a "catapult", rather, it however works like a "one time and one way" piston of an internal combustion engine works to ensure an intense fusion to achieve the purpose of burning fuel to produce friction or heat as an essence for the body's existence, where in, in a body like galaxy, existence is simply means as "floating in the space or firmament". And it goes as well as to the fission process and that it pumped or drives excess or refuse element out of the body in proportion, similar to an anti-oxidant or laxative food or drug works in human body works and that preventing the trouble of choking and or constipation or clogging in the system.*

With illustrations, the theory may had been emphasized well enough in Book 1, however, for the sake of those who had not been there, the question at this point is on how do the black hole manifest? And what's the truth behind the most controversial notion that black hole powerful gravitational actions, is so strong that even light cannot escape from it?

*As the theme of this writing, and that whenever a call to achieve the "truth" or its essence, say for the purpose of gaining knowledge, or wisdom or faith and peace in a way, one must be dependent on the law or on its principle. And for this, let me share the thought of Francisco Sanches [**Quod Nihil Scitur- That Nothing is Known**] and that he said; "If the only knowledge is, in fact, that which is acquired by demonstration, while its first principle are incapable of being demonstrated, then there will be no knowledge of the first principles, hence there will be no knowledge".*

The Black Holes are the ports located in the central region from both sides of a body like sun, especially that of a Galaxy, having a wide, perfect body condition [powerful or high speed revolution] that depict, rather satisfy the circumstances depicting the subject. It is the entry point of mainly hydrogen gases used to fuels itself. Initiated from the Big Bang, the self-fueling process, rather, the vacuum or suction effect or magnetic pull is carried out by the gravitational action of the body, and that is the massive rotation known as the centrifugal force, and that coiled and or warped gases as a result. And with the "unrestricted" operation is on progress, the galaxy body is tend to diversify or expand, gain more power or energy and heat that increase its revolution as well, rather, as a result. As the galaxy *[or sun]* increases the speed of revolution, it tends to **"stretch out the event horizons"** or the calibrated or proportional to speed's spreading of light element, or diversification of the so called post positive area. That contributed to thickens thus deepening the body structure therefore unleashes or depicting the Black Hole or space more. The Post Positive Area or Casing, the main reason or essential aspect of the body not to disintegrate its components or not to spread light gasses all at one time; the higher the temperature or speed is, the greater torque its secured, and that characterized by spontaneity, created the space in the central region, or vortex point and that causes the manifestation of the Black Hole itself as a result.

Furthermore, 11th of the 100 great scientists, an Arab mathematicians and astronomer, Al Hazen c.965-c.1040, was first to suggest that light was reflected into the eye from the objects one saw, and he proved that light travels in a straight line *[source 100 Great Scientists: Grand Dreams Ltd]*.

In this regard, the notion that a black hole is so powerful that even light cannot escape from it, is a real concern, gross or absurd, if not totally in contrast with the proposition of Al Hazen. While the fact that light can be block, or its luminous property may not suit well or not strong enough to cover such area, this treatise totally concurred with Al Hazen that light in any condition are not inclined or subject to mechanical vicissitudes, as bending or sucking. In this case, with a light emitting diode (LED) in a variable speed spinner, try to carry out simple experiment. By observing the formation or manner of light, especially a candle light that is more susceptible to an application of force such as blowing by the wind. In varying speed of rotation, one can perceive that the light differ in manner, and that the higher the speed of rotation, the more the lighting is being stretch out or literally left behind, thus project the hollow area in the vortex point and that factors such as deep and wide of the space, perceptible in a body of Galaxy, project a dark spot or space called a "black hole" by the scientist. And in addition, besides with the fact that a Galaxy is an independent body and floats in space (and that means you come from space and get through with this body, and expect you shall come back into space), thus, it's a silly thing, thinking that one can travel into another dimension through the black hole mainly because the inner part of the subject is in a fact a core wherein the nuclear production *takes place, and that an entity shall be reduce to gases even before coming half the distance to the point of entry.*

*As the nature of the black hole fully explained above [**a must see Book 1 for illustration and additional input**], and if not a clichéd, is that when the galaxy accelerated or increase the speed of its revolution, because of its light's gas characteristic, and that literally yield when the mechanical or centrifugal force, specifically, has been applied, tend to displace or stretch out the light, or gases' light's element therein, leaving the central region or vortex point hollow or empty. However, rather, spontaneously, because of the absence of a literal light matter in the region, thus facilitates refilling process of hydrogen gas that dependent on what the circumstances, the gravitational prowess or suction activity in particular, has had to offer as a consequence. Therefore, though whirlpool or maelstrom or vortex could takes place when or where ever the condition satisfied, in contrast to any proposition attributed to galaxy's black holes, it is actually a kind of them (point and or a space in the heart of a twist or upheaval), and part of the whole process and operation of body and its existence called universal gravitation.*

*In Book 1, the whole process and operation is simplified and depicted by helping oneself prepare a cup of coffee or juices as you like, or do a laundry on a top loading machine, uses a blender or simply flushing a toilet bowl. In this case don't try to go to other dimension by the black hole port, you will end up in hell. Should anyone remember an Italian beauty or the matador in Spain, helping oneself prepare a cappuccino, ever, is the best mimicking alternative. And this writing would like to share a note in English, and that be mindful of excessive foaming, it might overlap or override the concept [**a must see black hole article in Book 1 for the extended theory and or additional input**].*

The Origin of Sun

Incredulous or incongruous within polite or formal conversation, but no offense, the sole writing's purpose is to impart knowledge and express the full potential the idea has have to offer in order to counter skeptics upon mitigating global warming with the aim of preserving the earth, biodiversity and inhabitant or saving human life on its utmost concern.

If someone is thinking about the Earth and everything on it **(that speak about the Earth operation in general aspect, wherein abnormal phenomena such as thunder and lightning, air upheavals, earthquake and tsunami which is the outcome of a deviated or abnormal earth working pattern. And left unexplained, people dumbfounded with the awful scenario, and that beyond human control or comprehension, might consider these unusual or extraordinary events as an act of God. In the absence of Science on the ancestral epoch, as the "great idea" of creating God or mythical god that may assisted explaining the wonder of nature and or the natural world and its phenomena, this, in addition in ruling or governing a community, perhaps the idea [for fear that or out of fear] thought to be effective with minimal or less effort from the authority, as some parents ought to do to discipline a child [on tantrums]. Unexplainable, astonishing circumstances or mysterious event or marvelous nature creation, and that in the absence of mechanical or logical reasoning or interpretations** *[Philosophy once thrived on the ancient time, at least 1000 BC as per the record; The brilliant logical idea was in fact present, but in the absence of technological advancement or scientific knowledge, specifically the theory of everything, to support or compliment the idea, effuses rather eclipse it]* **and that through imaginative effort, thus pointed or attributed to deity or divine wisdom and or being, as the so called faithful or Theist believed. But at this point of time, things are unequivocally distinctive. In other words, remarkably distinguishable, the huge difference or disparity between the psychological aspect of man [say fear, comfort of the soul or life after death, the most enticing option] and the material or literal mechanical configuration and operation of the universe must be taught and learned by humankind, because the degree of human intelligence possessed, is somehow superior to other creation or being, should lead to habitant's ideal way of living, survival and existence. Noble deeds, happiness, co-existence, comfort of the soul, an ideal habitable or a paradise like dwelling place, are all this writing a dream to flourish.**

Coadjutant in a certain way, should have this writing made available and delivered in an honest and unmistakable way, a little earlier. Great thinker or reformist should not suffer for the things they thought would help humankind. Neither their effort should go in vain because they are help or trying to help; sorry for Jesus of Nazarene, also called as Christ, the greatest and remarkable one. In strict sense, was it just, in lay of noble purpose with the expense of the fact or nature?, nay, this is to say that nobody, a person or jury in the right mind will held a person accountable for a crime he/she doesn't committed. In this world today, once brought to life [born] it's just logical for, rather, that a child, must be declared free of guilt, from the responsibility of crucifying the Christ, neither the so called inherited sin. We have to cogitate on this thing, because it's apparent that it's the backwardness [unfaithful-ignorance of the fact and law], cover up or self-interest, if these things differ from one another, did. And unraveling oneself from the binding of assumed transgression and deplorable deeds, coupled with respect and gratuity in the benevolence of Nature [just to be clear, no veneration of the Sun], shall save the Earth and one's soul) are created by God, where in fact planets and their satellites were beautifully crafted by the Sun [spectrum], thus, rather, has at least the tendency, if not unequivocally, like the ancient people (Inca/Peru or Aztecs/Mexico or ancient Egypt), will end up on the Sun's worship as the deity itself. Of course, rather, if someone is talking about, or pertaining to a different entity or God, other than this writing is referring to. Nonetheless, this applies the same principle to the one that created the Sun, He or She is referring to a much bigger body which is the Galaxy in this case, and one can point out to the Cryogen Theory afterward. The truth may be find offensive to who advocate ancient belief, however, on this era, knowledge and the truth of the matter is a test of civilization's civilized manner and that to understand the smallest of things or abstract idea (spiritual) to the greatest matter that makes up the composition and operation of the universe, is a triumph of reason or knowledge and the ability of able creation, to understand, and we human being, however the capable, is just a tiny speck of the whole process.

*After the event of Big Bang as explained above, a Galaxy must be established. And as the Galaxy existence and diversification is on progress, so the making of the Suns are. In this view, rather, the fact that the operation of the body is in conformity with the very nature of producing another, as we can consider as an offspring, thus, right at the time that a Galaxy commence, a sun in the making is definitely on progress as well. Depending of the capability and or corroborative circumstances, the Galaxy for instance, produces potential Suns or millions of progeny in every seconds count (**See also the account/research of Jeremy Sanders of University of Cambridge, Institute of Astronomy – The image of Perseus Cluster Abell 426 shows a number of ripple-like structure [or the potent offspring or sun to be specific] around the core of the cluster**). In human aspect where a conceiving cell denied with the "essential nourishment" and the factor of "mechanical defect" or circumstances in general, might be denied to produce a child. In contrast, as long as the Galaxy is in operation will never cease producing as such. Though some of the cell or potential suns may conk out, some however are successful. Earlier on the theory, we have noted that Galaxy's self-reproduction process might ceased the evolution or origin(al), the way the Galaxy has been, which is through the Big Bang (theory).*

Producing a Sun is not that really complicated; emerging from the edge of the body or the equilateral discharge line, in fact it is just producing a baby or small whirlpool out of a giant one, which is their parent. And the question is on how they do it.

Since the theory could be figure out without difficulty, I tried not to shoot up the price of this book by eliminating illustrations, and I leave this thing, on Book 1 actually, nevertheless, modified and or improve Sun illustration would be easily handled. See illustration on the following as well as illustration and input on All But the World is Loving ISBN 9781434983824:

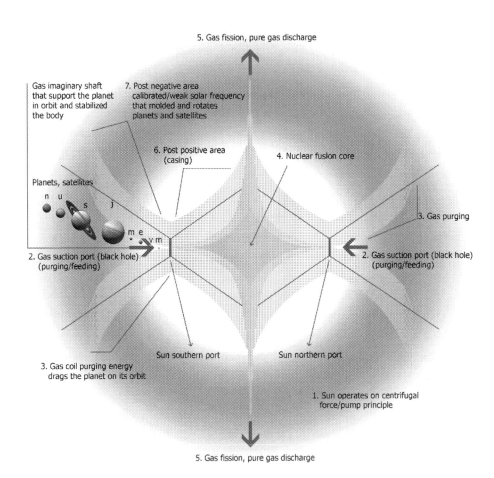

5. Gas fission, pure gas discharge

Gas imaginary shaft that support the planet in orbit and stabilized the body

7. Post negative area calibrated/weak solar frequency that molded and rotates planets and satellites

6. Post positive area (casing)

4. Nuclear fusion core

Planets, satellites

n u s j m e v m

2. Gas suction port (black hole) (purging/feeding)

3. Gas purging

2. Gas suction port (black hole) (purging/feeding)

Sun southern port

Sun northern port

3. Gas coil purging energy drags the planet on its orbit

1. Sun operates on centrifugal force/pump principle

5. Gas fission, pure gas discharge

SOLAR SYSTEM AND UNIVERSAL GRAVITATION'S
FLORES CONCEPT

1. *Sun or Galaxy operates (rotate) on centrifugal pump/force principle; coiling, warping, treatment (purging) and self-feeding of gases, as well as nuclear fusion and fission are some of essential operation for the body to produce heat, float and exist in the firmament. The operation in general aspect sustain the life of the body in almost perpetuity, or the un-relentless body's accumulative nature or diversification (accretion-one way operation enhance the growth or increase in size by gradual external addition thru fusion and or fission) in particular aspect, can be consider as the innate skill of perpetual universal gravitation and or unspecific tenure of existence.*

2. *Gas suction port (black hole as if the body or galaxy satisfy the criteria or circumstances) – out of the space, gas has been sucked and purified and directly injected to the chamber, and the actual form and circumstances (momentum, pressurized, dense, compact and firm) serves as piston to induce more or intense pressure for, rather, to ensure success on nuclear fusion as well as fission. In addition, rather, in one hand, the equilibrium of the operation is vital to stabilize the body in revolution. It holds the body (planets and satellites) on its orbit, literally, not to compromise or prevented the bodies from a possible vertical fall, unless or otherwise in the total absence of solar frequency and or the disappearance of the heat generating body such as Sun; dissolution of the mainframe, the Sun in this case would be a disaster, every entity under its rule or power shall scattered in limbo, much more, nay, imagine if the Galaxy end its life. And on the other, a [would be] solid, due to unrelenting gas's feeding operation, or the compressed gas serve as the shaft [of a bobbin] for self - stability and realignment.*

3. *Treatment of gases (purging) – immense pressure or high temperature (heat) all around the suction port serve as the heat exchanger between cold gases (from the space) and hot one that manifest from/in the body. The overwhelming heat on gas's exchange purified the element before injecting into the chamber. see item no.7*

4. *Nuclear fusion – suctioned and purified gases from both side of the port enter into the chamber (or black hole in galaxy) and meet at the core*

and splatters. The scenario is like two aircraft engine placed back to back and the exhaust provision is driven by the centrifugal force [causes by] the body's [one way] revolution.

5. *Gas Fission – gas's discharge to balance the body's operation and at the same time diversify. Nevertheless, in a body like Galaxy, fission combined with centrifugal force creates sun, consider as its progeny.*

6. *Post Positive Area – Immense temperature on this area bonded element, and that not to spread gases (or disintegrate body) all at one time, and that serve as the [flexible] casing; with that structure provides room to diversify. Accumulation of heat increase its revolution, power and energy discharge. The totality of the circumstances is an essence for nourishing bodies under its power.*

7. *Post Negative Area – calibrated temperature or weak solar output that manifest in this area paves the way for reshaping the planets and their satellites. Dalton's theory states that the disparity in temperature produces water [and instantaneously turned into ice] is correct in this case. And on the wide body of Galaxy, could be that of reshaping its paternal cell to induce creation of the body the original way (cryogen/ big bang).*

   Earth was caught in between the cold and hot gases or moderate temperature, and these circumstances provide room for biodiversity or human being to exist and or survive. And thus anyone of these circumstances, especially the hot form provision takes it course, shall have a devastating effect, therefore this treatise once again take this opportunity to remind people to contribute in mitigating or warding off global warming because if this phenomenon satisfy and exacerbate the condition of the planet to be attracted by the sun in advance or in "reckless" manner, and that shall experience mayhem or definitely a disaster, as a consequence.

Moreover, the fact that whirlpool needs a two opposing forces to satisfy and or commence, is like the incoming/downstream current of a river against the outgoing current from the sea of a high tide. Since a sun or galaxy's gas, it correlates well with the manifestation of air upheaval such as hurricane, tornado or typhoon to name a few, where in the earth stroke upon rotation, which this writing consider as the low pressure air that meet and struggle with the high pressure one that developed during orbit *[see Book 1 for additional input]*. The manifestation of sun is more likely to happen and succeed on the far end of the arm of the galaxy; the incoming frequency, or bombardments of energy, say a clockwise strike or Force 1 is simply to take on the preceding one which is the Force 2, making those currents to struggled and be pulled inward or with the element of overwhelming force, thus, making the current move on a circular rotation or *counterclockwise mode *[*F1 and F2 struggles by pulling or pushing each other and that means a manifestation of at least a balance force in between, rather in order to sustain, thus creating a whirlpool]* which is now against the initiator. And as the condition satisfied, inch by inch or little by little, the cell of a potent sun will develop into a full grown body that we call Sun, and this by the virtue of the initiator's circular operation or centrifugal force **(fission/disseminate)**, is naturally being pushed away (due to diversification) from its creator's body which is the mother galaxy. And as the sun established itself to live on its own, will therefore create its own family and which we can call the solar system and its community, the planets and their satellites and well composed out of gases as well and that made the same way or method **(circular/centrifugal force principle)**, the sun [itself] was created, and this explain on the following article.

Furthermore, out of the ordinary, rather a peculiar observation that this writing found out, is that if there is non- life exist on the other side of the sun, or sun's solar system southern hemisphere **(in this case, this writing assumed that the angle of projection or perspective is that our solar system is located on the sun's northern hemisphere, however changing the angle of projection denotes either)**, was the reason of ancient belief or tradition [of religions] to institute manner or costume, and that to discourage the left handed person to dominate or primarily uses the left hand especially on dining or taking food, for the superstitious belief was attributed to unclean or unworthy or unproductive, for the reason that it produce no life [at all] as we talk specifically on the subject above. In a point, the analysis of the ancient people *can be right* **(otherwise there might be someone living or something exist on the other side of the sun; so far exploration is limited on one side and outbound of the solar system. However if the Earthian are really serious finding the Earth's twin, they should travel at the other side of the Sun and this myth could be busted),** *but knowing the right, rather literally looking on the opposite side of the body, will yield the same observation. Myth maybe busted, but was it the same case on the Genesis' author observation that God made the woman out of the flesh of the man as the* **(original nebula of)** *moon out of planet, or a sun out of the galaxy? A crude idea or just lost in translation, or simply subscribe on the terms available on the field on that time, or can we confirm that religion on today, is that science on that time, or the religion then could be the science on today, therefore one? Nevertheless, this writing never meant to brag, but the assumption of scientist that the Sun's nuclear power will last at least four billion years is highly misconcepted. The theory of Sun's accumulation of power and energy, or universal gravitation and existence depicts the body existence for an unspecified time, therefore refute if not supersedes this notion. And lastly, we have to note however the possibility of planetary existence on the other side of the sun and this writing see that no problem with that, but astronaut must be very careful in crossing the discharge line of the Sun. The action of centripital force emanating from the body is like a vertical water sprinkler does, but it works like a circular cutter works, getting closer and or caught with the blade, their eggs might be reduce into halves.*

The Earth and Moon Origin

The Book 1 which is known to be the All But the World is Loving, was actually a modified title from the original Greek word "Ona Aepo Mia Archi" translated to me by the Greek consul representative named Papadopoulus in Jeddah Kingdom of Saudi Arabia, and that literally mean "Everything Under One Principle", and under the subtitle and interpretation of the principle that read as "All But the World is Turning" before it settled to the released title "All But the World is Loving", where in the writing found to be the *science's "gravitational" concept or principle is actually the counterpart of the word "love" or loving as dynamic or vibrant aspect" preached and the discipline in religion. And these vocabularies "signifies" "attraction" that comprehensible in both subject, the science and religion therefore consider in this treatise as the "link" between them *[a **must see theory** on **Universal Gravitation in Book 1 for additional input**]*.

In this view, before and or beyond the big bang, it is not surprising that one can assume that the very principle of the body's existence i.e. galaxy, sun, the planets and their satellites is through revolution, rotation or turning or spins, as one wish to call it. Thus, at this point, it is not really surprising to find out that the making of the Sun out of the Galaxy by this method is in fact the process of creating the moon out of creating the planet, where in the later entities favored "partly" from the theory of "fission and condensation". And nevertheless, in contrast with the widely accepted theory on today regarding the formation of the moon called "The Giant Impactor Theory", where in if we will work or apply the very principle of the earth and moon formation and operation that will be discuss on the following, the later theory is highly unlikely or least favored in here due to "grave" complexity or complication. Nevertheless, nay in a sense and honesty, in Book 1 however, moon formation's depicted the capture theory. And at this point, it is amazing to learn that out of six, and while five of them considered to be serious theories of the formation of the moon *[**the fission, the capture, the condensation, the colliding planetesimals or large chunks of rock and the ejected ring theory**]*, the one believed to be fabled or metaphor for credulity, which is called or stated that "moon is made of green cheese" as myth suggest, was fanciful indeed. However, the truth out of making cheese, is in fact the method of making the moon that is called "coagulation" from gas's material undergoing transmutation process and that the factor or circumstances was perfected by the solar system or of its influence by creator's revolution in general aspect.

The question in this case is not really on how was it done, but what would be the possible circumstances?

Let us view the sun in elliptical formation and or operation, like of a Ferris wheel work, standing on its edge. Characterized by the radial symmetry, in the south and northern side, imagine its extended uninterrupted circular frequencies like a shape of an ice cream cone or a trumpet (**And we have to note the implication of this frequency pattern [cone shape] and that the** *planet may tilt, as the earth is on 23 degree angle, and this notion may busted the myth that said the Earth could had been tilted due to comet's impact?).* Anyway, the further the frequency or light stretched out, the more it loosing and or getting bigger, thus, its magnitude or intensity's becoming weaker as a result. In this case, it is apparent that the reason behind on the outer planets that take relatively longer time of orbit compare with those bodies closer to the sun's core counterpart. And relatively Johannes Kepler, the German astronomer is correct when he stated that "the closer a planet comes to the Sun, the more rapidly it moves". However, the pitfall, nay, another theory this writing suggest, and that if the core of the planet, say the Mercury, adhere or fuse with its bed or surface area, would or may have different outcome specifically on its day by day rotation or may affect the frequency of revolution.

In this regard, rather, whatever the degree of energy in particular, or on what the circumstances has had to offer in general; say the distance from the sun's core, the rate of rotation or the nature of temperature are some, yet essential in determining or modifying factor. Initially, the cryogen theory somehow apply on this case, and the radiant frequency initiates the formation of the planet as well as the moons by creating or turning gases, the original nebula, specifically into maelstrom, and the hydrogen gases that undergone transmutations *[see also cryogen time theory]* created carbon dioxide or dried ice and that can be consider as "coagulation process" or the manner on how the Cheese is being made; clotting and turning, shapes the body passionately [one can consider the sun {hot gasses} as the patriarch, and the space or dark matter {cold gasses} as the counterpart]. The planets or moons in a certain point, or on the horizon between the heat of the Sun and the freezing temperature of the firmament, serve as the perfect breeding ground. Complimented from the solar energy's circular [spiral] pattern, the planets looks like a shape of an oblate sphere **[Rugby or American Football]**, bulging at the center mainly because it experience or encounter resistance or received more heat and creates more friction in the center compare to its pole side upon rotation. **This is due to the fact that spiral solar frequency that is set like of a cone shape pattern, induces the body's angle of inclination thus exposes' the planet median portion.** Little by little, time after time, rather, patiently and fine tuning, planets as the principal, and moons as a side product (excess) has been molded by the suns' frequency and "corroborative circumstances" has had to offer.

Nevertheless, nay in one point, this treatise doesn't discount the possibility, rather, most probably, if not most likely, that it was the moon was the first to form or the shell itself, or has been created barely ahead of the planet itself, and this provides room or protection for planets formation or configuration and that serves or speaks well like of its ob-gyn serves *[which I wish to include in addition to noble duties of moon; a must see Moon article in Book 1 for additional input, and that includes a modified yet an informative and genuine calendar concept- Athena Calendar]*, and this assumption pay a compliment that the Moon, despite, rather beside of its size, has a relatively harder surface, compacted or heavily built *[like an athletic person, owes to his rigid training or activity {and this include of its finest revolution that scientist has not identify or confirm so far} and this explain on Moon's duties and operation]* and thus, possess inflexible quality, and these in addition that this body stays aloft or afloat and or less dense, thus consider "tricky" or "slippery", compare with the "indulgence" of the Earth has received, thus, explained that Moon does not, and will not produce substantial iron core like of that Earth.

Nevertheless, nay, anyway, if the moons were just produced out of the excess of planet's original nebula is not surprising, besides the notions above, neither will make extra difference, however, we can dig much more on the comparison between the inner and incoming planets in this case, specifically as on why the planet Saturn on its current position's consist of at least 18 moons and rings of ice. However we can conclude that a legitimate moon has been form or created all along with the planet, therefore a buddy or the great bodyguard since then.

Furthermore, the scientist says that the question on where did the Moon come from or any theory which explains the existence of the Moon must naturally explain the following facts:

1. The Moon's low density (3.3 g/cc) shows that it does not have a substantial iron core like the earth does.

2. *Moon rocks contain few volatile substances (e.g. water), which implies extra baking of the lunar surface relative to that of Earth.*

3. *The relative abundance of oxygen isotopes on Earth and on the Moon are identical, which suggest that the Earth and Moon formed at the same distance from the Sun [**source:http//starchild.gsfc.nasa.gov/ docs/StarChild/questions/question38.html]**.*

*While items 1 and 3 clearly complimented and precisely depicted on this article, item number 2 has been expounded well in Book 1 (**on the following; the quadruple motions of Moon has been given a deep emphasis; besides the fact that the moon on it southbound oscillation, goes inward the sun therefore receives extra baking or exposure** [in specific point, we have to note that moon shadowed or cover up the earth; and that the sun's *circular frequency {*we should not be confused regarding the difference or application of circular frequency with the solar rays of light; specifically, while the former rotates the Earth and flips the Moon sideways, the totality or intensity of the solar frequency drags the planet and satellites on its orbit} discharge intended for the earth that would be blocked or interrupted, is the main reason that causes earthquake and or tsunami in a certain case, therefore these upheavals is in fact predictable before it could actually takes place], **its whirling rotation like a coin standing on its edge and **flipping on** [**moon speed of revolution is a little more than of earth orbit which is 104,000 KPH; citation on Book 1] **causes the moon to oscillates sideways like a figure skater that move a little upward on southbound, and sideslip on northbound operation. And as the Earth rotates, motions that mentioned above, pave the way for the moon to move forward and circumnavigate or commutes all around and opposite to the rotation of the earth as a result. And as the circumstances satisfied, may blocked/screened the incoming sun rays intended for the Earth thus earthquake takes place. In connection with this, rather to prove this notion, try the cosmic phenomenon [solar eclipse/earthquake]) that take place or darkened the sky in northern Europe [Svalbard, Norway; Saturday, March 21, 2015] and tremors in Papua New Guinea***

[Monday, March 30 2015]. *Wherein factors that constitute for the circumstances being satisfied could be that but not limited to the angle of projection, earth speed of revolution and orbit speed and [angular/perpendicular] direction [spring] or the distance between the trinity bodies [sun, earth and moon], moon oscillation speed and or the speed of light and projection [sun rays].*

Moreover, it is notable however, that inner planets like the Earth, possessed at least one moon and the rest has not at all. And while further planets like the Mars had twins, namely Phobos and Deimos, thus, this treatise conclude that planets may have moons as many as they can, but as the gravitation towards the sun is on progress, moons smashes and or annihilate each other for survival until the great, or the fittest remains or devout its services for the well-being of the planet before it submit itself to its creator, which is the Sun, again ahead of its guarded body or beneficiary, say the Earth **(or Venus if this tenet assumption is correct and that Mercury is in fact its moon),** and that reflects of moon's benevolence. Base on the notion above, this treatise therefore conclude, that definitely the moons, like on the planet Mars, in a certain point of time, shall collide and the fittest therefore survive. Was it not the reason on why is the moon has a relatively or substantial crater caused by the impact? And the inner planets have no moon at this point because it has been annihilated by its own planet?

Furthermore, inside the sun's cone shape frequency or spectrum, arrange the eight planets in sequence [see illustration on the origin of the Sun]; closer to the core of the sun is the Mercury, Venus, Earth and the outside planets were Mars, Jupiter, Saturn, Uranus and Neptune. And I have to note that while this writing convinced that the planet Mercury is a moon to or of Venus, nevertheless, agreed with Pluto as **[captured or adopted]** asteroid in the solar system, and that could become a planet. However, since it does not undergoes the process of the formation of legitimate planets, thus, might be hard to manage neither, or especially as to become a moon due to its complicated movement or duties and operation **[citations on the following or see Book 1 for moon's quadruple motions, an extended version of earth and moon operation for additional input].**

In this regard, since the sun's radiant and frequencies form like a cone shape formed, it is not really surprising, nay, this treatise's almost certain that this is the main reason on why the earth tilted 23 degrees on its axis, in contrast with the notion that in a certain time, the earth may had been collided with another body that may cause the earth of its tilting activity, wherein we cannot discount such possibility, however notion might be gross or wide of the mark, if not wrong indeed, this treatise can claim.

*In addition, inside the cone shape sun's radiant energy, it rotates and drives the planets on its orbit. The core of a planet serves as contact point in receiving signals coming from the sun. In other words, it is the similarity in temperature that keep them connected, or heat's force's pulling in [or against] heat, rotation against rotation, mass or force or power of a body against another body [and literally it's a blessing or an advantage on the planet's part that this activity takes place in a horizontal position, the main reason of the essence of the right or appropriate illustration of the body's operation], and it is notable that the planet is almost **[except one thing; that is to cool the planet]** helpless against the overwhelming power of the Sun therefore prevailed. At this point, the theme of this writing becomes apparent, and that if we fail to upend on exacerbating the Earth's temperature, its heat specifically, that clearly manifest on global warming phenomenon, will therefore submit the Earth into the Sun in a least possible time. Nostradamus said to be on 3797 [as the end of inhabitant]? Right or wrong, accurate or not, nevertheless this writing firmly believed that we have to beat the mark. Some but not limited to, of the indication that the Earth is moving towards the Sun and therefore experiencing global warming, are the intense air upheavals, frequent and powerful earthquakes, melting of ice, flood or tsunami, drought, deviated or shortened earth orbit pattern and that affects the season's farming thus altered food production that may pave the way to output shorted. And in a worst case scenario, is the *parting of the union between the Earth and Moon (*see Book 1 for additional and comprehensive theory). A rational person that perceived the threat of global warming is absolutely, rather in fact, those ideas that are written above are the sign or symptoms of an ailing or deteriorating planet and that unequivocally perceived and understood.*

The Moon's Operation (Duties and Responsibilities)

The fact that moon has one, and could be consider the only legitimate operation, but the circumstances paved the way to, or make it at least four sequential activities. However in Book 1, This idea tried to describe or portray the Moon's quintuple motions hoping to comprehend on the idea much easier by identifying a certain motion, that's inappropriate or consider being superfluous. This means that it wished, or to consider the "hyper activity" of the Moon will make it more controversial, and that may however uncover flawed theories (of ancient and medieval scientist) or belief in the formation and operation of the said body.

In this regard, one may wonder on why and how the Moon simultaneously projects a quadruple motion; the spins, oscillations, orbit and commutation in all around the northern hemisphere of the Earth.

*In the shrewdness of one of the great scientist in the world, this million dollar question unfortunately failed to provide explanation, and that said on Book 3 of the Newton's Principia, shows the law of gravitation at work in the Universe: Newton demonstrates it from the revolution of the six known planets, including the Earth and their satellites. However, He could never perfect the difficult theory of the Moon's Motion [source: **Encarta Encyclopedia Deluxe Edition 1999**].*

*Revisiting this idea in which the author believed had been prophesied by the French doctor and astrologer named Nostradamus (**a must see Book 1 for extended version and additional input**), is that in the author's experience, if there is someone that holds well on the theory of moon motion, however like Newton, technically unexplained, nevertheless carried out one of the most beautiful application of the operation of this body, was no less than the Prophet Mohamed of Islam, PBUH. Out of this, He developed an all year round of activities and that include the *Holy month of Ramadan, the 9th month of the Hegira calendar or the flight and exile of the Prophet, from Mecca to Medina in 622 marking the beginning of Muslim era, to the point that a **certain event of the moon and the star on the west [on a certain [mid-east view] perspective but perhaps it's the planet Venus] becomes the symbol of their faith (*In saying* *these in one point, is that in a certain time and on the right perspective, the said star was perfectly aligned, fall and or set almost inside the crescent shaped moon and may re-occurred overtime. While on the other, the Ramadan or the Holy Month of Islam depicts a purification and sanctification of the soul of a Muslim believer and or the follower of Islam. Nevertheless, nay in this view, holds the undisclosed anecdote or theory in mechanics or science and that the idea projects the planetary motion expressing, rather, concerning a very significant idea on global warming phenomenon and its consequence* (9th *month or September in Gregorian calendar is the awkward or summit point of orbit of these two bodies that may cause the moon being push deep or inner into the sun's core thus may parted its way eventually [if we do not mitigates global warming in general aspect or in particular, if we do not contend the Sun fatal attraction towards the Earth] and God forbid this event; we have to pray earnestly especially at the end of the Holy Month [equinox point [September] before the fall season] that the moon shall appear, and besides the triumph over fasting's sacrifices, therefore celebrate).* **And among other, while in one hand the Hegira calendar, and that a lunar month is consist of 29 and 30 days, and this describes the true course of the moon, and literally service pay is a fair labor practice; The Gregorian calendar on the other, which is composed of 30 and 31 days a month, wherein in 40 years labor, an employee could had been robbed by of at least a year of his end of service payment, depicts the opposite. Indeed the prophets teaching is a noble thing, but the interesting, if not the sad part is that some employer used to "play" on prophet's benevolence by paying employee's wage using the Gregorian calendar, and collects rental on their rented apartment by Hegira one; a must see Book 1 for The Moon extended theory, specifically the author's idea of Athena, a calendar concept depicting an intellectual and reliable information of earth and moon's tandem in motion, expressed as the queen and the lady in waiting in a royal and servant's affair).**

First and foremost, a Moon to effectively accompany a certain planet, say the Earth, must be in proportion, balance or with harmony to each other; In other words, the relation between parts, say the density in particular, volume and likely to its mass, must be in accordance with what the law is dictated. Specifically, since it is the planet that did require the moon, must therefore submit or in accordance with its standard, and the moon that relies on the earth of its orbit is one of those. Nevertheless a moon to planetary function, is like an outrigger of a boat, as one but sure not limited on this specific duty.

The question at this point is how do they operations matter and how do things really work out for both, and that, in relation with the Sun, for their existence?

Think of a Cue Ball of a billiard game that was hit by the stick on its left side, and that will give you a clockwise sidespin, and should have the outward rotation or sidle as a result. Similar to a coin standing on its edge, was hit on its left portion or side swiping, would yield the same result as a cue ball on the previous example.

Inside the cone shaped and or sun's circular or spiral frequency to be specific, imagine that it was the billiard cue stick, and that blowing or hitting the moon on its northern portion that causes it to spin, is the legitimate, primary or primordial motion or force of the Moon [that lead for the body to oscillates]. The next big thing is that since the Moon stays afloat, tend to move sideways or away from the Sun and upward in respect with the angle of frequency of Sun and shape or positioning of the Earth **(or southbound; moon is waxing and or full moon shape and angle of projection expose to the Earth)** and this is labeled as the Moon secondary motion.

We have to note at this point, and that the Sun's radiant energy to both Moon and Earth bodies is the same magnitude or similar stroke, but the application or purpose [due to dissimilar circumstances or distinctive characteristic such as mass], differ the outcome in a certain aspect.

Literally, to think that there is no banking point on the southern hemisphere, the question is on how the Moon could return to the northern portion, to the waning or new Moon phase? The scenario is like playing a lawn or table tennis alone, or without opponent to hit the ball from the southern side, how could a ball come back into the northern point?

Since the Moon stays atop of the Earth and this means that the moon is sitting in, in the like of skating rink which is in fact the slippery, stingy yet hard enough surface **(and that, not to break, moon's density is in proportion, or specifically, a lighter one or a weight that can afford to work with, or should I say that no moon [or servant] is greater than the planet [master] itself),** *the Earth gravitational field produces from its rotation as well as orbit. And we have to note that rotation of the earth is due to ceaseless bombardment of radiant energy coming from the Sun.*

Since the Moon, its density in particular is under, or highly influence by the gravitational field and or magnetic pull of the Earth **[And we have to note that characterized by spontaneity, moon's driven by or side sweeping by the Sun's radiant energy, where in this specific operation, in a strict sense, is independent of what relationship the earth and moon has have. Thus, define, or by the virtue of the Sun's frequency, Moon spinning's revolution per minute {rpm} is most probably higher than that of Earth orbit speed, which is around 104,000 kilometer per hour {kph} and or to double this figure is fine, yet, considering the mass of the Earth, being quadruple is not very discounted; The significance of this idea or assumption is that [Force on/of] Earth and or Moon orbit speed deducts from the speed of Moon's spin, will therefore the Difference of force makes, the like of those Russian ballerina or skater as you like it, gracefully spins and or dances atop of a like table or rink, the Earth gravitational field {considerably hard surface made up of gases obtain from the body's operation; see Newton's Third Law of Motion or Book 1 for additional input}, floats like a feather, hug like a python and the flexibility of this body is indeed invaluable. And with that quality, commits the Moon's {services} to the Earth for free, the reason, rather, not surprising that one's entices by benevolence, is being grateful on this body {adlib: the author beg to take, and that the depiction, representation or choice of words from a concrete, actual, literal and or flabbergasting performance and entity as Compliment, or meant to complement, otherwise for comparison purposes only, please.} A must see Book 1 for additional input],** *and a considerably light, sturdy and or massive Moon, and that where ever the planet goes, the satellite shall* *follow. In other words, the fact that the Moon is literally *engaged with the Earth [*that their diagonal, sliding and opposite direction depicts like of a mechanical transmission gear, or this moon's particular operation - circumnavigation, is like the great sport of skiing downhill and zigzag course], thus the Moon obeys the Earth, maintain its pace and or tolerances considered in here as the fourth or quartet Moon's motion [a must see Book 1; The Moon, for additional input].*

In relation with the Sun, when the Moon oscillate the farthest or summit point or of its southern culminating point, or full moon phase, and thus elevated, means that it is the also the [farthest and or highest] point the Sun's frequency can tolerate upon the Moon in respect with the Earth [gravitational field]. Thus, owe to Moon horizontal rotation (sidereal spins), the Moon will advance forward and diagonally, thanks to the virtue of Earth gravitational field [rink or platform] and its [opposite] rotation, and that from the elevated or inclined position, once again will cut or cross the Earth towards the northern portion or inner point of the Sun, or commonly known as the New Moon phase. These motions demonstrate that the Moon will circumnavigate or commute all around the Earth [with the virtue of its revolution towards the east] as the Moon's Third Law of motion. It is notable that the combination of First, Second and Third Moon's Law of Motion or the spins, sidereal or diagonal oscillation and circumnavigating the Earth, are the sum up of the perfect circumstances, wherein it projects the phases of Moon and the operation as an essence of an equilibrator or outrigger. Great evocation, but at this point, and that we can conclude that if these duties of the Moon is in fact essential or a pre-requisite for the planet to become habitable, perhaps human being and a viable planet like Earth is all alone in the universe thinking on how the thousand possibility of the initial engagement between the two bodies take place. Not discounting an erroneous proposition by scientist, and that if the Moon really causes the Tide, then there's no tidal event to balance the system in the planet denied with a Moon (we have to note that without Tide, then there's no night and day as well. And even a planet travels as if moving or orbit in a way, without compression will blow occupants out into the space and no atmosphere [for breathing] to support life). In other words, it's because that the incoming planets has a lot of moons, it doesn't mean it could settle right a perfect satellite like the tandem we have on the earth and moon, and that speak a million possibility of timing or chances of initial engagement or virgin conception.

Besides paycheck, the question at this point is what would be the essence of the Lunar indication that inhabitant of the Earth should care about?

*This will give us the idea that after the new moon phase and the body shows once again for another month or crossover journey, means that the system which consist of different sensors, such as thermal, density and or mass, revolution per minute (rpm) or the gravitation in general aspect, is healthy or normal, and works as if engaged into automatic mode. The hard part or thing however, is that delays on responding, specifically on resurfacing out of new Moon phase is a total concern if not tells at least a bad omen, specifically Moon closing in to the Earth event. And that, if the Moon submit totally to the sun, its creator, Earth shall be left behind without the moon and this could be problematic, and that can be consider as the beginning of the earth worst scenario and perhaps the beginning of an end as this treatise assumed that it is a replicate of what had happen between the planet Mercury and Venus, where in the former is most probably, if not the fact, was actually the moon to the later [**Note: Regarding this proposition, Author can be reach through the publisher if additional information is required by any individual or institution**].*

*At this point, hail this treatise is to the essence of the great religions; the Judaism, Christian and Islam specifically, Prophet Mohammed, PBUH for instituting prayer in every phase of the day, and fasting especially during the Ramadan, the 9ᵗʰ and Holy Month of Hegira calendar. Indeed, the sacrifice and the power of mass prayer may move the great or essential things in the universe. Things connived, rather, miracle happens on the right place and in the right time (**see also Quintessence concept**).*

And a certain point that this writing consider is that the 9ᵗʰ month of Gregorian calendar which fall on September, the equinox or in one of the solstice time of the year, or on the summit point of the Earth on its orbit, is in fact one, if not the most critical point, wherein, the Earth and Moon relation could break due to vulnerable circumstances. We have to note that earth and moon orbit is the later fourth motion. Specifically, *naturally repels, but since the body works only by natural sense, thus no assurance or total guarantee neither and that [awkward positioning of the duo particularly on this month is like two balls on gravity feed], will not collide eventually. Nevertheless, though the actual scenario is feeding horizontally, solar attraction is in fact planets and satellites are working or racing to get inside the funnel which is the cone shape radiant frequency we have discussed above [thermodynamic or electromagnetic conduction]. And the blessing or the good thing however is that the Earth is in rather good position than its satellite, the Moon, but in case that the later, or the duo opt to live independently or by themselves, is nothing but a tragic scenario and end (if the earth came closer to the moon, touch or collision could be very violent and pushes the later inward. In this case, pray with Muslim brothers during the holy month of Ramadan for the atonement of sins and this may yield the life after. And on September for the Moon to turn out and in of the system and that bequeath a better and ideal Earth and could be perfected of an all-season and or all-around planting trees). The fact that the Earth will descend on this month or season could left behind or abandon the Moon that might had anchored on the much stronger gravitational pull of the Sun [*Due to exacerbated heat of the earth, mainly because of global warming, might help to push the moon inward and might stays there if the circumstances that define the distance or spacing between the trinity bodies; the Sun, Earth and Moon has been altered in favor of the great body which is the Sun. Thus, one, or a compelling scenario, is that inclination to the north will describe a zeroing angle, therefore northern portion (of the body of water) will experience floods ahead of the southern counterpart. It is notable at this point, that looking back on the principle of the formation of the planet or Earth specifically, is that gasses takes over as the primordial element, then precedes by the ice sheet, earth or land masses, and afterward, the floods or water takes place, wherein on its current position is "ruling the Earth" that we must be wary of its "strange behavior" or definitive consequence such as floods and tsunamis. Otherwise failed to comply may have the trial that the planet Venus and Mercury, as the later consider as Moon to the former, has been get through, and that with the irrefutable fact of these planets, rather the undeniable fact or scene due to global warming, we** *are losing the battle against the fourth element which is the fire and or heat and that if we do nothing against this threat.*

And this treatise once again take this opportunity to remind everyone to contribute in helping to resist and ward off the global warming phenomena in order to prevent a worst case scenario, or at least to delay this thing will be a triumphant for the inhabitant of the Earth especially those in the future generation; they are our children, please do not deprive them of a safe environment neither cry in vain mainly because of our lapses and irresoluteness. A must see Athena Calendar concept in Book 1 for additional input].

The Earth

In Book 1, an opening statement on article, The Earth, The Global Warming and The Revelation, described this creation filled with enlivening or exalting emotions. While the author tried to impress and inspire readers like an artist that touch other's life or emotions of their work of arts or masterpieces, but at the back of my mind is like a painting of falling leaves or sunset, or perhaps a child waving goodbye to her or his love one, definitely, what I've been through in the past when I left my children behind to work in Saudi Arabia, and that inspired with sadness. I'm not quite sure if I found the word's right for everyone, nevertheless, with the utmost concern of the nature or environment, I tried to rewrite it in here hoping to touch lives, motivate or prompts to action in preserving its beauty and essence.

The Earth; It is our planet, our world, our habitat, home and our treasure.

It is wonderful and amazing indeed.

With the Sun's spectrum on it, it can be consider as splendid body in space of having excellent condition.

It is awe-inspiring and perfect.

It is a fine creation, one can tell, and verily, a paradise to those who really appreciate and pleased with the nature. An author from India said: It is marvelous. Well, you are all to your words to magnify, describe and/or cherish the beauty and value of this magnificent creation.

*As we discussed and found out that the planets and their satellites was created by the Sun, is made up of gas nebula, and that with the help of corroborative circumstances, creations or formations were carried out through the sole process and the very principle of the operation and existence of body or matter in the universe which is commonly called the Revolution (Turning or Rotation). Thus, rotations, spins or swirling that form and shape and create the planets and satellites and of the suns from the course of the galaxies, could mean one thing, and that from the slightest degree to the current point of operation, like human being on conception, nourished, stimulated and strengthen, and that [**elements or**] body's revolving since then or of its very beginning. In other words, element (gases) was beautifully crafted by the Sun spectrum, turning this entity or gases nebula to a fine creation we call planet. Planet in a certain point of time rotates and drags to its orbit by the Sun spectrum.*

*Well the body or planet that was caught in a habitable point of space or time can be considered as the greatest gift to habitat, or of mankind. It is a miracle; and that the span of millions of years to enjoy this endowment, what we human being, or tenant as you like it, of this planet, considered as the highest (degree) of creation, can give back in return or as gratitude being the residence guest of this planet; is it the body's destruction or preservation? Well, the answer is apparent if not overwhelming, and that this point of our life is just loaned from our lender, the Mother Earth, (**indeed we must be grateful but to pay or to exalt the creator which is the Sun in this case could be gross if not absurdity one can consider but who could blame the Inca or Aztecs or Ancient Egypt for the degree or magnitude of their gratuity**) therefore we should hand this treasure of life as polished, and without the blemish of corruption and handed down with utmost care to the next or future generation.*

We human being has an intellect; was it difficult for us to set aside pride and learned that the paradise we living in, or pleasure that environment benefited for us, is also the paradise that our children's desire and would like to *experience? In this case, we should or have to learn to pamper the environment, biodiversity or the planet in general aspect because this is the earth we living in and our descendants to foster. The main factor of global warming and threat to the planet existence is the oil and gas production and the deforestation. Carbon gas emission consider as pollutants could roughly make a three to eight percent contribution. It is a funny thing that my Swiss made shoes cannot stand with the endurance I had been through on keep coming back in Philippines different institution's concern with environment and research. Besides with the fact that I dig dip on my pocket shouldering a 40$ bill sending a copy of Book 1 to His Excellency, The United States President and that from a 400 pages book hoping only to tell them at least a thing or two of global warming consequences [US carried out fracking activity instead which is logically exacerbate the earth frailty condition]. Nevertheless, when it comes to global warming, the democrats in the houses, this writing believe outperform their counterpart.*

In one hand, due to increment on planet temperature would lead a supposed massive face of attraction towards the Sun. And a few hundred kilometer side sweeping of the earth inward or towards the sun's core, means a pungent air upheavals, and the brunt of this kind of phenomena has been felt in the Philippines on the last quarter of the year 2013 when they experienced the strongest typhoon so far. While on the other, besides with the fact that layers of the earth supports itself from preventing "massive" thermal convection or the transfer of heat from one point to another (oil and) gas production is indeed compromised the buoyancy of the earth **(When it comes to global warming, analogy between human and the earth makes no difference except that the former has brain. I don't want to think that the thermal sensory element of the planet is more astute than human thinking. In a certain case, deficit or lack of oxygen in human aspect could result in a brain damage or stroke. Due to operation or compression to be specific [the upper layer of the earth, the shell or bed, works against [the opposite way] the core; in this instance the liquid core or liquid coal serves as lubricant and the rugged activity between them produce gases or pressure via squeegeeing], though earth has a natural mean to refill gases, gas production or gas's escapes is like making a hole or poking in a balloon filled with gases, and that will gain more weight or increase its density and sink as a result of in proportional** *activity or production. **Gas is one if not the most essential element the Earth naturally produces on its operation, the compression upon rotation as well as orbit. Gas help the planet for its buoyancy, and besides oil, this element or degree of layer could or would be the great help insulating the earth surface from the core of the body therefore production and depleting of the said element exacerbate the heat transfer in this case). In other words, rather to be specific, continuing such activity in the earth, orbit pattern would be altered, and that coming short on the peak of the orbit standard, will exacerbate heat that may induce drought and forest fire as the country of Australia and Indonesia and or partly in America has been exposed to, which we can say due to circumstances or condition, the vulnerable part on this point of time. While on the other, due to higher density, orbit on the bottom point (solstice) will create a slack or sagging pattern and that exacerbate freezing temperature as North American experiencing on the first quarter of the year 2014.*

*Earth preservation or mitigating global warming is not that hard as other may think of, but requires balance approach, coordination and implementation; Say reduced the oil production and increased the price as to stabilize economy; this is to come up with the oil producer or oil producing country to maintain stability or to enjoy the same standard of living because they are the first to deny and or the hardest cry's foul when it come to this matter. Carried out the alternative on fossil fuel wherein green technology on private cars is mandatory. And bank on renewable energy source: solar energy, hydrothermal or geothermal energy, wind or water **(current)** and the long list of human potential, technical innovation and ingenuity and creativity can be harness and sustain.*

In addition, Tree is life therefore daunt deforestation and or illegal logging. In other words, as far as the planet and biodiversity existence is concern, tree is the most significant and essential entity on this world; like of those ice's freezing temperature, some of its function (or being the main factor) is to create/emit cloud or cloud seeding that is in charge on the atmosphere, protecting us from the harmful solar energy discharge. And the [mineral] water [refuse or heavy element] produced on transmutation process that goes into the river bed and that plunge into the ocean [current circumnavigation] is a source of fresh water supply to cool the surface of the earth against the core of the planet and its volcanic activity in response to its operation and or feat of the sun **(a must see Book 1 for the comprehensive theory of the essence of tree)**. *Preserve, protect and or treat and nurture rainforest (and support like of the project/foundation of HRH Prince Charles of England) as the life giver of your own community.*

Furthermore, digging on the metaphysical concept of planet and their satellite's origin and existence, is that due to the revolution of the sun, re-shape and molded the body out of the original gas nebula or element (air). In a very short period of time or instantaneously become water, then become dried ice then create core then create water and earth and water.

Now the game on these transmutation processes is like the world' greatest wrestling show on earth and that is the team event; the duo of the earth (land masses) and trees against human (intellect and survival and or progress or greed), water, fire and air, and its apparent a discrepancy or one-sidedness in this case. While the trio of water invaded or overrun the earth, air flattened and or fire consummated the trees. And the worst thing is that human being carried out those things the trio combined. Those things that supposed to protect us, we cannibalized, and this is the sad and most regrettable reality. If things go that way unrestricted, would become worst sooner or later. In other words, rather the point is simple; after crushing trees and subduing the earth or conquering the mainland thus weakens the human defense mechanism, the trio of water, air and fire shall turn their back to pound and or slaughter human being. On our experience on nature cataclysm, one can tell if, rather, if these phenomena, gather its momentum, takes off, and sure take its place, and feeling the brunt right now. And all with the concept written in here is to support and compliment this idea and that to defeat skeptics in any subject that matter; science, religion or philosophy. This writing's quest and or its utmost desire, is to tell people to protect the earth from massive oil and gas production and unnecessary human activity. Daunt deforestation and plant trees and preserves rainforest and ice deposit, the first line of defense against [global] warming. And this leads to balance the system therefore protect us from the harm of elements such as water, fire and air. And fans can enjoy the show of the great world's wrestling stars.

A must see theory on earth's engineering and natural sciences on The Global Warming and the Revelation on the concluding article.

The Principle of Thunder and Lightning and Air Upheavals

Propelled mainly by air, a massive and dynamic body planet like the Earth and much more of the planet Jupiter, of its principle of operation is in, can develop great air upheavals and disaster such as tornado, cyclone, hurricane and or typhoons. The observations made by the atmospheric scientist like Vilhelm Bjerknes (Restless Earth pp.78) asserted this fact as the outcome of confrontation between the cold and warm air masses, wherein in one point this treatise's totally concurred but could had been perfected incorporating Coriolis and Kepler theory. However, the principle of the "updraft theory" alone, also called as steam engine theory, that causes or brewed air upheaval specifically, contradict the other, in this case. The fact that a square foot container on its boiling point and has progressive temperature, produce a three to five millimeter updraft, and for that reason, indeed, will require a great pressure from a certain source of heat in, or beneath the surface of a great body of water, an open sea in particular, for a great air disturbances with a great magnitude to manifest and sustain the whole duration of the event. Nevertheless, updraft principle or its origin, or the manifestation of a whirlpool in the earth atmosphere to be specific, is quite interesting and this treatise aim's to share additional information as far as the metrological subject or service is concern. The questions in this case is that where in the Earth the massive warm and cold air came from, and how the circumstances developed, or how do the condition satisfied?

*To claim that this principle is not that hard to prove even to those non-mechanically incline or non - technical intuitive mentality can be a good start. And on this case however, is that it does need the primary or secondary level of education of the application of Newton's Third Law of Motion which is, rather essential in this case, and that says "when a matter or an object move, an air at the same time generated, while the force that acted on one way, an equal force commence on the other." In addition, nay, to satisfy the demand for the flawless structure or intrinsic and functional element, the Gaspard - Gustave Coriolis **(1792-1843; French mathematician, mechanical engineer and scientist)** force or effect theory, which we can consider as "very academic" nevertheless, is very helpful indeed to the point that is consider as the fundamentals of the Big Bang and Universal Gravitation or the inflationary principle of a body such* *as Galaxy and Sun. However, in oceanographic and meteorological principle, its observation must be characterized by careful, exact evaluation that if fine details left unexplained, may lost its applicability or significance as the Coriolis effect theory alone, in strict sense, may lead in understanding the nature's phenomenon half of the truth about it. In general point however, the beauty of its method and practical applicability, the movement of the storm in particular, impresses the like of this observation, but it is strange to find out that the most essential aspect of the subject had been left undeveloped or taken for granted or neglected. Specifically, in the absence of the general natural sciences theory, or the theory of everything in general aspect is disheartening to the point that it indeed compromise the safety and or the very existence of the Earth, our planet, let alone, rather, the exposure and or degree of hazards from the nature disaster could, or may had been exacerbated by the unfounded claim or assumption made by some, or most of religious preachers (**in saying this is echoing Jesus Christ's as He said no one in them can turn black hair into gray**) about the "wonders of nature", or the awe inspiring beauty of its creation. In addition, the then inexplicable mechanical law of nature, the disturbances or violent agitation such as thunder and lightning that causes air upheaval. And most probably this might be the reason of the religious foundation and other welfare community or institution with the same objective, as John the Beloved mentioned in His book, the Revelation, where in the concept and supposed devotion of the church is to help those in need, the orphan and widow especially those people who suffers and or the afflicted by the nature catastrophe. And the catch's or the gratuity of this noble deed's the comfort or salvation of one's soul to the point of a shot or a promise's of life after death to or for the most Faithful. In a certain case however, someone may had been retard or hinder one's view, nevertheless, the reason on telling these things, is not to demean the moral teaching of any religious advocacy nor creating or believing in religion without God, but hope to help make clarifications anew in case of any obscurity between (**the real concern regarding**) the "beauty of its teaching" or the comfort or salvation of the soul in particular, and that in conformity with the truth about nature, human being and environment, or creation's natural sciences. Nonetheless, the theory is important as the fundamentals and proponent of planet's operation, biodiversity and its existence in general aspect.*

The Guard, Door and the Unwelcome Visitor

On the 24 hours per day revolution and the 360 days on its orbit, Earth as a massive body, generates force or power and its energy as a result from the ceaseless solar frequency spectrum. Specifically, out of the space or gasses, rather, unrestricted, vulnerable or aloft, the Earth circular movement or the 24 hours rotations produced air and that we can consider low pressure, yet, thick and stingy [gummy] voluminous gasses. And this, in strict sense, or in general gravitational aspect, could be considered as the "magnetic field in a sense, or radiation belt in a profound concern." This radiation belt is in fact the space resistance, produced and developed upon rotation of the body and that serves as the mantle of protection or defense mechanism around its frame, and that works like a windshield of a car or an aircraft works. And depending on the body's configuration and efficiency in general aspect, will determine the shielding's gas' that may form, shape or may appear. As far as the force is concern, this particular shield or magnetic field [radiation belt is like an aircraft fuselage and being pressurize give us inhabitant room to breathe] which is made out of low pressure air, is considered malleable or weak, yet stingy and or tight in a certain aspect just enough to frustrate or eludes intruder. Specifically, rather, reinforce or consolidated with the combination of air resistance from body's revolution itself and with the "high pressure air" being developed and or encounter during planet's orbit. In other words, though low pressure air protects the earth surface or territory against a much stronger foes, which is the mixture of layer of gasses that was mentioned above, it is however vulnerable in a "strange" or particular way. And that, rather, the more a shield becomes harder, the more it should *fortify itself to resist but brittleness as factor tells the opposite in contrast **(*conditions such as, tilting or earth deviated from its course where it sets an angular contact making the low pressure air durable wherein a sustainable high pressure air turn its back and create a twist, penetrate and sink into the earth atmosphere [low pressure area] and that would become the air upheaval; see illustrations on the following).** *Since Earth air defense mechanism is consider low pressure against a pungent air resistance during orbit, it is more susceptible **(brittle and crunchy)** to intruder which is in this case is the high pressure air (space resistance) produced on earth orbit. And the scenario looks like, rather, works like a predator works, hunting on its (human) prey relentlessly, and that was held or trapped inside a hole or a stingy glass's chamber* *which is the dynamic Earth [thus] covered with radiation belt in this case (**A must see Book 1 of the same article's title for additional input**).*

*At this point however, it is noteworthy not to be confused regarding the task the Sun exerted against the earth, wherein one hand, the Sun's spectrum that initiates the "pressure" pushes the Earth outward, and the gravitation or magnetic pull that originates from the Sun's core [great speed, swift and or smooth] pulls the body inward and this makes the principle of turning the [aloft] earth as a result or its consequence. And with the Earth engulfed to the high magnitude sun's magnetic field [cone shape chamber], the synchronizing and simultaneous operation of pressure and magnetic pull, causes the body to rotates and hold or keep on its track and *dragged to its orbit respectively in response (***swinging or hurling in the air by a man, Earth Orbit is like a stone on a [flexible] slingshot/string, and at the same time pulling by the string little by little by its initiator which is the sun in this case; see Book 1 for the extended version of this theory**).*

In this case, it is noteworthy to consider the general aspect of the operations as innate, or the natural planetarium and solar concept; set up, task, maneuver and control, and it is amazing that this model without manner or attitude, works through or by sensing Temperature alone, nevertheless, fulfilled with the corroborative circumstances. According to British Biologist Thomas Henry Huxley (1825-1895), dubbed as "Darwin's Bulldog" or the ardent supporter of British scientist named Charles Robert Darwin, author of the "Theory of Evolution", and I quote:

This distinctive character of our time lies in the vast and constantly increasing part which is played by natural knowledge. Not only is our daily life shape by it; Not only does the prosperity of millions of men depend upon it, but our whole theory of life has long been influenced, consciously or unconsciously by the general conception of the universe which have been force upon us by a physical science.

The notions of the beginning and the end of the world entertained by our forefathers are no longer credible. It is very certain that the Earth is not the chief body in the material universe, and that the world is not subordinated to man's use. It is even more certain that "Nature" is the expression of a "definite order" with which nothing interferes, and the chief business of mankind is to learn that order and govern themselves accordingly.

*Moreover, this scientific "criticism of life" presents itself to us with different credentials from any other. It appeals neither to authority nor to what anybody may have thought or said, but to Nature. It admits that all our interpretations of natural fact are more or less imperfect and symbolic, and bids the learner seek for Truth not among words but among things. It warns us that the assertion which outstrips evidence is not only a blunder but a crime. Scholarly and pious persons, worthy of (all) respect, favor us with allocution upon the sadness of the antagonism of science to their medieval way of thinking, which betray an ignorance of the first principle of scientific investigation, an incapacity for understanding what a man of science means by veracity, and unconsciousness of the weight of established scientific truths, which is almost comical (**Excerpt from "Science and Culture", an essay of British Biologist Thomas Henry Huxley; source: Microsoft Encarta Premium 2005**)*

Furthermore, though the Earth on its constant revolution that produces the low pressure air, has the ability to deny intruders, how could a high pressure air satisfy the condition and somehow manage to sneak and penetrates into earth's surface, and since it is considered a high pressure and against a low pressure one and that would breed air upheavals, and what tells about it when the frequency of manifestation is concern. Specifically, why no air upheavals every minute?

*The fact that the earth is so vulnerable to mayhem or air upheaval in particular, the equilibrium [**Quintessence**] or the state of natural balance, play [it or] the part so well. Factors that improved or perfected an ideal stage or condition, include the distance of the planet from the Sun, revolution, its size; mass, weight, diameter, and mechanical properties such as heat, coldness, lubricant, coolant, hardness, flexibility etc. and the general aspect that influence or affect this stability or symmetry is the Temperature. Therefore this treatise suggest and conclude that we have to subdue ignorance regarding the truth of the nature, and in very particular, the challenge, difficulty or problem that the global warming is laying down upon us, whether it is man-made consequence of action, or the natural course of planet and or both, but one of the most important thing is we do our share in helping the body existence, and do the best we could on our part in order to save the planet, biodiversity and humanity. We have to note that due to solar attraction, things that get bad, mainly because the Sun has no intellect, shall become worst and is irreversible.*

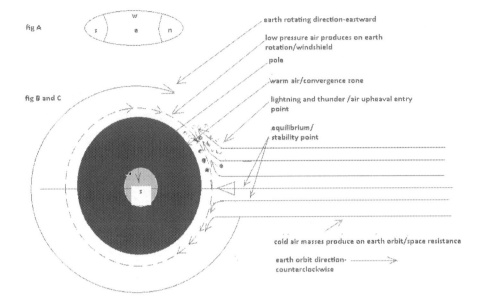

fig A

fig B and C

earth rotating direction-eastward

low pressure air produces on earth rotation/windshield

pole

warm air/convergence zone

lightning and thunder /air upheaval entry point

equilibrium/ stability point

cold air masses produce on earth orbit/space resistance

earth orbit direction- counterclockwise

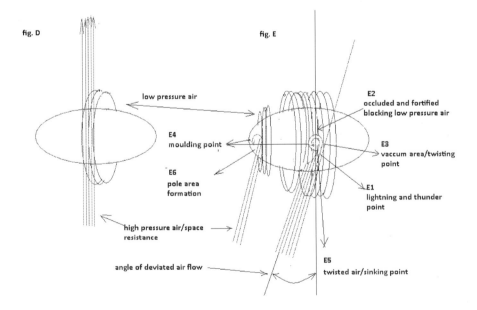

fig. D

fig. E

low pressure air

E4 moulding point

E6 pole area formation

high pressure air/space resistance

angle of deviated air flow

E2 occluded and fortified blocking low pressure air

E3 vaccum area/twisting point

E1 lightning and thunder point

E5 twisted air/sinking point

On the couple of illustrations above, designated by letters A to D, is the basic operation of the earth, the rotation and orbit and its consequence. In fact, however the model's basic, its function is the prime application of Coriolis theory of force and effect. An extended or uncut theory of operation was actually explained in Book 1 of the same article.

And to present here a concise idea is that when the Earth rotates, the air resistance developed against the direction of its rotation, and its taking place all around or all over the earth atmosphere and all of the time, wherein the *unrelenting operation is in fact procure a million possible or potential storm or thunder storm and lightning flashes, every second (***And to imagine an interruption of frequency on this particular task, is another thing, and that would be best explain on tsunami and earthquake articles**).

As an additional task, when the earth *orbits (***earth orbit is around 60,000 mph or 104,000 kilometer per hour, and takes little less than one billion kilometer in one year or one complete cycle, ascending and descending in an almost perfectly spherical pattern, the 360 days or 360 degree and that constitute a degree each day and so will become the parameter of a perfect frequency and cycle. Say a variation or deviated orbit pattern, specifically, nay, perhaps the shorter the annual days of orbit it goes, the problematic the life on the Earth - see Book 1 for Athena Calendar concept and or tsunami article)**, the air resistance developed as well. The dual and or consolidated air resistance from rotation and orbit, hovers all around the earth atmosphere and that from the equilibrium or stability point, the air resistance splits on different direction and could have meet on the other side or on the opposite side of the entry point, struggles, and that when the circumstances satisfied, specifically on fall season, creates a twisting motion and that when sustain, since fall or downward earth orbit direction, subscribe to an *updraft pull, and that air twisting motion extended to the surface of the earth that becomes the air upheaval (**fall season air upheaval manifestation - back entry point**). The appearance of this kind of air upheaval is in addition with the common cause of entry on the earth atmosphere, which is the "front entry point or the head on clashes and violent struggle" (**thunder and lightning show time**) between the masses of low and high pressure air, and if the condition satisfied, that paves the way for the air upheaval to manifest.

The Tides

*Though the author, with all honesty has not, or never been obtain a copy of the book's Galileo Galilei's Dialogue Concerning the Two Chief World System's, which was dedicated to his patron, Ferdinando II de Medici, Grand Duke of Tuscany. And that the concept of the tenet compares the Copernican with the traditional Ptolemaic system. Bestseller, and there was no question that the Copernican side gets the better of the argument, and this article, anyway and or nevertheless dedicated to Galileo, for the author understand how hard he has been through on defending his idea which was widely disputed, where in, according to the history that Galileo fall short as Einstein commented, in providing mechanical proof as the former hoped for, thus, failed to convince the authority and thus suffered on the Roman Inquisition on 1615 (**found vehemently suspect of heresy, force to recant and spent the rest of his life under house arrest; source Wikipedia**), to the point that convincing the impartial reader remains a contentious issue at that time. As a result, much more on this were being considered incorrect until, rather, up to this point in time, where in the Academics field held the notion (of the classical Tide theory) from some of the great or prominent scientists or personalities, such as Ptolemy [**as well as Tycho Brahe in this particular subject**] that was said having derived from ancient observation, perhaps from Babylonian astronomer, Seleucus of Seleucia, Wang Chong of China 27-100 AD, Johannes Kepler, Isaac Newton, Pierre-Simon Laplace and their advocates are some of them, that considered Tides, were explained more precisely by the interaction of the Moon's and the Sun's gravity, or specifically, is cause by the gravitational pull of the moon in a body of water like oceans where in this writing, like Galileo firmly believed incorrect. However, as far as this writing is concern regarding Galileo's account on this matter, which is far reliable than the notion of those prominent person listed above this treatise can argue, wherein he considered the activity of Tides as the required physical proof of the operation of the Earth (**heliocentric against geocentric model**), however, nay, unfortunately, unable to provide the corroborative theory or fundamentals that explain everything against a formidable skeptics, and that, unfortunately, the authority on that era, the church. In one point, the ingenuity of his theory on his time, however (**the Earth moves around the Sun**), it was said that on general evaluation was considered a failure, and as this writing* saw it, especially on the matter that he considered that the *Sun lies motionless at the center of the universe (**this notion was in effect or an accepted fact until today and even reiterated on the book written by Stephen Hawking; without the fundamental of the theory of the origin and operation of the Sun, it appeared, rather, it seems that a body like the Sun was well understood working like a capacitor charge for a specific consumption or period of time [which is incorrect], wherein, scientist claimed that the Earth may exist for another or around 4 billion of years, which is not a bad thing or assumption for us inhabitant living on today, but not of course on those guys after 4 billion years. But the thing is, unsupported concept or conjecture like this weakens the philosophy of life or the state of science, metaphysics and even religion, thus become vulnerable to error and that may compromise human as well as the planet's affair. A must see Book 1 for the comprehensive theory of Sun and Galaxy operation and that includes the fulfillment of Isaac Newton's theory of Universal Gravitation)**, and cannot provide the lucid explanation on the notion that if his theory is correct, there would be one high tide per day. In another, as this writing see it, one but significant factor when he undermined the essence of Kepler's idea, his contemporary, regarding the [elliptical] orbit of the planets, wherein this case, unaware, or denials of the significant of one's theory, that somehow may accolade or compliment his own, therefore may weakens as a result. In defense of Galileo however, is to lay down question on why the authority subscribe to the ancient theory (say account on the Bible's Old Testament) where its concept has more defect and hold with imperfect comparison compare to what they obtain using an advance method of experiments and investigation? **(a must see theory on Tides in Book 1 for additional input)**.

Tides define as the periodic variation in the surface level of the oceans and of bays, gulfs, inlets and estuaries **(is correct, but)** caused by the gravitational attraction of the moon and sun **(was a carnal error [due to interpretation of ancient writing; say Greek philosopher, Bible] if not a gross incompetence, this treatise could claim or argue)**.

We have to note that there is no question that the Sun causes the Earth to turn from the very beginning of its existence. To prove the argument, say on the planet Earth with water in it, turning loose item, especially a fluid or liquid characteristic, specifically water with high density, will then fall or settled at the bottom **(180 degree)**, and this "settling or pouring out" condition clearly manifest of a high tide scenario on the bottom point or 90-180-270 degree, wherein the water from approximately 45- 90 and 270- 315 degree angle has fall or poured in, in the former thus creating a low tide on the later **[the question on why is the water never spilled outside the earth atmosphere during revolution has been vividly explained in Book 1 and soon will give additional input on the following Tsunami Article]**, while its counterpart, the water in the ocean stored in a basin like container which is on the top portion **(0 or 360 degree position)** of the earth, projects a relatively calm and the normal or minimum water level a basin can hold or contain.

In this regard, nay in one hand, while from the high tide, going low **[ebb tide]** to *normal tide level **[*slack tide that projects calmness]**, depicts on or from the 270 to 360 degrees, a quarter turn of the earth in a clockwise manner. On the other hand, normal to low tide, going to high tide **[flood tide]** level will be on zero (0) to 90 degrees position. And this will give us conclusion that from these points, 270 to 0/360 to 90 degree position, is a low semidiurnal tide. It is notable however that point 0/360 degree is the slack or calmness tide. On the opposite side we can observe the counterpart which is from 90 to 180 to 270 degree position, projects a semidiurnal and high tide level and wave is on full potential mode or state, specifically on 180 degree point.

And it is noteworthy that tides timing activity is on progress, rather varied in each every seconds count and progressively, mainly because of the earth dynamic activity or rotation. While the Earth orbit or creates seasons, serves as the timing's main factor, this was perfectly corroborated with the Earth size or area and revolution **(rpm)**. As a result, without going into the sea, we can understand that on *February and September 21 **[*reset as necessary]** as these was the equinox point (summer solstice) of earth orbit, and that in one point, the "calm tide" on the month of February (winter season) will be on 12'00 o'clock noon and high tide must be on 12'00 midnight. On the other, the month of

*September projects the opposite indication which is 12'00 o'clock noon on the high tides and the low/calm tides should be on 12'00 o'clock midnight. Basically, rather, we can conclude that if the water recedes from one point, say in ocean basin, will therefore fill up on the other side of it. In other words, low tides on high point of the Earth and high tides level on lower area and this, the potential or magnitude of tide depends on the degree of Earth angle or revolution (**a must see The Tide and The Wave Theory on Book 1 for additional input or soon on the theory of Wave on the succeeding article**).*

Furthermore, though this argument could be proven only to planet like earth, we have to note that if the circumnavigating of the moon causes tides, then a planet with water but without or denied with a moon, therefore has no tidal event. It's strange, because if another planet with a sun tandem [without moon, but has water] is absolutely not suitable neither capable of supporting life. Tide is the cause of the rotation of the earth. And the tide timing activity is the earth orbit or seasons. The basic principle is that the pull of gravity, and that the water always settled at the bottom. If a planet that has water and sun but no rotation, sure will create friction on a certain point especially those area that expose to the sun, and temperature will shoot up to the water boiling point. If there's no rotation that define the spacing or distance between the bodies, therefore no invisible shield, the pressurize air that protects the surface of the earth, therefore no atmosphere to breath and therefore not capable in supporting life. The fact that the moon is just a quarter of the mass the earth has possess, therefore when it comes to gravitational aspect, the latter is more rugged or powerful and pungent in this case, thus exercise authority over the former. What the moon can do in a certain case is to block the incoming solar frequency towards the earth, and this create the earthquake therefore this phenomenon is in fact, rather, clearly predictable; see the following article on earthquake and or the duties of moon in Book 1. And to think that the moon imposes authority during high tide, with the water density or billions of tons of weight of this element, and I don't mean to brag, but if this is correct, during high tide, men could be weightless and perhaps flying, and could be a good thing in a certain case, but be wary not to be caught on transition period, you will drop dead soon on low tide. Indeed, rather this writing firmly believed, and that with the astuteness of Saint John the Beloved, he could be leading the church in a more noble way than his guardian and could be predecessor.

The Wave

Without setting foot in college, initially, I learned Earth Science from a hand out of a brief open sea diving course and the rest was experience and cogitation through a reading habit or self-study method. On my point is that though Wave and or the like of Tide theory has been produced through academics artistic effort, specifically extensive studies and or observation, however, rather, don't mean to brag, but was really concerned regarding the "weakness" of the outcome of the theories or the assessment of the subject matter.

To produce a Wave, was said to be the air moving over the surface of water has to somehow transmit its energy to the water, so, if the wind gets stronger, the waves will get higher, and the most accepted notion was proposed in 1950's, the Miles-Phillips theory [see also Dr. Tony Butt article- How Waves Are Generated or The Book of Knowledge by John Farndon and Angela Koo, pp. 291].

The total explanation of this article was in Book 1 actually, but I love the whole article rewritten in here, yet, I settled and manage to have some quote from it in order to aid us in discerning some essential point. What this writing mean is that the theory on Tide sure will compliments the Wave property, one way or the other and these entries will depict or emphasis the real nature of Tsunami on the succeeding article.

"A single stroke of the Earth upon revolution, wherein a common knowledge or observation is that it creates a lot of reactions especially on the body of water such as bay or lake, sea or oceans, which we can consider, rather, as far as the dynamic aspect or motion is concern, a vulnerable matter, mainly because of its fluidity or liquid characteristic. Next to, rather, alongside with orbit, Earth in a relatively normal cycle or compression, reaction in particular, can be consider as major proponent made to benefit the biodiversity and or the inhabitants on the earth. It provides us air to breath, water to drink and hot core to warm us as if the heart of a human being, which is one of the most essential component or factor in energy production, were some of it. And from this view, Wave operation as a certain reaction, therefore, must be in accordance with the nature's law of operation. In other words, law of nature or chronology of its

operation comes one after the other or definitely in sequence, in which one can view from its fundamental up to the summit and or the other way around, and that Tide or Wave in particular, or Nature in general aspect, in a sense is simply comprehensible.

The fact that the Tides activity possessed the dynamic aspect of the body of water, its motion is actually the Wave. The question in here is how does it work?

*Basically when the earth rotates, it tends to carry or move the water along. And since the shape of planet's round, the circular force or motion of the earth and that creates an angular formation upon turning, literally, makes the water fall from the shoreline. And because of its Pressure or Density, were supposed to settled in the bottom, thus emptying the shoreline area. And depending on the angle of deviation (**the higher the angle, the bigger amount of water displacement, the bigger the wave and the stronger the wind it produces, or directly in proportion which is true the other way around**), will therefore pushes and races the proportionate amount of water from the *__middle-surface__ (*__surface because the water is under pressure by its own weight or density and held by the gravitational pull by the Earth [orbit]__) point of the body water or sea, going into the shoreline for compensation or to cover up the losses, and simply we can call the operation as the basic or natural or renewable water Displacement and Leveling cycle. It is noteworthy that the same principle applied whether the activity of tides is on low tide mode or pulling or displacing of water from one point, and or high tide mode or filling up on the counterpart. And this cycle were repeated from time to time. In this case, it's apparent that any interruption or abnormality from the normal cycle will create an unprecedented threat, such as water surge or tsunami and this would be explain on the following article. Either way, the racing of water, with much pressure on high tide mode more than its low tide activity wherein the water is receding. The calibrated water shifting mode (a proportional but may not be limited to Earth diameter and or surface area, angular deviation, planet's rate of revolution [RPM] and or solar frequency discharge) is like pitching a glass of water from a bucket into another and back into it in a circular manner (shoreline-bottom-surface to shoreline). And that the movement of water that* *is visible from the surface is called Wave. The Mass or Density of water is dependent on the tidal mode or earth angle, and that high tide propagates bigger and or swelling waves and that may depend on seabed configuration as additional factor or circumstances, and the low tide mode tells receding or waning wave in contrast.*

It is noteworthy knowing that the renaissance or classic idea, and that says the blowing of the wind causes the wave, where in without attributing *air disturbances [i.e. **storm, typhoons, hurricane, and however manifest during earth maneuver on orbit; see Book 1 The Guard, The Door and The Unwelcome Visitor article for additional input]***, is in fact the opposite indicative. In other words, rather one could be found that in a normal situation, it's actually the "wave" that causes or propagates the wind in contrast. The scene is similar on, rather, with striking a hand fan; a fan at rest could produce no wind at all, so the water that is calm, thus, when the water start to move repeatedly in a certain direction, it is fanning or blowing the wind into that direction or in respect to the forces developed or position's established.*

In addition, the real essence or factor affecting the circumstances is the finely regulated movement or shifting of water due to ideal earth lateral surface area and that is proportional with the rate of earth rotation which is highly dependent on Sun's frequency, distance and or capacity that gives the Earth a perfect, calibrated, coordinated or synchronizing earth angle in respect with the rate of revolution, thus, water undergoes smooth transition period or settled on its course, in most of the time, the usual or ideal manner. And the great question at this point is that what would happen if the wave or tidal cycle were interrupted or disturbed, specifically, if the water pulled hard from the shoreline and gone deeper into the middle of the sea, and at the same time or in addition, the mid-surface water that should compensate in a certain or on the right time, however failed to carried out its task? And what does it takes for this thing to happen? The succeeding article wish to satisfy these queries.

The Tsunami

1. *Tsunamis happen when a big seismic event shakes the sea floor and causes the sea to ripple. Seismic events include earthquakes, volcanic eruptions, massive landslide dropping into the sea, and a huge landslide under the sea, or even an asteroid, meteor or comet impact. The vast volume of sea water and tremendous amount of energy create waves that can travel 800 km/h [500 mph], as fast as Jet Liner [source: Preciosa Soliven, The Philippine Star January 20, 2005].*

2. *Tsunamis can be generated by any significant displacement of water in oceans or lakes, though are most commonly created by the movement of Tectonic Plates under the ocean floor, during an earthquake. But they can also be caused by volcanic eruptions, glacial carving, meteorite impacts or landslides.*

3. *Commenting on the impact to Japans' people and economy on its recent tsunami disaster [11 March 2011], Professor James Goff, co-director of the Australian Tsunami Research Centre and Natural Hazards Research Lab at the University of New South Wales says: "it is a horrendous tragedy, caused by a completely unpredictable event".*

*As we have learned the principle of Wave and Tide from the previous articles, right away, we can define a Tsunami [**as well as the earthquake; citation will come shortly after this article]** in this case as a disturbance of a normal wave and or tide, as well as the current pattern that may lead to very destructive manner. Definitely, Tsunami is the outburst of the "compressed" sea or ocean water [**that was affected and was satisfied of the circumstances, in the frail of significant, or the absence {or screening} of solar frequency in a certain case]**, cause, but not limited to the moon's interpolation between the earth orbit and moon oscillation and commutation, or the trinity bodies, the Sun, Earth and Moon operation in general aspect.*

*Usually, rather, a *common tsunami, (***because a greater tsunami, as far as this writing believed, is the interruption of water current at the bottom of the ocean circumnavigating the Earth. Naturally, with the*** *aim of cooling the planet and that the current under the ocean that works like a radiator in a car works, thus eluded friction that may cause the breakdown of engine or any heat propagating machineries [in this case is the operation of the Earth's core] Blockage or any interruption [derailment or deviation of current pattern due to abrupt or sharp turn upon the Earth orbit] or delay of the ocean current, whatever might be the causes, is the most dangerous scenario that propagates Tsunami),* but not limited to the then sucked shoreline's water that is about to resurface in a certain time to complete a Wave cycle, but instead, had been pull hard by the density of water in particular, and the gravitational action (**breaking in or slowing down Earth revolution; see Book 1 for additional input**) in general aspect, due to interrupted cycle, sending it into the bottom of the sea and or compressed, and that could be the main factor contributing, rather that paves the way and or unleashed Tsunami. It might be cause by the delay of Sun's frequency cause by the interpolation of Moon, which is in fact, also the main cause of an Earthquake. In, or from a normal mode of tidal activity, *it* **is noteworthy that when a water, the tide or wave start to move, there's always an angle of inclination involve and that is a factor of compression; the steep the angle of the {earth or ocean floor or} water basin is, when literally fall, the harder the water compresses and this in addition with the very crucial timing factor, which is in this case, the longer the time** [it is said that it takes 8 seconds for the solar frequency to reach the earth], **and or "hardened or solid degree" of the interruption of frequency, the higher the severity or gravity of the event. And as far as the damage is concern, and that, could be more devastating. And one of these, which this treatise believed was the Asian Tsunami on 26ᵗʰ of December 2004.**

With the fact that the earth was categorically far from the sun, or on its solstice point of orbit on winter season, to be specific the month of November, December, January or February, which is the time that the Earth is vulnerable to such phenomenon or solar frequency interruption, thus, the degree of event is might be severe [but not limited to] compare to other or rest of the season.

At this point, the Earth in dynamic aspect, try to imagine the probability or principle of matter formation. When the earth rotates, say eastward, air or space resistance of course, shall work westward. While the mountain top goes to the east, the body of water will move to the west in contrast, however, besides tidal and wave activity in particular, a fluid or water were subject to the law of density in general aspect. In other words, underneath, the ocean convection current that circumnavigate against the shell of the Earth and serves as coolant or as radiator works in engine's car's work, will make the difference as far as the severity of Tsunami is concern, only or if this Convection Current could had been badly interrupted, is like a series or column of oil tanker or train traveling in a considerable but the same speed, and that, in any reason (however gross or superfluous, we cannot discount the probability of swelling of the seabed or volcanic activity, but most likely to be the frequency or speed of the tanker we have mentioned above) **could had been interrupted from the frontline, thus compacted or compress, and derailed. In this case, it is apparent that the principle of an earthquake manifest in here as well, and that makes the gravity of the event more devastating as the duo can work simultaneously. In short, while in the feat of solar frequency, the shell top of the earth works eastward** [solar frequency operation is like racing two fingers in your skin], **the ocean convection current works the opposite way, therefore, interruption of the solar frequency that dejected or deprived of the operation of the shell top of the earth, prove the Earthquake and the interruption or blockage of the convection current demonstrates the presence of Tsunami. The scene is like those items on top and sliding against the way of a conveyor belt, interruption on the belted region, whether the power source or mechanical parts on conveyor's fault, sure transporting items will experience delay or mayhem. And when the essential solar frequency is restored, the then compressed water which was of course pressurized, will move to find an outlet to equalize or level the situation, thus, along with the wave, will be discharge aggressively and or violently back into the shoreline which is what we call Tsunami. Depending on the tiding mode, say high tide, may exacerbate the event and that those that are weak point or less in resistance may causes unprecedented damages in** *that certain place especially infrastructure closer to the shoreline, until the disturbances gradually fades away or specifically, the compressed water is evenly disseminated and that waveform pattern and frequency may return to its normal cycling mode.*

We have to be transparent or lucid on this event; the earth and water in the ocean basin resemble the water on a cup assembled in series all around a shaft, and that was rotating and at same time hurled 360 degree in the space relentlessly. The moment that the frequency of Earth rotation has been interrupted, much more of its orbit, is obvious as turning the cup upside down in a low cycle or weak frequency, as well as on deceleration of speed on hurling or literally its orbit. In this case, rather, as a result, troubled would manifest worst on the place wherein the "excess" water from the angle of inclination the basin can hold (mid part of the earth; at least 45 to 315 degree), shall meet, and that is the bottom point. And if, we could imagine the scenario on the total absence of solar frequency (synonymous to the death of Sun), those inhabitants on this point (bottom) are the first to drowned and freezes in the space, while those on places facing the body's orbit and that in 15 seconds time, will be blown away on the opposite side, hurled and then freezes in the space as well. In conclusion, we are trying to prove that any of these bodies, particularly the Sun and Earth, and that delay, stand still or ceased on its operation, reflects the above circumstances or consequence, otherwise, nay, therefore myth or superstitious belief attributed on this event could be busted with the veracity of this argument.

Moreover, this treatise doesn't discount the possibility of the classic idea, the items no.1 and no.2 in particular, from above, to be the cause of a Tsunami, however we can find out that it is highly unlikely to be the reason of such phenomenon not just because of the degree of the event, but it is applicable only in a certain situation, or very particular to be specific. And this mean that Asian Tsunami of December 26, 2004, wherein its magnitude was so vast that it covers or affected several countries in this place. And that those notion from above these treatise believed, were likely to fail mainly because it will not generate adequate force to overcome water density or weight as resistance as the

Tsunami travels hundreds of kilometers before it reveals itself in the shoreline. In other words it needs an apparent and or a tangible reason, or a great, or substantial [source of] force in particular, in order to overcome resistance (the density of water itself or any other factor, say distance and or area), for a Tsunami, with a great magnitude, to manifest.

The great question in this case is on how the Tide or Wave being interrupted, or how do disturbances like Tsunami or storm surges takes place? And in addition, the item no.3 which consider this event as completely unpredictable **[as this will be explain on the following article – The earthquake and additional input on Moon operation]**, is the thing of the past [incorrect] this treatise maintain, and what is the truth behind this claim? - A must see theory on Tsunami, Earthquake and Moon operation in Book 1 for illustrations and for a comprehensive theory and or additional input.

The Earthquake

In Book 1, Earthquake like Tsunami, described as phenomenon that occurs specifically in the interruption or disturbance, or in weak solar output. Nevertheless, though I emphasized that these phenomena could be working independent to each other, with the "awkward" operation of moon and earth "against" the sun as one and definite factor. On a certain point, God forbid but time will come that these upheavals may however manifest simultaneously, more than that of individual event or incident, mainly because of the rapid expansion of the water bodies from which is the outcome, or the trouble of global warming; Specifically, disparity in temperature produce [plenty of] water, thus, global warming Earth's inducing more heated gases, will therefore meet the gases' atmospheric temperature, which is cold, therefore precipitation is on full potential, and that bring about rains that causes the Earth to flood. And in this case, it is not surprising to experience severity of rains only in a matter of days and that would take a month then.

What would be the essence on verifying and or identifying earthquake frequency? More than anything else's to save life, is unequivocal advantage. Leaving the earthquake uncheck in particular, or unmitigated thus unabated *global warming in general aspect, gravitational attraction, specifically downsizing or zeroing the distance of the Earth from the Sun, shall increase the solar frequency indulgence towards the Earth. In this case, rather, in addition, awkward or close up distance of Moon and Earth that more likely to screen intense frequency [planet exposed on this condition {in the event of accident}, is a serious matter like of a car on a full speed], is therefore an increment to a more devastating earthquake, tsunami and air upheavals. Intensity of an earthquake with a magnitude of 6 or 7 on a Richter scale then, might be superseded with a common magnitude of 8 or 9 and or even higher nowadays and it apply, or expect the same thing in category of air disturbances. Once again, let me take this opportunity to say that mitigating global warming is all cure to our troubled planet.*

*Since or with the virtue of its operations, specifically the rotations and orbit of the earth that relies mainly on the solar frequency output, the dynamic aspect of the interaction in between, makes the surface layer of the earth [shell or bed] to curl as a result (**conk out or perk up; as fine as the sun's mega frequency, the Earth dynamic condition is folded like of a finely corrugated brick or roof. Solar frequency is extended or connects down to the core of the Earth [and since the earth Core is confined, thus vibrates or bounces back in response to the feat of the Sun] and this serve as the Link between the couple. And in this case, it is notable that the Earth bulges where in the pressure concentrated, which is in the center of its axis, however, minimized on its pole side]. **Thus, interruptions, partial and or complete, of the solar frequency, cause mainly by the Moon interpolation in **corroboration of the satisfied circumstances such as weak solar output especially during winter days because basically the Earth is far and or away from the Sun on this point of time or orbit, and that depending on the degree of event or (partial or full) time factor, and that the longer the time of interruptions, the intense or extreme discomfort is, thus, **in a certain point of the Earth** would make, or experience the mainly surface layer to return to its static or neutral condition (**earth on static condition [normal and or at rest] - layer is tense or stretch out; wile earth on dynamic condition layer is compressed or curled due to bombardment or extreme pressure from the solar output).** And that is the bad thing on, or about the absence or reduction of the solar frequency that* *reaching on the Earth. The event horizon literally experiences pushing/shoving and pulling from the backside, and pull/retraction from the frontal area. In general aspect, the event horizon [of the earthquake which has weak or has an interrupted solar frequency - epicenter of event] experience tension from, or in between the boundary of the area that is under the influence or on normal frequency condition, thus, in intense cases, breaks this belted region or portion of the Earth shell. And it will experience aftershocks upon restoring order [of frequency], otherwise, normally shakes in minor or tolerable, yet abnormal event.*

The question at this point, nay, the geologist hypothesis that may had been misconstrued [due to the absence of fundamental theory, say the quadruple motions of moon and sun origin, existence and or operation], is that if the moon interpolations is the main culprit of Earthquake and Tsunamis phenomena, these event would rather takes place every month at least or perhaps every two weeks in rather morbid cases. This statement or query is in fact correct in observation and principle, but the conclusion, unfortunately defective this treatise could argue, as the essence of this fact will make the difference between the notion in here, and the classic geological concept, particularly of an earthquake.

*[**Since the moon revolves around or circumnavigate the earth, and at the same time projects its phases, the disturbance or interruption of solar frequency can be satisfy depending on the lunar inter-position, which is base or dependent mainly on earth orbit point or pattern. In other words, rather, to be specific, if the earth orbit is **downward or fall/winter season,** and that the moon get caught ahead of the earth orbit path [**moon on new moon's phase is on the bottom of the earth**], the solar frequency intended for the earth of that certain point of time that has been screened on moon interpolation, is therefore absent and that cause the manifestation of an earthquake and or tsunami where ever the circumstances satisfied. This is true the other way around, or if the earth orbit is **ascending or on spring/summer season,** that means Moon, in new phase is located on **top of the earth** before its orbit. We can comprehend on the basic principle that the moon before the earth orbit could be problematic, but not at all time. At this point, rather initially, or without the aid of instrument (say, [Rahman] Spectroscopy), in the previous event (**Solar eclipse on North***

Pole; March 21, 2015 [in a relatively normal orbit pattern, new moon phase could trigger an earthquake on north pole and subsequently on bodies corresponding position] Svalbard Norway, Earthquake on South Pole March 30, Papua New Guinea, to Nepal/Indian continent April 26 earthquake [moon southbound oscillation hit Nepal and after two weeks, May 13 and 12 again on Nepal and Japan respectively, and this takes place on moon northbound oscillation wherein the case of Nepal was indeed rare, but hitting twice in a month is not impossible to happen. From this point of view, one can tell that moon southbound flight or full moon, rather, considering the factor that the moon is closer to the earth, could be dangerous. On these current events, Moon phases are almost on a relative point and that was a quarter position, nevertheless, considering the distance in between the body plus the orbit factor, apparently, will tell a perfect condition to satisfy and or trigger an earthquake]; we have to be wary about the 2015 Earth orbit pattern or phenomena, specifically, the phasing of moon against the earth orbit on, or that started on the spring season because it wholly satisfies the factor that contribute in making earthquakes. What we inhabitant could wish or pray is to change the angle of projection and circumstances), we can assume or conclude, if not totally concurred, that since the operation or spiral solar frequency distribution to be specific, comes or fly from North to South only [but of course if one is living on the other side of the sun, it could be true the other way {in this case, explorer should try to prove if there's planets and inhabitant on the other side, the deep and or inner portion of the sun]; with an angle of inclination, rotary solar frequency distributed on a one way spiral pattern], therefore the solar eclipse on the north pole, will most likely to yield an earthquake on the south pole. And this with the slight degree of angle in consideration due to, or mainly because the solar frequency appears like, or in a cone shape pattern, and that means concentrated from the north and a little loose on the southern point. We have to note however, that even though no event of solar eclipse has been takes place or recorded (especially [far or remote] northern hemisphere or north pole earthquake), nevertheless, if the factor or circumstances mentioned above has been satisfied, earthquake however may takes place anyway. In other words, a partial or near miss chances **(that is normally happens in the middle east; and the idea on this** matter answer the question on why this part of the world experience less earthquake [nevertheless, we have to note that land masses is critical or too dangerous to have one], in comparison to other places that is vulnerable to this unfortunate event) *which is hard to detect, however, rather, therefore is not being discounted* (on this little concern, I wish people or authority should not lose heart in this case, because what is more important is that people should be forewarned of an apparent, rather a would be devastating, yet impending event of the mayhem especially on places frequented by earthquake, therefore saves life. Obscure and or in concise statement, this writing believed, and that the fact that the middle eastern ancient dweller learnt, or well verse on the operation or relation between the trinity bodies of sun [essence of solar frequency] and earth [topology and science], and moon [motions] in particular, may however had a great advantage in this case. Specifically, free or less earthquake middle east, wherein the moon movement in general, and *positioning in particular [*require citation or computation- except from the solar frequency interruption during new moon phases {but more likely to hit and create great havoc during full moon and semi-diurnal phases because Moon is closer into the Earth},* that more likely creates a moderate to powerful earthquake. A southbound oscillation or full moon phases that is potentially devastating, in a sense, mid-point or a certain point on this area, though it's not totally free, but less likely to experience a large scale earthquake at least at this point of time, mainly because the high frequency and pressure condition, the moon doesn't reach the tipping point that may satisfy the condition such as the angle of projection or trajectory; and it has the same notion when it comes to air upheavals, high pressure denies the penetration of air upheaval but relatively dangerous to have one]* in relation to sun spiral frequency, wherein despite of the fact of the absence or lacking in, of technical support [instrumentation], ancestors was rather skillful and impressive of scientific observation of natural phenomena [marine, metrology and geological sciences; however come short of interpretation and the "critical" absence of fundamental theory, that in strict sense compromise one's safety and lead a person away from the truth in general aspect], and that the present generation is benefiting from this cogent or outstanding ability a person has had at the time). *Was it too* *obvious to say that solar eclipse on the earth southern hemisphere, therefore yield no earthquake in the northern hemisphere [see also Moon's theory or Book 1 for additional input].*

As far as Earthquake and Tsunami is concern, the perception of solar frequency is simple as imagining a compressed or pressurized air/gas blowing your body or skin, and that tend to expand to the full capacity the air has had against, or solar frequency has had to offer, against the capacity of the earth or skin has had to resist. Thus in human aspect, interruption or screening of [air] pressure depicts a normal condition, but circumstances in the wide body like Earth wherein its operation is under control of solar frequency discharge, tells the opposite in contrast, or its the earthquake that manifest in an abnormal solar frequency interaction, rather normal condition in a smooth operation.

So therefore we can conclude that earthquake and tsunamis phenomena, in contrast with the classic idea, are indeed predictable by either mathematical calculation or Raman spectroscopy's instrument [upgraded] to be specific. And in addition, rather, it is notable that if we failed to comprehend and live according with the dictates of nature and its reason, and the principle of matter and the essence of technical instrumentation and innovation, then, rather, perceive on today that is highly unreliable or unrealistic, but who can discount the possibility of the accuracy by analogy or comparison or observation made by a preacher, and conjecture by divination or myth uttered by a quack or village doctor, wherein attributing superstitious belief in the event of solar eclipses, creates confusion if not a terrifying predictions to the point that attributing natural phenomena to human trait, event such as war which is purely human affair, in a sense, rather somehow, may have a truth in it, especially if one is guilty of a misdeed, therefore believe? A must see Book 1 for the Dynamic Body Chart or Athena's Universal Calendar concept and its additional input.

The Global Warming and the Revelation

To complete an inspiration from the divine beauty of nature, or the trinity bodies that set forth a finely tune operation and that causes biodiversity and humankind to exist, is the way the Nature protect us (Nature or entities such as heavenly bodies, like humankind, holds the idea or philosophy and that fundamental of [perpetual] existence is the control of [body] Temperature, as Aristotle said 'Moderation' is the greatest virtue). And that, as gratuity or gratification, the question this treatise ought to possess is how could we able to help the Earth or nature to preserve its beauty and life or Temperature in return? And in particular, why or what [the book of] Revelation or somehow the prophecy of French Doctor named Nostradamus had something to do with global warming?

When the Sun exerts "fine" solar frequency to the Earth, it turns or rotates the body, the 24 hours daily operation. The circumstances of this event provides the planet protection, wherein, rather as result, molded a malleable or stingy yet a literal wind shield (that works like a windshield of an aircraft works). And one of those purpose or benefit is that to safeguard the internal system and or the composition or biodiversity that made up the Earth. In addition, the formations of the Earth defense mechanism, shielded or safeguarded us from the intrusion of foreign objects, as well as preventing us from being blown away out in the space due to (the planet encounter) with the high pressure air that were produces on Earth orbit. Mainly cause by the solar frequency discharge, and that sun's centrifugal or gravitational pull or forces, or its elliptical operation that could be visualize or resemble like of a vertical water sprinkler and works like of a ferry's wheel works, drags the Earth on its orbit.

In other words, rather in this case, during Earth orbit, the high pressure air produced on this operation is constantly looking forward for a feeble portion of the Earth defense mechanism to penetrate. And if that so, rather succeed, is what we call air upheaval such as typhoon, hurricane, tornado or cyclones that gives inhabitant a hard time working with and or coping up with the mess. As I've mentioned in Book 1, relentlessly, air disturbances or high pressure air was like a predator working in hunting of its prey that held up in a hole. To make matter interesting, rather worse, with the Earth orbit speed of 104,000 kph on it, and that, if the earth were interrupted on its operation, and specifically the stoppage from revolution, and this mainly because of the total absence of solar frequency, and this could be the worst possible scenario; could be that, but not limited to a great earthquake, of course total darkness shall takes place, and *rupture on the earth will pave the way to extreme volcanic activity followed by tsunamis that will wipe out inhabitants. And in addition, the disappearance of the windshield produces on earth rotation will finally commence and pave the way for the extreme air upheaval that will blow everything out of the Earth surfaces, and that within 15 to 30 seconds time we are all dismembered or gone with the wind and hurled and freezes in the space or firmament. Apparently, scenarios pathetic a person could ever imagine.*

*In this case, it is notable that since the trinity bodies of moon, earth and sun that works like of a compound gear works, and that any abnormal activity from one of these body's demonstrates, might depicts a trouble in the other, especially if the source of disturbances originate from the primordial body, or the Sun in this case, nevertheless, discomfort or distress could be felt only on an inhabited planet like the Earth we are into. Miracles happened on our own perspective or view, but when it comes to nature activity, everything is possible and it just a part or as a consequence of its "plain" activity, but prayers of the faithful, fortunately makes things connived in a certain occasion. However, we should not mix, rather being confused of reality with fantasy, because we human being, cannot play with nature and that everything we had in reality is our faith (**intelligence**) and desire and hard work. Of course our time is different from the time of the writer or author of the book of Joshua (Old Testament) written on chapter 10:13-14 with reference to the book of "Jashar", that says the Sun stood still and delayed going down, and the Moon stopped, where in one, or at this point in time, no one would take it literally because of the possible or imminent doomsday scenario, as the consequence of the reason or circumstances mentioned above. Nevertheless, this treatise were once again, would like to express its desire to inform academics or governing body to recheck the methodology of meteorological principle or fact about the nature's operation. And in so doing, we can develop or provide an advance or a much better instrumentation and analysis against nature's disturbances and that we'll earn us protection and security, therefore fortify damage control measure, and this minimize harm and injury or emotional or psychological set back due to loss of life and property or on both. A must see Book 1 for the meteorological arguments such as lightning and thunder principle, updraft theory on air upheavals, where in this treatise maintained that classical information were flawed if not* divergence from the fact of nature's operation. It is noteworthy that nature's principle that in conformity with fact, precedes one after the other, or primordial elements or operation accolades the summit, one way, or the other way around, thus disregard notions proven to be gross and unnecessary.

Early on this matter, we had mentioned that when it comes to approach on climate change or the global warming, is that the fatal if not the grave mistake that governing body were succumb or cuddling to, (is like the great men of the past who suffers inequities, was denied, if not the conscientious denial of the authority itself) is the absence of the essence of the Theory of Everything, specifically, the idea on global warming that explained the systematic or linear approach on trouble shooting the said phenomenon. Besides the deforestation which is one of the vital aspect that consolidate (**however, is not the priority on mitigating global warming, thought to be the sole reason that proliferate global warming; adlib: an article on Saudi Gazette/The New York Times dated September 21, 2014, headed and that say "To save the planet, don't plant trees" [by Nadine Unger, an assistant professor of atmospheric chemistry at Yale, is one of the dumbest if not the worst proposition this writing had ever know so far, denying the planet to recuperate from the brunt of global warming. I don't mean to brag and I'm sorry for this word, I just wish they should have dig deeper on the subject and should have known better of the circumstances]**), the authority or policy makers, was keen in adopting measure to limit the carbon gas emissions only, or somehow continuing talks on setting national caps, which is not, as far as this treatise is concern, the only and or the real culprit on this matter. Because the reason of the problem and the idea of solution that involve right there, though this were not bad enough we could say, but the root of the problem literally lies down under and remain, this writing can argue.

Unequivocally, the question is that, if we do succeed to implement climate agreements, that most countries especially those heavy oil and gas producers and polluters do, and that refuse to accept the pact if not a cold reception in the first place, the main reason that the deal has been elusive or delay significantly; partiality or predilection is one but not limited to a great factor; deal could be tight in one and generous to other and that may somehow, requires a drastic *measure for the plan just to be adopted and let alone to be efficiently managed; do we think that the idea on limiting carbon gases emission alone, on the mitigation of global warming or offsetting heat on the planet or climate change, will do the job the way the organization wanted to be, or will it serves its purpose accordingly or effectively, where in this treatise with the best of knowledge and belief, do not think so, and why is that, and what's the essence to argue? (this writing was before the global warming summit on France. Like Pope Francis who encourages the world to work against global warming, policy maker could have a very specific agenda, say: 1a. Massive reforestation is the most vital solution. Each country, a quota of 20 million trees in one year may not hurt economy that much, thus, may not require a bigger budget from outside source. 1b. daunt deforestation; selective logging is a best alternative and control or persecution on illegal loggers and timber illicit trade is a must [they are one of the collaborator of the wrongful death of the planet, biodiversity and or inhabitant]. Invest and develop on producing forest fire fighting machine such as jumbo firefighting aircraft and countries must consolidated when, or where ever there is concern of a [huge] forest fire.*

*These are the questions, or the essential theory, that to tackle the climate change effectively, must naturally explain the fact, specifically, the engineering or mechanical operation of the Earth in respect with the human activity that denotes the difficulty of a partial knowledge; half- truth, cover up or denials and depicts the danger of a flaw and inappropriate solution, as well as the uncertainty of the outcome as the pessimist may contend. And the fact that the convenience of the success of any possible alternative must be presented in honest or unmistakable concept, and that easily perceptible in case of any impediment that might be put forward, are somehow tough and stressful and indeed "complicated" for those who actually want and dedicated to save the Earth. But for **Gorkan Jung**, a Turkish globe-trotting enthusiast, travels a thousand miles to show the world of his desire to protect nature and live a healthy life. Aware or not, he might be promoting peace in the world as well. And hail this treatise to those who devoted their time and effort and carried out the task. This writing's aim's to help somehow. Simply plant a tree in every places he visited, and sure a little help and his effort would have a tangible impact.*

This is a great statement, but doesn't mean to brag or to be rude, and that the fact that we owe too much on scientist and or physicist on their essential contribution in the field, as Stephen Hawking said they are the bearer of the torch of discovery in our quest for knowledge, is indeed correct. Unfortunately, rather, perhaps the Theory of Everything as a vital factor, turns out that most of them, rather, not even one are free from error and or true, neither one could achieve a hundred percent accuracy this treatise can claim. And that what we're trying to say is that base on the tri-dimensional theory presented in here and in the Book 1 as well, carbon caps emission policies is the least effective way on mitigating or combating global warming, unless, rather, of course before we know the real cause of the problem that proliferates it. In other words, climate crisis demands a much higher level of public awareness and action than those currently exist or the theory that being held. As this treatise believed that we are approaching a near critical point of a drastic climate transformation, the information therefore must be organized, systematic and applicable in a relatively wide, complex or complicated variety and variation of circumstances. The essence of the Theory, however assumption at this point, must be consensus or an accepted principle, thus, rules and procedures devised to analyze, predict or otherwise explain unequivocally the nature or behavior of a certain phenomenon, and this knowledge or belief should guide our action or judgment towards a reliable or effective solution. While it is true that climate crisis represents or portray a threat to biodiversity and to all living things in particular, and or the habitable planet in general, solutions is in fact a unique opportunity to help improve and enhance living standards worldwide through cleaner environment, more sustainable technologies, products and services like of the essence of a renewable energy.

In this notion thought to be crude or theoretical in nature, nevertheless, devised and suggests a "three dimensional" approach to combat and upend the increment of global temperature, where in the system imply, however difficult might be, nevertheless will demand the global adaption or submission over the integrity and veracity that is in fidelity to reality, or faithful to the fact thus, in strict sense a non-negotiable idea, these treatise being advances, rather, a compelling reason that this idea possessed and ought to present to the people of this world.

So as far as the solution is concern, since industrialized or advance country are on the defensive mode mainly because of economic anxiety and or interest, nevertheless part of the process, though acceptance is indeed the hard thing, but this treatise firmly believe that we are compelled to do so, but the real concern or challenge lies in the information campaign on how it would carried out the task effectively, and that is against the ignorance and or impediment mark by obstinacy and or stubborn, wherein a moment spend in argument, is a moment they are putting life in grave.

It seems to be inexpugnable for no one is willing to sacrifice the comfort or way of life that someone enjoys on the current trend; say the wealth brought out by mining, oil production (oil cartel) and deforestation and these in all the expense of the planet. And since non-renewable, rather, takes relatively much longer time to naturally produce the elements more than spending on our "need", and that reserve are fast degrading as a result, basically the theory of production, supply and demand. The self-induce or natural ability of the planet to cool itself as in the radiator of a car built for the engine to last and at least eluded breakdown is in fact leaking badly. And apparently, the threat of global warming is undeniable in this case, is a matter of choice between a burning house against an elegantly crafted white wedding dress or a well-organized wedding day ceremony. This is the social problem that is emotionally and psychologically attached to an individual, and plays a great role of inept attitude, thus depicts a "retardant global warming mitigation epidemic".

In this case, implementing solution on global warming troubled spots, where in developed and industrialized country is concern or fearful about sacrificing the way of life or their living standard specifically, where in, it is correct in a certain time or aspect especially on transformation period, but with the advantage on the field of science, engineering and technology, fortunately anxiety or the solicitudes emotion is non- binding or a non-permanent element. Factors such as poor planning, delayed implementation and that abrupt solution however, may possess difficulty or contribute to the burden on its citizens as a consequence, thus cautious is essential.

Definitely to bring about anxiousness to the people of this world is not this writing's cause, but, overcoming anxiety about the trouble of global warming *through the acquisition of reliable and essential information is the core of the idea. And that a gambit move against an "unseen" but cunning or tricky speculative opponent, which is the nature cataclysm, that may proliferate through or by the atmosphere, lithosphere and or the *aerosphere [***also spells yposphere; means beneath the surface; this particular word or vocabulary may not be an entry in dictionary yet**], thus, the three dimensional approach in each respective point were elucidated in here as prelude of troubleshooting method or alternative and hope to impedes backlashes from nature's catastrophe if not to upend the undesirable incident by implying "defensive" attitude.*

*And since nature catastrophe, specifically earthquakes and tsunamis, are *indeed predictable [***except earth self-inflicted tremors or landslide** {due to massive mining and oil production as well as deforestation, and that shall provide space that loosen the earth compactness' particularly on the underneath, and that may create an unprecedented opening or sink on the earth surface as a result}, **in contrast with the classic or accepted idea and belief that it was totally unpredictable were incorrect**], thus, upgrading defense mechanism or sensory elements in respect with the nature of a calamity is a must in this case. But, or in the global warming mitigation, we are all, and expected to fair and clean fight, and to those who believe in this idea, we will ensure that there is no "low blow", because Nature, more than anybody on this world, doesn't tolerate cheating and induce unprecedented or heavy penalty for this.*

To begin with, an agreement and that say a massive drive and campaign on reforestation, preservation and thus impediment or tight policy on deforestation is a must; citations shortly on the following. In addition, fifteen year time shall stop producing fuel powered private cars is really a good start. It is far better than setting a limit or cap on carbon gas emission without the knowledge of the true nature of global warming saga, which is not very practical, or not equipped or unprepared to meet a contingency situation, the reason why heavy polluters or industrialized country hesitates, whether emotionally or economically at this point in time. We have to note that solar energy, hydro and volcanic activity, are more than enough to power, in general aspect, human consumption. Harnessing or utilizing this potential source of power shall be a part and or plays the significant role of solution and that economic development in general or energy security in particular will be ensured. And this is a lucid thing, and that this treatise hope that oil producing countries should realized, rather, can survived without depending much on oil cartel, for the reason that preserving nature will mitigate global warming and downgrade the impact of natural calamity. Though phlegmatic, Global Warming response must be realistic, accurate and effective to the point that it totally eliminates the source or sources that proliferates climate change from our side or on the human's earth's responsibility. And from this point, this treatise believed and hoping that everything, as far as the global warming mitigation is concern, must follow and can maneuver as necessary. Global warming solution's and or nature preservation is not just a political mandate, rather, to be the highest form of the law of the land and no country, community or individual shall except from it.

Global Warming – The Atmospheric Level

*Governing body such as the Kyoto Protocol tried to iron out difficulties and yet struggling to ratify or reach an agreement regarding on setting the national caps on carbon [monoxide] emissions. Though this treatise has no intention to undermine or demean the purpose of the idea **[if and only the principle applied was correct and or an appropriate]**, the irony is that, while they are too late to implement the solution, too, as this writing see it, those Solons whose assumptions was based on the "incomplete assessment" of the totality of global warming phenomena, may not work effectively as intended or as expected as well, this treatise can argue. Nevertheless, if there's an irony, must have the funny side as well, and that, the world's four country's biggest carbon emitters; China, the United States of America, India and Russia (except India, the rest are on the world's top oil producer) are all capable of space exploration, thus can colonize other planet like Mars, and that, rather, in case if the Earth itself is unbearable to live due to, or exacerbated by global warming, was mainly because of their technical lapses and their "corroborators' activity" if these things differ from each other. And since we are all enjoying the fruit of a material world, and that seems no problem with that, but in expense of the Mother Earth is a different thing. And the utmost concern and or the bad side on this case, nay in strict sense, Earth defilement may extend as far as, or shall not except even those indigenous people living on the remote area and that has nothing to do* *with the advance technology of the world from the brunt of climate change in which we are responsible. And since we are all "succumbed to this temptation" therefore, we are all, in this generation, liable on this offense, hence, this treatise would like to invite or encourage everyone to initiate reform and give their share to bring on solution. And no offense, if religions play the part that impedes or hold back the attitude, or mentality of people and that take things of global warming for granted, because of their sincere or conscientious belief, whatsoever, must however, nay definitely, take a stand to educate people of the essence of biodiversity or nature, for no one in this world, this writing believed, would love to live or resurrected in a place or planet with a temperature feels like hell.*

What and why is that on the atmospheric level?

The idea that any formation of clouds is in fact a form of cloud seeding is correct. Basically, rather naturally, like and along with rainwater, cloud seeding is a product of the disparity in temperature. And though it is a pollutant and is harmful, however it is notable that the carbon gases emission (carbon monoxide) is one of those. Say a cool and forested area or a snowy mountain against the volcanic or solar activity produce ideal gases or clouds, and that due to its lightweight characteristic settled in the atmosphere (and rainwater as heavy or refused element broke down as spring or mineral water; [it dispel the myth that water comes from the other planet] the process, circumstances and factor are unique in this case. Treat rainforest or trees or ice deposit as life giving body therefore must preserve its essence). And in this case, cloud is notable of its different layer, level or point or property of gases depending on its rarity. The cleanest of them is on the top spot. Now since carbon gas emission, specifically the carbon monoxide is a product of the abrupt disparity in temperature and thus we cannot deny the fact that it is a form of cloud seeding. And the serious consequence however is that carbon monoxide is a poisonous, thick and heavy element that is detrimental to living thing's respiratory system. Since it is heavy, it stays on the lower part of the atmosphere which is closer to the surface of the earth and the problem start and lies on at this point where in the scientist findings that it blocked the solar outgoing rays is correct in this case. Aside from this, transformation process (rarefication), like and most likely, with or without the rainwater along, the heavy or refused element i.e. lead, returns to the surface as pollutants. And notably due to contamination, this kind of rainwater wherein once consider as one of the cleanest, is fit for consumption no more. And in addition, since heavy and polluted gases stays on the atmosphere, and that earth rotation causes it to commute, thus no one are sure how far it would go, or how large the area that could possibly be affected. And the conclusion that rare viruses may form out of this harmful element, or with the synthesis of this pollutant with another, to form another kind of bacteria that sure cause diseases, could be true in this case.

And with all of this, how could we stop seeding or emitting the thick or heavy polluted gases that comes mostly from industrial and power plants, and how about those machines from the transport group that creates lead's smoke's belching. In general aspect, how could we implement solution?

*To tell it straight forward, and that we do emit smoke mainly because we feed raw, crude or untreated, or wet or liquid fuel abruptly and that all reacts heavily on feeding or burning process and that yields smoke as a result. Unequivocally, the health safety design is generally taken for granted. And the problem lies on the consequence of massive production, and should had been, rather power plant fuel with carbon, must be designed on efficient fueling process. While the best disposition of this problem is natural, renewable or the green energy discipline, solutions may vary from a critical one or say a sudden break away from this outdated method of power production, and though it was good and absolutely the essence or cure for a damaged environment, however, we do not imply rather compel of an abrupt transition because unprepared, or unproven or inefficient alternative may turn out costly if not possessed with the higher consequence and risk. Another thing is that if we cannot refrained ourselves from using a fuel or a coal fire powered plant, say a tight, to the point of a budget deficit, nevertheless, we can adopt a "temporal" yet efficacious idea or solution and that is literally providing the plant or machinery with a lengthy, or long winding fuel or coal purging or drying and heating facility before it actually feed into the chamber for fusion. We have to note however that even though it may possibly turn effective, say heavy smoke might be refined, still it denotes the word temporal [**of course it is not a total solution**], because it may induce* *heat that somehow may propel the disparity in temperature that may bring out rain as a result or flood as its consequence.*

Scientist and or expert proposed like of a carbon captured solution and that smoke would be going to store underground for a certain purpose, is not totally a bad idea, but it is not or may not be practical either, this treatise could claim. Mainly because, as this was mentioned on Book 1, that it is more likely of a smoker, and that to prevent a second hand smokers had to inhale or swallow the smoke and that it applied the principle mentioned above. And that is the proliferation of heat from underground and surfaces that may require a substantial maintenance budget as one of the series of its consequence, not discounting the possibility of health hazard and risk upon leakage and or over capacity.

Giving in to the benefit of the doubt, in this case, owing to the reliability of engineering technique or design, let assume that this solution has been implemented, yet, the global warming persist, therefore turn out that it is not the total solution and shall require the authority to look forward for the other causes, or reasons to believe that it may have come from other sources and area, and that may point out on the earth surface thus propose alternative and this treatise hope is not too late to come up with this idea.

Global Warming on the Surface Level - Mantle of the Earth

*One of the most important and essential aspect of global warming is that to prove to everyone that it is real and taking its place (**and we have to note that depending on entities vulnerability it takes toll or discomfort gradually and cleverly or in discreet manner [hiatus happens intermittently], thus people must be knowledgeable of the fact that when it comes to global warming, the [4] elements of the planet, the earth, water, air and intensified fire, are interconnected and or work simultaneously or reciprocally, wherein the increment in air temperature could be the most critical one. These might create, but not limited to intensifying fire that destroys rainforest and inadequate supply of mineral water warms the ocean or seawater, increase earth temperature thus pull***

harder towards the sun, carbon gasses or air pollution or airborne diseases, viruses, respiratory system diseases, thawing of glaciers and or floods are some of it. And this scenario, subduing the land thus forced migration [exodus], dry spell, water scarce and food shortage and eventually extinction. It's a great statement, but the comfort of living or indulgence the natural resources has brought to us, and that we'll have to pay the price eventually, of either by ourselves, or of the future generation's tender life); *we all know that the planet is so vast that seems to individual that the capacity of men is very limited to reverse its trend that people may tend to ignore it. This writing hope, for those who believe in the future, and the future we intend to extend or pass off to the next generation, and that we have to note that solutions may take great effort, patience and or time, thus this writing suggest that we should waste no time and must act now.*

Besides, with the fact that emotional attachment or psychological presentiment, say apprehension on economic meltdown that may sacrifice the way or comfort of life, owed or in expense of nature, is the critical reason of the standoff, thus impedes and or miserably delaying remedy's deliverance. Nevertheless, at this point of the earth, where in the inhabitants thrived and enjoy the beauty and pleasure of nature, and we are witnesses that this point clearly manifest transitions as well, say landscaping, water intrusion, the tsunami and/or flooding, pungent air upheavals, violent earthquakes, a fast vanishing ice deposits, endangered species extinction and the brunt of deforestation. The authority in this case, being the first and foremost body, must commit itself or required to have a stand on these things or their respective issue and concern. Say for life's a treasure, and nature and its function that in fact govern us inhabitant, therefore prioritize or ahead of anybody or anything else's. I mean, and to tell it straight forward, the authority, say the UN climate panel must procure and equipped with the proper tooling, put their balls right in the right place [mean to wittingly assess the trouble, come up with tangible solutions and the authority to implement and sustain], nay, as bestowed by the knowledge of the Truth of the matter and commissioned by the authority from within, the governing body, must faithfully discharge its mandate, therefore saves the Earth.

Basically, the surface's first line of defense against a natural or a man-made global warming is the ice deposit, where in, when it comes to the disparity or changes in temperature, is one if not the most vulnerable entity. As we have mentioned above, and that besides rainforest, cloud-seeding originate from this point to naturally counter a solar flare or radiation as well as earth volcanic activity, is unequivocally the reason we must preserve it and this to achieve a habitable environment or to balance the system in general aspect. And as the scientist concluded that melting of ice will induce more water that may turn into flooding and that may reduce land masses in which human were once inhabited, is one of the troubles of global warming. In strict sense, rather in fact, the global warming in general aspect, is the outcome or side effects of the transformations or the continual struggle specifically, in between the elements, the [air], earth, water, and fire, where in totality, the earth against the power or tremendous pressure of the sun, which was however claimed, unfortunately unsupported with this kind of theory, nevertheless, unequivocally if not precisely unfolded as early as 500 BC, by Heraclitus, an ancient Greek philosopher. In other words, the statement is huge, and when an individual is concern, the reality is immense for it is just a bit of the whole circumstances the human being would involve itself, but we must try for our own good, survival and existence.

Furthermore, the rainforest that works similar to ice deposit, specifically the cold mountainous area that emits, or literally another source of green gasses that form the cloud to shield us from harmful solar radiation, could be the last bastion of defense coming from this position. And the great questions would be that; for it is mainly the source of ocean water that serves as "*coolant*" upon earth operation [*a must see **Book 1** for additional input particularly on its **mechanical operational aspect**], what if we lost trees and rainforest or ice deposits that cool the atmosphere and lithosphere level which is the essence of biodiversity and planet existence, do we have the reason to believe that global warming is nothing but a farce? In Book 1, it was greatly emphasized the essence of a tree where in, rather since its role or duty on the existence or preservation of the earth and its biodiversity is much more than that of other entities can do, including or such as human being, is therefore the tree's significance must be treated to the utmost and this clearly depict that deforestation in general aspect, or an unauthorized cutting of trees is definitely a crime against humanity [**a must see Book 1, the article of the Essence of a Tree for its expanded theory**].

And if we succeed on rainforest and ice deposit preservation, and the trouble of global warming persist, may come from another source, thus, besides vanishing of ice's deposit and rainforests, we'll try to work on all the possibilities that enhance the increment of global temperature. In this case, the third dimensional theory uncover the idea on what it causes for the ice cap to recedes more than that it should be, or while in one hand the frequency of forest fire is on the rise, why it induces too much rain on the other?

The Global Warming on the Aeposphere Level

*Aeposhere or *yposhere which means the underneath of the surface of the earth [*entries may not be found on the standard dictionary yet]. It is a common knowledge that the earth is consisted of different layers before it reveals the core. Each layer on its respective point has its own particular function. Generally, either in response to the Sun and its solar feat, which we can consider the highest or the authoritarian ruler in the case of the sun earth interaction. Locally, since core's confined, in "respect" or in reaction with what the circumstances or consequence the Earth operation against the feat of the Sun has had to offer, must deal with the fact of the system. Knowledge [of abstraction and methodology] is essential to counter the threat or misconception originating from this point. In other words, to give an idea on what the dynamic earth structural concept were, is to uncover its definite function as well. To tell it straight forward, since dynamic, is that definite layer or definite structure of the earth when disturb and or if the condition has been satisfied, of either nature or man-made activity, might be accompanied with trouble directly, or indirectly [eventually] or as a consequence.

Dynamic Earth Structural Concept

Basically, earth's consisting of different layers, and of different properties, however, like the function and an appearance of a mechanical bearing, it can be sum up into three main parts, namely;

1. The shell or outer ring or the hardest layer that serves as conveyor bed or belting.

2. *A wedge or pellet and that made up of liquid, such as water, [liquid] coal and liquid core **[magma]** that serve as lubricant and or bearing that lessen the friction upon the interaction between the shell and core. And this portion, the liquid element produces gas's pressure that work like a squeegee work in a confined area.*

3. *inner core or the inner ring and or shaft that is made up of a hot iron ball that produce pressure **[volcanic activity]** and or bounce back and or in response to the feat of the sun's nuclear power. A must see Book 1 for illustrations and additional inputs or expanded version of the explanations of the subject.*

The Shell

Shell – or the crust as the rigid or the (brittle) outermost layer of the earth, and that includes the mountainous area and seabed. Basically, this portion of the earth receives the mega frequency coming from the sun. In one point, since the earth stays aloft and not supported with anything, the uninterrupted sun rays bombarded on the earth causes it to turn or rotates of around a thousand miles where in the earth diameter is in proportion in equivalent to single day of its operation. And on the other, the intensity of the sun's nuclear power drags the earth on its orbit with the speed of around 104,000 kph or 60,000 miles an hour. It is notable that any interruption of the sun's frequency on anyone of the earth's dual function or the accuracy or precision of earth operation, definitely faces a consequence or two and that earthquake or tsunami are some of those. Earlier we have mentioned on the article of Global Warming and the Revelation and that on the Book of Joshua 10: 13-14 commanded to delay the settings of the sun where in the scientific view or technical aspect of this case, claim were totally absurd knowing that delay or interruption on the frequency of the Sun would have a devastating consequence or doomsday scenario. As a result, Earthquake shall take place at least, or worst on stoppage of the earth rotation in just 15 seconds of a time, will blow anything on what has the east have, going into the west, and what had the west have will be blow out of the space and there freeze.

*Furthermore, for it is a fact that elements, the air, water, fire and earth are in constant transformation or struggle in each other, the hardness in particular or the property of the shell of the earth in general aspect, relies the theory of the planet existence where in the biodiversity benefited and enjoys its durability and dependability at its most. Since the earth is dynamic, the actual activity on this case is that this outermost covering or layer of the earth consider as the bed of a conveyor belting, is in fact being coil or wrinkled [**conk in on indiscrete manner**] in response to the sun's spectrum or being folded by radiant energy of the sun's nuclear power's mega frequencies. And as a result, it bulges on the convergence point as resistance to the pressure incurred during operation where in the earth material properties such as hardness and elasticity, that works more than enough if not in proportion with solar power, preventing the body from self-disintegration. However it is notable that the total operation or creation of planets, is in fact a hardening process or coagulation, like of a cheese being made; from gas to liquid to solid and to liquid and or gas eventually, as the planet is subject to extreme purification process before being submitted to its creator which is the Sun in this case. And in this case, reaction of the Earth works like a conveyor belt that works in a fine, quantum or indiscreet yet sluggish manner, and that scenario in case of frequency interruption that mostly cause by the moon *operation [*moon interpolation that blocked the solar ray] is an earthquake or stampede as it pushes the neutral point [**earth static point-conk out**], or struggle [**aftershock-conk in**] to revive the "dead point" of the system with in at least 8 seconds, or depending on factors [such as the speed of the moon interpolation and or with regard to earth orbit direction or pattern] that may affect the time of travel to reach the earth of solar frequency, after an interruption [**a must see Book 1 for additional input**].*

In addition, to know how the surface of the earth past-slide with the rest of the layers, is to know what lies beneath that help to work, or to consider the shell to work as conveyor belt or bedding.

The Wedge

Whatever we had acquired in life, it's a nature's providence; this is concise, yet, great or ambiguous statement but unequivocal principle of life. This is the fact, the reality, the truth and or the wonder of the goodness of nature in general aspect that in strict sense, the compositions extend beyond our limited capability to think and to know everything and each detail. Mainly because life in one point, is too short indeed, and that frustrate and make impossible for us human being to achieve an omniscient or total knowledge, let alone the incorrect fundamentals of the primitive or ancient people that wasted our time and somehow lead us to confusion. For doing the principle right in the beginning should induce a better life on today **(on the account of the prophets, reformist, philosopher, scientist and thinker, such as ancient Greek philosopher Socrates, as well as Copernicus, Galileo, Spinoza, Darwin or Jesus of Nazarene also called as Christ, the greatest of them, who was consider as the son of God for his greatness and peculiarity. The problem lies mostly on the ignorance or incompetent authority that stands "dead-ma" [conscientious ignorance] or simply just didn't care on the case, and that one could assume, if not apparent to these great men's gambit, a cover up of a certain belief and race and reputation? Factors like these weakens the authority's moral orientation and could have violated or failed to secure the right of an individual. And overlooking the essence of Nature, could be the generation's greatest mistake?).**

On the other, because of its greatness and its ability to exist in a long period of time, the quantum mechanics of nature and or its element become a viable substance for biodiversity, particularly or especially for us human being. And this come to think or note on this writing that we must savor the nature's allotted time for us and that is today, the present time or the habitable era. If, rather, one can say that if it is an orchestrated or God's grand design, so be it, however we have to live with the reality we are into as Jesus of Nazarene said; "knock and the door shall be open unto you" and that is to help our self.

Well, in technical sense, or on scientific general aspect, this is to say that any disruption to the normal course of nature and its innate activity, and that sooner or later, aware or not, will, have to pay the price and may cost us our tender life.

*The fact that the layer of the earth called Wedge or the Pellet, and that composed of the liquid coal which is the "petrified state" and the liquid core or magma serves as lubricant to disunite the shell from the main core of the earth and that permits the shell [**of the earth that works like of a squeegee**] into Conveying and that thwarted friction that proliferates heat [**pressurized and working through, excessive gasses released through the relief ventilation or opening, commonly known as volcanic activity or eruption**]. **It's logical that Wedge, once removed or exhausted, unites the then separated or adjacent layer which is the shell and core.** And this action, this writing firmly believed, mainly the cause of thermal convection or the transfer of heat or pressure from the core region into the surface area which is the Shell in this case, and that unmistakably creates or definitely the main cause of climate change or in totality the source of global warming phenomenon. And that were exacerbated by the fact that increment on the temperature on the part of the Earth could lead into the fast-pace of gravitational attraction from [heat to heat exchange] or going, or in between the body of the Earth and of the Sun.*

*Abrupt attraction of the Earth towards the Sun, will give trouble as it begets an intense or pungent air upheaval (**see Coriolis Effect and Copernicus of Heliocentric theory or Kepler idea that planets or element moves faster near the chamber of the Sun**). And on this perspective, a trained eye or the expert can clearly depicts the trouble as well as the most effective solution not only on global warming trouble, but also a big factor or help that delays or can foil the massive love or attraction coming from the sun, and these by ceasing the activity on this *state (***the exhaustion or the massive production of gas and oil or the petrified elements and or components; specifically, these activities were loosening the **compactness of the earth [**that may induce more sinkholes] and that may increase the volcanic or magma's activity or the thermal convection process or the transfer of heat from one point to another [down under or from the core region into the surface of the earth] that produces more hot gasses that proliferates into* *the atmosphere, and this is to cause more rain [due to the disparity in temperature] therefore floods. Punctured Earth [as if a needle poked a balloon or compressed gas deficit or loss compression in a worst case scenario, like an aircraft engine that loss its ability to compress gas] and or depletive gasses and massive water adds to the burden of Earth orbit as if a massive body like elephant, drags and cannot go height; Earth orbit takes off and or gain momentum in virtue of the Sun spectrum and relatively takes a longer time. In this case, as far as the Earth orbit is concern, Density is critical or additional weight is a real concern mainly because it will changed pattern, if not, alteration of orbit, and this may expose the planet in a compromising, or worst, dangerous route and situation. Citation required or see Book 1 for additional input). And the massive reforestation and or rainforest preservation drive, without a doubt, are some of the great factor, if not precisely will do the task effectively on reversing the trend of climate change, especially on the surface and atmospheric level. In general aspect of the theory and factual circumstances of the subject matter, and that underneath and or unseen and tricky, eliminating highest common factor of global warming, specifically, daunting oil and gasses production, shall protect, or secure us from the brunt of impending catastrophe; A must see Book 1, All But the World is Loving for additional input.*

The Earth's Core

Core or the heart is the vital organ of human being [or living things] and so the earth as well. The heart on its task, receives signal from the brain, so the earth that receives solar frequency from the sun, rotates and drag on its orbit. The core and heart, and or the body itself have no thinking, thus "emotions or reactions" responded only by sensing on what the temperature or the frequency has had to offer; human being in strict sense, govern by this principle as well. In other words, rather, specifically, in a low frequency state or circumstances, the temperature should be low and so the pressure is [proportion], while the increment on any of these condition or entities would tell the opposite in contrast.

Well, this is to say that the core of the earth connects with the sun through the solar unrelenting discharge where in the whole process consider as the sum of the *gravitational attraction between these massive bodies – a must see Book 1 on the author's genuine and unconventional theory on Gravitation [**the fulfillment of Newton and Einstein theory on gravitation**]*

*In this case, where in the earth receives signal from the sun, generates pressure "into" the core. And since confined, vibrates outward in response, and this activity or process or circumstances produced gasses and pressure well. And so to speak, the impulse of the core, works like a heartbeat works in a human being. One can consider the whole operation as a simple process, however, contributory elements or factor (**compounded or synthesis**) and circumstances in general aspect is quite contrived and or complicated, the reason this writing believed that the theory of this element should be given a deep emphasis.*

*So imagine on how the planet or the earth that have it surface or shell conveys all around the core separated with the layer that serves as lubricant or film- the wedge, which is consist of liquid coal and core, works. The main concern is simply that the system works in a perfect manner, or the manner that the circumstance's has had to offer. And that imagine if there's no sun and its solar frequency, there would be no [perfect] planet and planetary motions. In a vibrant planet or earth, imagine an interruption on the solar frequency, an earthquake and tsunami will manifest. Imagine the shell's conveying belt's damage [**by unregulated mining**] may procure an artificial earthquake. Imagine a gas filled planet or balloon that escapes gasses [**due to gas production**], sure it result to a dense planet and that will compromise planet's buoyancy and that affects seasonal temperature and may obtain harsher air upheavals due to abnormal orbit pattern and speed [**past or massive pace of attraction between the bodies, the sun, earth and moon shorten the biodiversity or the habitable era. And thought to be great, and that an awkward point between the Earth and Moon may cause to parted ways. As if this theory is correct, reflects the same manner of planet Mercury, as this treatise consider the later as moon to Venus. Furthermore, the circumstances, unambiguously projects an earth turbulence state and could be the beginning of the end of the lives of the biodiversity and inhabitant. At this point in time, this statement could be consider exaggerated, for the circumstances may not come abruptly, but for a trained eye, may always**]* *notice the abnormal activity or strange manner or pattern the body is showing. And as far as the middle east experience is concern, and that, if the author's assumption is correct, Prophet Mohamed PBUH of Islam may thought about this *thing on Ramadan {*one, if not the total concept of the virtuous deed; delay of the resurfacing of moon is a total concern of system's trouble indicative especially on the end of}, the holy month {while in one hand, earth and moon orbit on 9ᵗʰ month should be on the equilateral summit point which is September of the Gregorian calendar, February on the other, is the bottom equilateral point which is the cause or reason of Chinese or Persian new year celebration. And because of this, fall season or bottom point specifically, and that, as far as the earth orbit is concern, consider as the graveyard point [descending] or area, thus emanating from this season projects an spring or new life for the planet in general aspect, therefore rejoice; see Athena Calendar concept on Book 1 for additional input} therefore fast, pray and noble deeds on the whole aspect and be save].* Imagine an ill or ailing [bleeding] heart and or a disturbed earth core; due to pressure, little by little its main element or magma/blood might outpour, and the hollow or loosen core, pave the way to loss compression [which is vital, but not limited to buoyancy/blood circulation] the organ's main function. And therefore the body that stops the heart/core from beating, thus stops blood/magma circulation, pave the way to the increment of body temperature [friction's heat - global warming/fever] and die as a result. Like of those water/current [underneath] of the ocean [feeds by the river], it helps to combat increment on the earth bedding or shell upon operation. And this writing concluded that to stay in control, or to keep the body or machine of its normal operation, the Temperature must be well regulated or moderated. And the question why the body like Galaxy or Sun doesn't require a water or fluid to lubricate its own system, is a wrong conception. It is because besides the fact that the body parts itself diversify [self-diversification and a philosopher claim that a sun is an epitome of a perfect body], indeed it's the cold's space or atmosphere, corroborated with centrifugal revolution/operation are the great and perfect factors that keep the body away from excessive friction or heat thus eluded breakdown or dissolution. We have to note, rather conclude that a totally hot or cold [only] firmament or environment will result to a death or a non- functional universe. In this case, change's life, life's change and therefore change's constant.

*Moreover, imagine the [shell] conveying system, deficit, of or totally without the wedge or lubricant **[due to oil production]**, and that case, the core might adhere to the shell and ensure friction **(or heat that the planet rotation will become shorter as a result)**, that pave the way for global warming to the point of ending the habitation and or biodiversity, and further, of the planet hardening process to the point of its death because of the rapid pace of gravitational attraction of the Sun. And as I've mentioned in Book 1, imagine a planet without the trees or rainforests,, as well as the ice cap deposit. What or who do we think will carried out the cloud seeding that make us the rainwater and cloud that protect as from the ultraviolet harm and excessive sunlight, or from air upheaval which is intensified nowadays. And the transformations that induce rainwater for us human and wildlife as well, to drink, or as a marine sanctuary, usage on medicinal purposes, farming, recreation, industrial application and one of the most essential function today's on power generation. But it doesn't end here for the utmost purpose of this liquid that plunge into the trees, and see as spring or mineral water, and that goes to the river bed and or tributaries and some of them goes to the lake and most of them end up to sea, yet its purpose just started in there. As the earth turns, it mixed and goes well with the seawater and that circumnavigate the earth and works like the radiator of an automotive works, and this prevent the proliferation of heat coming from the volcanic activity in particular, specifically, from the pressure emanating from the core, or the gravitational response from the solar energy discharge in general aspect.*

Imagine exhausting 80 or 100 million barrel of oil per day and other minerals including gas, sure we are loosening earth durability and or compactness. And assuming that a ton of raw material per barrel of oil and million pound of gases exhausted from a certain point or from the earth whole area, therefore, one or a Mathematicians [the 20th century counterpart of Prophet or Nostradamus] can have the idea of the saturation or "dispersion point", that in turn, rather this activity is in fact the process of creating artificial earthquakes and sinkholes that nobody is safe from its wrath [the oil someone else's had siphoned, might be from his/her neighborhood]. Likewise, the fact that freezing temperature [on ice cap deposit] and its ability, as well as rainforest, to hold water and gradually discharge, sustain biodiversity or inhabitant of the region, and on this case, *rather in the contrary, the quickly vanishing of ice cap deposits and deforestation, is apparent and definitely that some parts of the world's facing water scarce. We have to bear in mind, that without producer [or on offsetting the balance application of nature], or deficit on water supply is not just a regional concern but global discomfort mainly because the freshwater injected into the ocean's to maintain the temperature of the Earth upon operation is one of the vital aspect of this concept. And that since the disparity in temperature [hot gas emanating from the earth meet the cold gasses counterpart at the atmosphere] induce an intense activity of rain or water, is literally we are sinking due to floods. And the intense or an overwhelming temperature or heat, drains the water abruptly therefore experience or suffer from drought. We have to note that without the natural elements (**the trees or rainforest and ice cap deposits as the front line defense**) producing water, the seawater will boil and eventually would dry up leading to the end of biodiversity and so the death of inhabitant and the planet itself.*

Imagine these things or scenario taking place and in fact started, and that unabated, or left unmitigated, no doubt that I'm a big fan to John Lennon as He said; "imagine all the people living in this world", exactly, it's a hellish scenario. In this case we have to learn to read the writings on the wall, such as Nostradamus 1503- 1566, the French physician and astrologer, author of Centuries [1555 the book of prophecy] as he prophesied that the end of the world will take on the year 3797. And that was 17 hundred years closer from now. One may believe and other might ignore it, but since we have the lead about it, the global warming that taking place, the idea on this treatise is Michael Jackson's "Beat It". As we can see on how we are dealing with the environment on today, is on how are we treated or taking care of the children of the future generation. And it is no secret that the great responsibility lies on those great and or developed countries thus must lead the charge. We must ensure, rather should try our best for the next generation wouldn't cry in vain for our inaction. Somehow, try to learn from the FOX movie entitled "The Day After Tomorrow" for it is the least of the natural catastrophes we could experience (adlib: The author is waiting for the movie that depicts the struggle and survival against extreme air upheavals, earthquake and landslide or sinkhole, floods or tsunami and a boiling sea water and or the sea of fire as volcanic eruptions. For the meantime, this letter suggest of the superheroes should do in order to prevent or avoid or delay these kind of wrath. Throughout the year, Batman must initiate in planting trees all over the earth. In this case, besides its habitation that provide human with food and shelter, it supports the nature to produce water, an element that break down the increment of temperature or help cool the earth down from its unrelenting task, the revolution and orbit as well as the excessive solar energy discharge. The same way or alongside, Spiderman must carry out the task extensively. Gradually or at all cost, they must prevented people from destroying their inhabitant like trees or rainforest and the earth itself. The law must consider these offenses as against humanity therefore need appropriate and or stringent measure. [Gas] Liquid or oil and the like of the element [{that consider} as layer] is like the blood of human being. Bloodletting due to injury, of oil and gas production, increases the planet temperature {therefore creates virus or diseases [variation in temperature breeds an element]} thus increase the chances of solar gravitational pull upon the earth {see also Kepler's theory - the body move faster as it gets near the center of the gravitational pull or force of attraction - core}, and so compromise its buoyancy that have significant effect upon the planet revolution and orbit, the earth dual task induces by the Sun. And that may create powerful and frequent air-storm, earth-quake, sinkhole and water-tsunami upheavals, among others. Absolutely, these scenario or the complexity of the dual operation of the planet give Superman a hard time, or task that is next to impossible to accomplish and that is by pushing the planets outward. One by one, or one after the other, we have to note that planets move inward or towards the core of the Sun, wherein the solar discharge or gravitational pull of the Sun, of which the planets and its satellite like moon has or being created, is the reality of existence. And nevertheless, the essential aspect of knowledge, or the present and imminent danger of the general operation or transformation process, possessed by the global warming theory in a certain aspect [or local level of the concept one way operation and mono principle of origination or creationism], of the vast and enormous universe, is the fact or the truth upon the existence, operation, dissolution and resolution or the perpetual cycle of the universe in general aspect, that human being must learn, in order to give others a choice, or an option for those who want to deal with the essence of life and survival in the world we live in, and thus have the better chance to survive).

Together, we have to opt on green technology such as hydrogen fuel powered car, renewable energy and these as we minimized and ceased the gas and oil production afterward. Daunt deforestation and be an advocate of rainforest and ice cap deposit preservation. Planting a tree or trees, is like or synonymous to saving's someone's life. We have to bear in mind that the love for nature or environment could be the greatest love for the planet's inhabitant and or humanity. We shouldn't forget that, the fact that we shape the world we live in, comes with the great wisdom, leadership and responsibility. And that whatever the degree of consent might be, a certain belief or knowledge, career or advocacy or worst is the ignorance of the principle of living the natural way or naturalism, must be aware of the logical pitfalls and that may cover up those who actually destroy the earth and its environment. Misleading information, historical inaccuracies and or stern belief of a flawed principle and subreption, could lead oneself being a victim of pride and selfishness therefore denied of bliss. Ignorance, rather sincere ignorance and conscientious stupidity, as Martin Luther King Jr. said, is the most dangerous thing in this world, and when it comes to nature that in fact govern us, is no excuse at all.

And lastly, braced yourself knowing the Truth that John the Beloved, considered in here as the true vicar of Christ, revealed; No one has ever seen God; [and that] God is *Love (*literally an attraction or an overwhelming [pressure, pulling] force of a [perfect] body such as Sun or Galaxy. And this theme serves as link, defining or unifying idea of science and religion; however used in different occasion or time, the word "love" [religion] and "gravitation [science - Isaac Newton]" denotes the same meaning as "attraction" therefore, nay vocabulary, that used chiefly as comparison to support a point of view; see also All But the World is Loving, The Universal Gravitation, for additional input), but if we love one another, or whoever lives in love, lives in union with God and God lives in union with him. My children [we know that the Son of God has come and has given us understanding, so that we know the true God]; keep yourselves safe from false gods! This little phrase is synonymous in telling to be an advocate of peace thus avert war, do not destroy the environment therefore preserve our planet and habitat; do not condone but suppress extremism thus promote justice, moderation and co-existent; and do not be the anti-Christ, and *that is being against the maxim, or of the teaching of the moral philosophy or religion, and the beauty of science in it, the fundamental of creation and law of the universal and perpetual existence. The essence of wisdom and knowledge ward off evils, are therefore the triumph of reason and of humanity.*

*Whatever you are in and believing, try to consider this invitation, and that for the sake of our future generation, believes on this idea, and without delay, carried out the appropriate measure; plant a tree and be a superhero, because you and me, or we are the one, who could actually save the Earth. In this regard, rather in gratitude to mother nature, let's celebrate the "Save the Earth Day" (on from "fall" season) by planting trees all around the world [**at least twice a year but not limited to the calendar concept of Athena, Gregorian, Hegira, Hebrew, The Persians, Chinese, Buddhist etc.**], on the first day of the month of "Summus" [September 21, the Gregorian/Shawwal 1, the Hegira] and Celebrare (on spring or as a Flower Festival; February 21/Rabbi2 1]. See also All But the World is Loving [1] for the Athena Calendar concept, a true parameter or the real depiction of the Earth revolution, orbit or seasons. And on this common desire and prayer, please help us God.*